Texts and Monographs in Computer Science

(Continued at the end of the book)

Suad Alagić

Object-Oriented Database Programming

With 84 Illustrations

Springer-Verlag New York Berlin Heidelberg
London Paris Tokyo

Suad Alagić
Department of Informatics
Faculty of Electrical Engineering
University of Sarajevo
71000 Sarajevo, Lukavica
Yugoslavia

Series Editor

David Gries
Department of Computer Science
Cornell University
Upson Hall
Ithaca, NY 14853
USA

Library of Congress Cataloging-in-Publication Data
Alagić, Suad.
    Object-oriented database programming/Suad Alagić.
        p. cm.—(Texts and monographs in computer science)
    Bibliography: p.
    Includes indexes.
    1. Database management.   2. Object-oriented programming (Computer
science)   I. Title.   II. Series.
QA76.9.D3A46   1988
005.74—dc19   88–13988

Printed on acid-free paper

Typeset by David Seham Associates, Metuchen, New Jersey.

9 8 7 6 5 4 3 2 1

ISBN-13:978-1-4612-8137-5   e-ISBN-13:978-1-4612-3518-7
DOI: 10.1007/978-1-4612-3518-7

To Mara

Preface

The major topic of this book is the integration of data and programming languages and the associated methodologies. To my knowledge, this is the first book on modern programming languages and programming methodology devoted entirely to database application environments. At the same time, it is written with the goal of reconciling the relational and object-oriented approaches to database management.

One of the reasons that influenced my decision to write this book is my dissatisfaction with the fact that the existing books on programming methodology and the associated concepts, techniques, and programming language notation are largely based on mathematical problems and mathematically oriented algorithms. As such, they give the impression that modern program structures, associated techniques, and methodologies, not to speak of the formal ones, are applicable only to problems of that sort. Although important, such problems are of limited applicability and scale. This does not apply to books in which modern concepts, techniques, methodologies, and programming language notation are applied to systems programming. But, even so, this does not demonstrate that in entirely application-oriented problems—those in which modern computer technology is most widely used—modern programming methodology is just as important.

This book is meant to be a step toward providing a more convincing support of such a claim and, thus, is based entirely on common, what one might call business-oriented, problems in which database technology has been successfully used. However, as far as I know, that usage has little to do with what in my opinion belongs to modern trends in programming languages and programming methodology. From the research point of view, the integration of data and programming languages, and the associated methodologies, is certainly the major goal of this book. But, at the same time, its goal is also to demonstrate that such an integration has very important large-scale implications.

Another important reason for my decision to write this book is the situation in the database area where the proliferation of high-level, nonprocedural languages (such as relational languages) and other nonprocedural tools has established another wrong impression in which again, although for a different reason, the results in the development of modern programming language concepts, notation, and the associated methodologies do not seem to matter very much since so many things can be done nonprocedurally anyhow. Application programmers are offered interfaces of modern, high-level, nonprocedural languages and quite often old-fashioned programming-level tools, where the interface of the two is hardly (if ever) conceptually and notationally attractive.

Although modern nonprocedural database tools allow attractive solutions to problems of increasing complexity, this book demonstrates that there are many of them that require a good solution on the programming language level. Furthermore, some common application-oriented problems require the full power of integrated data and programming languages that comes from concepts like relational model and recursive procedures, exception handling, and attractive screen management—of course, with the condition that we apply the established programming methodology criteria to procedural solutions of such problems having to do with elegant, modular structure, correctness, adaptability, efficiency, etc.

This does not mean that I am not in favor of nonprocedural tools. In fact, we have carried out the development of such tools associated and tied in with the programming language notation used in this book very far, in order to implement a complete database programming environment. The existence of such nonprocedural tools influenced the decisions about the required features of the database programming language used in this book considerably.

As far as the notation is concerned, the database programming language used in this book has been derived from Modula-2 and is thus called MODULEX. It differs considerably from other proposed database extensions of languages like Pascal and Modula, as well as from other proposed database programming languages. Whereas the previous proposed extensions of Pascal and Modula, such as Pascal/R and Modula/R, are relational oriented, MODULEX is object-action oriented. It supports the relational model as a particular case, and explores the concepts of the definition and the implementation modules as defined in Modula-2 to obtain a simple and powerful object-oriented extension of that model.

In spite of the fact that all the power of the relational model and the associated languages is offered in MODULEX, as well as its object-oriented extension in terms of modules, the programming language is kept

small and simple, just as Modula-2 is. The adopted extensions are kept
to those that are absolutely necessary, and consequently, the book should
be simple for readers and programmers with some familiarity with languages like Pascal and Modula. This approach to the programming language design makes MODULEX quite different from other proposed database programming languages. Indeed, rather than adding a number of
new and fancy features that such languages have, MODULEX explores
the power of the existing programming language concepts. The concept
of a module as defined in Modula-2 plays a crucial role in this respect,
and its appropriate interpretation leads to a particularly simple object-
oriented extension of the relational model.

Representation of objects as modules is one of the major original contributions of this book. MODULEX is essentially designed by adding the
entity set type and the associated action-composition rules (such as
foreach) to the standard collection of programming language abstractions.
These extensions are defined in such a way that they offer the power of
the relational model and the relational languages in the programming language framework. Imposing modules on such a unified relational and programming environment produces the desired object-action-oriented environment.

In view of the above described approach to the object-oriented database
programming language and its environment, the programming methodology
presented in this book is, of course, object oriented or abstract data-type
oriented. By this we mean that the cornerstone of our approach are object
types whose properties and actions applicable to instances of those types
are encapsulated in the definition modules of those objects. In comparison
with the relational approach, users of those objects are still permitted (or
may be allowed if appropriate) to state arbitrarily complex queries upon
such objects, but other applicable actions are restricted to those specified
in the definition modules of those object types. The actual representation
(implementation) of such objects and their associated actions is separated
from their definition and from their users as well. The object types in
typical database application environments quite often have relational
representation.

Conceptual modeling of application environments presented in this book
is based on a collection of standard abstractions: aggregation, generalization, covering, partitioning, and recursion. They all have simple algebraic
interpretation, as do the usual data abstractions in Pascal-like languages.
At the same time, the relationship with the associated action-composition
rules in such languages is easily established. The relational representation
of the chosen collection of standard abstractions enriched with those rules
and the structure of modules has been developed carefully in this book
in an object-oriented style.

The graphical representation is a departure from what is customary in
databases, and is based on the algebraic interpretation of standard ab-

stractions; so, an arrow simply denotes a function—what could be simpler and more consistent than that?

There is no question that the chosen framework of a single, small, and simple database programming language has its limitations, in terms of presentation of some important features of modern database systems. Although many typical integrity constraints are specified nonprocedurally in the MODULEX screen language, particularly those related to the relational representation of standard abstractions, the programming-language-based presentation in this book demonstrates how they are enforced procedurally.

This explains the role of the relational model in our approach. In fact, one of our major goals was to reconcile the relational and object-oriented approaches, and I have just given a brief and very general description of how this is achieved. Thus, in spite of the object-oriented methodology applied in this book, the presented material is to a large extent also relational-oriented programming methodology.

Perhaps it is a pity that this book is not more formal (i.e., mathematical) since virtually all the presented material has nice and sound mathematical foundation. This applies to standard abstractions, the relational model, action-composition rules, modules, and formal verification techniques for actions. Only the very basic mathematical concepts underlying the presented material in its entirety are given, in an informal manner, and I must admit that the reason for this is my desire to reach a wider audience, who may be uninterested in the underlying mathematical concepts. Therefore, the underlying concepts are used only when necessary in order to make the definitions more precise and clear. The basic formal theory of the relational model is also presented under these same limitations.

I hope this book presents a new way of teaching about databases. Indeed, introductory programming language courses based on languages like Pascal and Modula-2, and the familiarity with the very basic notions of modern mathematics are all that is required to use this book. It is my hope that readers with this background will find this book appealing, since it is entirely based on the programming language notation. I also hope this book will present some of the most important conceptual database problems to people whose work is in programming languages and programming methodology, in a manner that is much more appealing to them than the way databases are usually taught. The research on integration of data and programming languages, and the associated systems, has certainly a lot to offer to both database and programming language areas. It opens up a large number of new research problems whose solutions have practical large-scale implications.

Perhaps the exercises are the best part of this book. They expand the material in the main body of the text with a number of more advanced concepts, techniques, and methodologies. Some of the most attractive and rewarding examples and problems are given in the exercises. Working them out is the only way to master the underlying methodology presented in this book and enables one to make quite a number of discoveries on one's own. The presented selection is large enough so that lecturers teaching a course on this subject can make the appropriate choice of assignments to their students.

This book has been written alongside the development of the MODULEX database programming environment, which, in addition to the compiler of the database programming language, has as its major feature the associated high-level, object-oriented, definition, query, manipulation, and control screen language. The MODULEX screen language is designed in such a way that it fits in the unified object-oriented framework, based on the database programming language presented in this book. In addition to object-oriented and relational-oriented queries, it supports conceptual design in the sense that it makes the automatic generation of the definition and the implementation modules of object types possible, together with the associated actions from the specifications given in the screen language. At the completion of this book, the MODULEX database programming environment has already been running on the VAX, and its reimplementation on the personal computer is also planned. Readers interested in the described software tool should contact the publisher (or the author) of this book for further details.

The material presented in this book, as well as the MODULEX software environment, grew out of my research project "Extended Relational Database Programming Environment," which was support by the National Science Foundation under grant JFP/708. I would like to express my sincere appreciation for the work done by my research assistants Miroslav Kandić and Dragan Jurković. This applies not only to their contributions to the implementation of the MODULEX system, but also to their extremely valuable help in reviewing and editing the final version of the manuscript.

Sarajevo, Yugoslavia   SUAD ALAGIĆ

Contents

Chapter 3
Design Methodology   123

Chapter 4
Standard Abstractions   189

Chapter 5
Input/Output Programming   249

Introduction

1 Objects

In order to satisfy users' needs, database technology requires the design of a suitable representation of its application's environment. This representation is called a *conceptual model*. A conceptual model of an application environment is thus an abstract representation of that environment that contains only those abstract properties of the environment relevant for the information requirements of its users.

Our approach to the design of a conceptual model of an application environment is based on a collection of abstraction techniques. The most fundamental technique is classification of relevant objects in an application environment into a collection of object types. A set of objects is regarded as an object type if all the objects in that set share the same set of relevant properties (*attributes*). The relevance of a property of an object is, of course, determined by the purpose of the model. A particular object then becomes an instance of an object type. For example, in a university application environment, object types would be STUDENT, PROFESSOR, COURSE, DEPARTMENT, etc.

In order to apply the classification abstraction, we have to specify precisely the properties shared by a set of objects that belong to the same type. For example, such a specification for the object type STUDENT might look like this:

Object type: STUDENT

Attributes: Student identifier
            Name

```
                Level (undergraduate, graduate)
                Address
                Phone
```

An attribute of an object assumes particular values that also belong to a *type,* that is, to a set of objects that share the same set of properties. For example, the type of the attribute Name is a set of sequences of characters, and the type of the attribute Level is a two-element set.

It follows then that a new object type is defined in terms of other, already defined object types that become attributes of the new object type. We say that an object is an *aggregation* of its attributes. Aggregation is in fact another fundamental abstraction in the design of conceptual models of application environments. Its importance comes from the fact that an object type is defined as an aggregation of its attributes. In general, given object types E1,E2,...,En, we define their aggregate object type E in such a way that E1,E2,...,En become components (attributes in a particular case) of the object type E.

To clarify, we will use the programming language notation. The fact that an object type E has object types E1,E2,...,En as its components is expressed in terms of a record type. Such a type definition for the object type STUDENT has the following form:

```
TYPE Student  =  RECORD Student#:  String7;
                        Name:      String30;
                        Level:     (undergraduate,graduate);
                        Address:   String35;
                        Phone:     String7
              END
```

In general, we have

```
TYPE Object = RECORD Attribute1: Object1;
                     Attribute2: Object2;

                          .

                          .

                          .

                     Attributen: Objectn
             END
```

where Object1, Object2,..., Objectn and Object are object types.

The graphical notation used throughout this book is based on the mathematical interpretation of aggregation and has the following form:

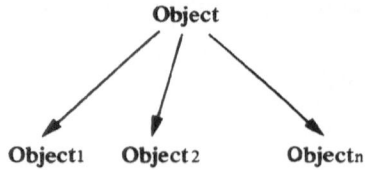

The mathematical interpretation is in fact very simple. The set Object is the Cartesian product of sets Object1, Object2,..., Objectn; that is,

$$\text{Object} = \text{Object1} \times \text{Object2} \times \cdots \times \text{Objectn}.$$

Indeed, an instance of the type Object is a tuple (a1,a2,...,an) of values of attributes of that instance:

$$\text{Object} = \{(a1,a2,...,an) \mid ai \text{ in Objecti for } i=1,2,...,n\}.$$

Given an instance o of the type Object, its components are denoted in the programming language notation as o.Attribute1, o.Attribute2, ...,o.Attributen. So, for example, if s is of type Student, its attributes are denoted as

s.Student#, s.Name, s.Level, s.Address, s.Phone.

Selection of a component of an aggregate object (attribute of an object) is also called *projection* and is of fundamental importance for the aggregation abstraction. In fact, we can interpret Attributei as a function (projection)

$$\text{Attributei: Object} \rightarrow \text{Objecti}$$

defined as

$$(a1,a2,...,an) \rightarrow ai.$$

The relational model of data is largely based on the above simple observations. In order to represent an application environment, it requires only classification and aggregation abstractions, where the latter is used only in a particular form where all the components of an object are simple. An instance of an object type is represented as a tuple (a1,a2,...,an) of values of its attributes, so that a particular set of objects of the same type is represented as a set of such tuples. But such a set is formally a relation. For example,

RegisteredStudents = StudentIdType ×
                     NameType ×
                     LevelType ×
                     AddressType ×
                     PhoneType

is a set (a relation) of registered students, where the type of that set is StudentSet defined in our programming language notation as

TYPE StudentSet = ENTITY SET OF Student.

The above genuinely simple and natural representation implies the following requirement: Given representations o1 and o2 of two distinct objects of the same type Object, we must have

$$o1.\text{Attributei} <> o2.\text{Attributei} \quad \text{for some } i=1,2,...,n.$$

In other words, two distinct objects of the same type should be represented by two distinct tuples of values of their attributes. In order to guarantee this condition, it is sufficient if the two tuples have different values of at least one attribute.

The above reasoning makes obvious the importance of an attribute (or a set of attributes, in general) whose value determines a unique object of a given type. Such an attribute or a set of attributes is called an *object identifier*, or a *key*. In a relation that represents a particular set of objects of the same type, there is thus at most one tuple with a given key value. The requirement that each object type in a conceptual model of an application environment must have at least one key hardly needs any further justification. We simply need to know what actual object of an application environment each tuple of a relation represents.

2 Actions

A conceptual model of an application environment is meant to satisfy information needs of users of that environment via queries stated against that model. An example of a query would be

Print the names of all registered graduate students.

This query would be expressed in the programming language notation used in this book as

```
FOREACH s IN RegisteredStudents
WHERE     s.Level = graduate
DO        WriteString (s.Name); WriteLn
END
```

where s is of type Student and RegisteredStudents is of type StudentSet.

Set-oriented queries are typical for the relational model of data. In fact, in addition to the representation of sets of objects as relations, the relational model also offers a collection of general-purpose operators upon such a representation that act upon that representation in order to produce results that satisfy specific information needs of end users. Projection is one such operator, and the other involved in the above query is restriction—selection of a subset of a set of objects where each object in the subset satisfies a given condition. The result of the above query is expressed in the usual mathematical notation in terms of restriction and projection as follows:

{s.Name | s in RegisteredStudents and s.Level = graduate}.

A model of an application environment is of course useless unless we can specify actions against the model that would produce some useful effects. This trivial observation indicates that a representation of an application environment in terms of classification and aggregation of types of objects in that environment is an extremely simplified view of the environment that has to be enriched by actions that may be performed on the represented objects.

Actions associated with an object type in fact correspond to activities in the application environment involving objects of that type. This means our approach to conceptual modeling presented so far has to be refined in a crucial way. An application environment is still viewed as a collection of object types, but the essential part of specification of such a type is a set of actions upon instances of that type that correspond to the actual activities involving those objects in the application environment. For example, conceptual representation of the object type STUDENT would now be completed in the following manner:

Object type: STUDENT

Attributes: Student identifier
                 Name
                 Level
                 Address
                 Phone

Actions: Enroll student
                 Drop student
                 Change level
                 Change address
                 Change phone

The refined object-action approach to conceptual modeling of application environments requires specification of a set of actions associated with objects of the same type as the most important specification of that type. If we carry out this approach to all its consequences, then an object type may be defined entirely in terms of actions that may be performed upon instances of that type. Indeed, we already observed that attributes of an object type in fact correspond to projections. If we accompany a set of actions associated with an object type with a set of projections (e.g., SelectStudentId, SelectName, SelectLevel, SelectAddress, SelectPhone) to the attributes of that type, we obtain an entirely action-oriented definition of an object type.

Although the action-oriented definition of an object type has a sound mathematical basis, it is not unusual for programmers to deal with an object entirely in terms of actions that may be performed upon that object. In fact, the whole point, is to forbid explicit manipulation of representation of an object by the clients of that object and force them to use a predefined set of actions given in the definition of that object type that are guaranteed to manipulate the actual representation correctly.

So far we have defined object types in terms of classification and aggregation abstractions. There are some obvious primitive actions associated with these abstractions. Other actions associated with an object type will then be defined starting from these primitive actions and by applying appropriate action composition rules. Primitive actions associated with the classification abstraction are

(i) inclusion of an instance of an object type into a set of objects of that type;

(ii) exclusion of an instance of an object type from a set of objects of that type;

(iii) checking membership of an instance of an object type in a set of objects of that type; and

(iv) modification (update) of an instance of an object type—this is in fact the assignment action of programming languages.

As noted, the primitive action associated with aggregation is *projection*, that is, the selection of a component (attribute) of an instance of an object type. Using projections we can specify updates of particular components (attributes) of an object by performing assignment to those components. For example, the action ChangeLevel performed on an instance s of the object type STUDENT is specified in the programming language notation as the following assignment statement:

$$s.\text{Level} := \text{graduate}.$$

Most actions associated with an object type are not simple. They are obtained starting from the primitive actions and by applying a predefined set of action composition rules. For example, three typical actions associated with the entity type STUDENT may be decomposed as follows:

```
EnrollStudent:   Get student data;
                 Check validity;
                 IF data ok THEN
                     include student
                 ELSE Write error message
                 END

DropStudent:     Get student identifier;
                 Find student;
                 IF student exists THEN
                     exclude student
                 ELSE Write error message
                 END

ChangeAddress:   Get student identifier;
                 Get new address;
                 Find student;
```

```
IF student exists THEN
    assign new address
ELSE Write error message
END
```

In the above abstract decomposition of the actions EnrollStudent, DropStudent, and ChangeAddress, the primitive actions are Get (read), include, exclude, assign, and Write, whereas action composition rules are sequential (denoted ;) and conditional (IF-THEN-ELSE).

A conceptual model of an application environment of any complexity will consist of a collection of interrelated objects together with the associated actions. Decomposition of those actions will then require the full range of action composition rules of modern programming languages. Consider, for example, the action EnrollStudents associated with an object REGISTRY. Its decomposition will have the following form:

```
EnrollStudents: REPEAT EnrollStudent;
                UNTIL   AllStudentsEnrolled
```

where EnrollStudent is the action whose decomposition was performed earlier. In the above decomposition, we used the repetitive composition of actions of the REPEAT-UNTIL form.

FOREACH composition was already introduced. Its fundamental importance comes from the fact that database technology deals with large sets of objects. FOREACH composition is thus used for expressing set-oriented actions, queries in particular. In addition, even actions on particular objects (e.g., DropStudent, ChangeAddress) include a find action that selects the desired object instance given its properties (values of its attributes). Search for a particular object given its object identifier is, of course, preferable, but quite frequently the identifier is unknown, and we have to inspect a set of candidates for the desired object instance, which is obtained by some qualification condition the candidates must satisfy in order to qualify for the consideration.

It is very important to distinguish between two semantic levels associated with a composite action of an object type. From the viewpoint of users of that object type, all actions associated with that type should appear simple in spite of their possible complexity. All that matters to those users is what an action accomplishes and how it is invoked. The details of how exactly that action performs its task are not and should not be of any concern to its users. Of course, the creator of that object works at the lower level and is required to decompose actions associated with an object type in such a way that they perform their task correctly.

The two semantic levels associated with a composite action of an object type are captured by the programming language notion of a *procedure*. A procedure is a composite action that has an identifier and parameters. Users of an action specified as a procedure invoke that action by its identifier and supply the required parameters that are specific to a particular invocation. For example, in order to perform the insertion (inclusion) action, an instance of an object must be supplied, as well as a set of objects of that type into which the given object instance should be included. Likewise, the exclusion (deletion) action requires as its parameters the identifier of an object instance and a set of objects of that type from which the specified instance is to be excluded. Updating the value of an attribute of an object requires three parameters: object identifier, the set of objects where the given object is to be found, and the new value of the attribute.

The above reasoning is illustrated for three typical actions associated with the object type STUDENT:

Object type: STUDENT

Actions	Parameters
EnrollStudent	Student, Set of students
DropStudent	Student identifier, Set of students
ChangeAddress	Student identifier, Set of students, New address

Invocation of an action is performed by a *procedure call*, and its decomposition is given in a *procedure declaration*. The procedure declaration for the action DropStudent would have the following abstract form:

```
PROCEDURE DropStudent (student#: StudentId;
                       set: StudentSet);
BEGIN Find student;
      IF student exists THEN
         exclude student
      ELSE Write error message
      END
END DropStudent
```

3 Abstractions

So far we have only dealt with particular objects. However, a conceptual model of an application environment of any complexity and scale will in fact consist of a collection of interrelated objects. In order to develop this potentially complex model structure, we rely on a number of standard abstraction techniques used to compose/decompose complex objects and classify various possible relationships that may exist among objects in the chosen application environment.

Two standard abstraction techniques were already introduced: classification and aggregation. Indeed, it is hardly possible to discuss conceptual models without mentioning these two abstractions. We now explore aggregation further and then introduce other standard abstraction techniques.

Classification of objects in the chosen university application environment reveals object types that are aggregates of other object types. An example is the object type LECTURE whose attributes are the object types PROFESSOR and COURSE:

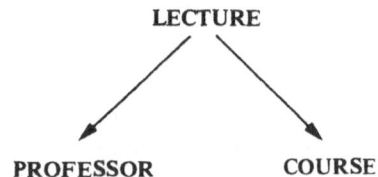

LECTURE

PROFESSOR   **COURSE**

To be more precise, LECTURE is an aggregate of simple attributes such as Day, Time, and Room, and of the compound attributes PROFESSOR and COURSE. In the programming language notation, we would have the following representation:

```
TYPE Lecture = RECORD Subject:  Course;
                      Lecturer: Professor;
                      Day:      (Mon,Tue,Wed,Thu,Fri);
                      Time:     String5;
                      Room:     String3
              END
```

This natural and customary representation from the viewpoint of programming languages (a record with embedded records) has also been studied from the viewpoint of the relational model, and it has been discovered that it causes some problems. As a consequence, the relational model does not permit an object type (such as PROFESSOR and COURSE) as the type of an attribute of an object (such as LECTURE). An alternative representation takes course and professor identifiers as attributes of the object type LECTURE so that we obtain the following:

```
TYPE Lecture = RECORD Course#:    CourseId;
                      Professor#: ProfessorId;
                      Day:        (Mon,Tue,Wed,Thu,Fri);
                      Time:       String5;
                      Room:       String3
              END
```

But this relational representation also has its problems, which are revealed when we consider decomposition of actions associated with the object types LECTURE, COURSE, and PROFESSOR. The problems are precisely due to the fact that the aggregation relationship is expressed linking objects by values of object identifiers that behave like pointers in programming languages. For example,

(i) inclusion of a new lecture requires checking whether the course and professor instances specified by the values of the attributes Course# and Professor# of the object type LECTURE actually exist in the current sets of objects of type COURSE and PROFESSOR; and

(ii) exclusion of a course or professor requires checking whether there are scheduled lectures of that course or of the professor. If so, some appropriate action must be performed first, such as the replacement of the professor by another or deleting the lecture(s) altogether.

These conditions are referential integrity constraints and should come as no surprise to programmers who deal with data structures linked by pointers. In view of the importance of relational database technology, programming methodology for dealing with the above type of logical relationships expressed in terms of object identifiers will necessarily be treated in this book with due care.

Generalization is another abstraction technique of fundamental importance for the classification of objects in an application environment into object types. It is in a sense dual to aggregation. Given object types Object1, Object2,..., Objectn, which share some common properties and differ in others, we can define their generic object type Object in such a way that Object has attributes common to all Objecti for $i = 1,2,...,n$. Objecti becomes a subtype of Object. Conversely, given an object type Object, we can introduce its subtype Objecti in such a way that Objecti inherits all the attributes of Object and has, in addition, other attributes specific to Objecti. This type of refinement (decomposition) is called *specialization*. For example, given the object type STUDENT, we can introduce its two subtypes UNDERGRADUATE and GRADUATE as follows:

Object type: GRADUATE

Attributes: All attributes of STUDENT
Program (MSc or PhD)
Advisor
Department

Actions: Enroll graduate
Drop graduate
Change program
Change advisor
Change department

Object type: UNDERGRADUATE

Attributes: All attributes of STUDENT
              Status (full time or part time)
              School
              Year

Actions: Enroll undergraduate
              Drop undergraduate
              Change status
              Change year
              Change school

The graphical notation for generalization used in this book is also dual to aggregation (all arrows are reversed):

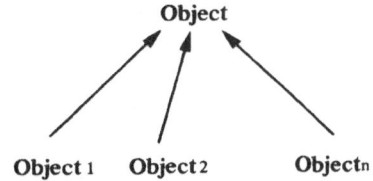

It is justified by the fact that the type Object is equipped with a collection of injective functions $Object_i \rightarrow Object$ for $i = 1,2,...,n$. A function $Object_i \rightarrow Object$ in fact corresponds to the is-a relationship. In other words, an instance of type $Object_i$ is an instance of type Object where the latter is formally obtained by projection to the attributes of Object (i.e., by dropping all the attributes specific to $Object_i$). For example, a graduate student is a student. Given an instance of GRADUATE, we obtain an instance of STUDENT by dropping the attributes Program, Advisor, and Department.

Although it is certainly possible to consider a more general case, we confine ourselves to the most important type of generalization in which object subtypes are disjoint and the full property inheritance holds. The latter condition simply means that each subtype $Object_i$ ($i = 1,2,...,n$) inherits all the attributes of its generic type Object. This should be familiar to programmers and corresponds precisely to the situation in which a record type has a number of variants:

```
TYPE Student = RECORD Student#: StudentId;
                      Name:     String30;
                      Address:  String35;
                      Phone:    String7
               CASE   Level:    (undergraduate, graduate) OF
                      undergraduate:
                      Status: (fulltime, parttime);
                      School: (Arts,Sciences,Engineering,Medicine);
```

```
            Year:    (freshman,junior,sophmore,senior)  |
        graduate:
            Program:      (MSc,PhD);
            Advisor:      ProfessorId;
            Department: DepartmentId
    END
    END
```

This representation, however, is not adequate in the context of relational database technology. Not only is its immediate representation in the relational framework not possible (i.e., STUDENT, GRADUATE, and UNDERGRADUATE are represented by separate relations), but GRADUATE and UNDERGRADUATE should indeed be treated as stand-alone object types that may be accessed independently of each other and of their generic type STUDENT, as in the following relational representation of the object types STUDENT and GRADUATE:

```
TYPE Student = RECORD Student#: StudentId;
                      Name:     String30;
                      Address:  String35;
                      Phone:    String7;
                      Level:    (undergraduate,graduate)
        END;
```

VAR Students: ENTITY SET OF Student;

```
TYPE Graduate = RECORD Student#:       StudentId;
                       Program:        (MSc,PhD);
                       Advisor:        ProfessorId;
                       Department#: DepartmentId
        END;
```

VAR Graduates: ENTITY SET OF Graduate

In spite of the fact that subtypes of a generic object type are represented separately, their relationship to that generic type comes up in action modeling. For example, in order to print a complete record of a given student consisting of all generic and specific student data, it is necessary to join tuples from the sets Students and Graduates with the same (given) student identifier.

Decomposition of actions associated with the generic object type and its subtypes brings up this relationship and also requires some well-known action composition rules in programming languages that we have not mentioned so far. In order to illustrate this point, consider the following decomposition of the action DropStudent associated with the object type STUDENT:

```
DropStudent: Get student identifier;
             Find student;
```

```
IF Student exists THEN
    exclude it;
    CASE level OF
        undergraduate: DropUndergraduate  |
        graduate:      DropGraduate
    END
ELSE Write error message
END
```

The above decomposition illustrates an integrity constraint associated with generalization indicating that an instance oi of a subtype Objecti is not permitted to exist in a database unless its corresponding generic instance oi of type Object also exists in the database. Consequently, when the generic student data are excluded (deleted) from the database, specific (graduate or undergraduate) data are excluded as well. The latter is expressed by a selective (CASE) composition of actions in which one out of a finite number of actions is selected for execution depending on the value of an expression of a simple type (a particular attribute in the above case). The above example exhibits once again the importance of action modeling that captures essential aspects of the semantics of an application environment.

Aggregation abstraction is based on the Cartesian product operation. The underlying set operation for generalization is *disjoint union*. In a disjoint union of object types, a distinct copy of each object type participating in such a union is maintained. Given an instance of a disjoint union of types, we can always determine the subtype to which that instance belongs (and the corresponding subtype instance). For example, given an instance of the generic type STUDENT, the value of the attribute Level determines whether the given instance is a graduate or an undergraduate student. It is interesting to observe that adding an attribute that plays the role of the type discriminator is also the Cartesian product operation.

The next abstraction we consider is called *covering*, and is based on the power *set operation*—construction of the set of all subsets of a given set. We say that an object type E is a *cover* of an object type M if every instance of E corresponds to a set of instances of M. E is called the *cover type*, and M its associated *member type*. Note that the actual set of instances of M associated with an instance of E is not determined by the definition of the model. An example of covering is

DEPARTMENT

Cover (FACULTY)

where a department is viewed as a set of faculty members.

Covering is *not* partitioning the set of members into disjoint subsets, and so, in the above example, we assume a faculty member may belong to (be associated with) more than one department. Consequently, instances of the object type DEPARTMENT are identified with subsets of the set of all faculty members. Although a department may be associated with an empty set of faculty members, we expect to obtain (cover) the set of all faculty members when we perform the union of sets of faculty members associated with particular departments.

A more realistic approach to conceptual modeling, both in this particular example and in general, is the application of both aggregation and covering (to obtain *cover aggregation*), so that a department is viewed as an aggregate of simple attributes such as name and location, and of compound ones such as a set of faculty members, a set of courses, a set of personnel, and a set of students:

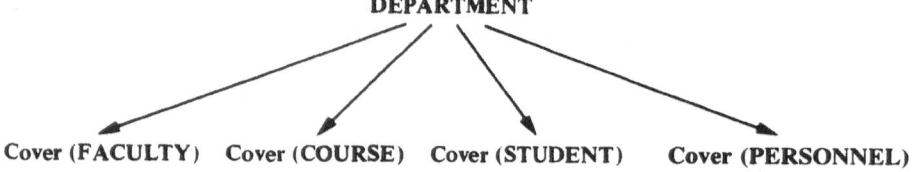

DEPARTMENT

Cover (FACULTY)   Cover (COURSE)   Cover (STUDENT)   Cover (PERSONNEL)

The immediate representation of the fact that DEPARTMENT is a cover type of the type FACULTY would lead to the following type definition:

```
TYPE Department = RECORD Name:     String30;
                         Location: String30;
                         Faculty:  SetOfProfessor
             END
```

Programming languages (such as Pascal or Modula) recognize the importance of set types, but for reasons of efficiency of implementation, their cardinality is severely bounded and their elements are required to be of a simple type. Neither of the above conditions is satisfied in the above example where the type of the attribute Faculty is in fact ENTITY SET OF Professor. Consequently, the above immediate representation does not satisfy the requirements of the basic relational model.

We can easily devise two alternatives, one that is closer to the philosophy of programming languages, and the other conforming to the basic relational model of data. The first representation is obtained taking the type of the attribute Faculty to be a set of simple values—identifiers of objects of type Professor

```
TYPE Department = RECORD Name:     String30;
                         Location: String30;
```

Faculty: SET OF
Professorld

END

where the cardinality of the type of the attribute Faculty is not bounded as in the usual programming language approach. This is indeed an immediate representation of the covering abstraction. However, object identifiers behave like logical pointers, and their manipulation requires a lot of care well known to programmers. Problems that may occur are in the database area called *violations of integrity constraints*. For example, if a faculty member is fired, all references to that faculty member should be excluded or replaced by references to existing faculty in all departments in which that person was a member.

The relational representation of covering is based on aggregation. It is obtained by introducing a new type, call it MEMBERSHIP, which is an aggregation of the object types DEPARTMENT and FACULTY.

MEMBERSHIP

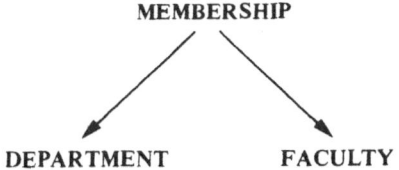

DEPARTMENT   **FACULTY**

The attributes of the new type MEMBERSHIP are department and faculty identifiers, so that the restrictions of the relational model are satisfied:

TYPE Membership = RECORD Department#:   DepartmentId;
                              Professor#:   ProfessorId;
                              TypeOfMembership: (full,adjoint)
END

This new representation opens up some other possibilities such as introducing the attributes of the cover-member relationship. The referential integrity problems, however, obviously remain in view of the fact that the relationship is expressed in terms of object identifiers.

Now consider a frequently occurring situation in which a faculty member belongs to (is employed by) one and only one department. In other words, we have the following functional relationship:

f: PROFESSOR → DEPARTMENT.

This relationship introduces partitioning of the set of faculty members into disjoint subsets, one such subset per department. Given a department d, its associated set of faculty members is determined via f as

$$\{p \mid p \text{ in Professor and } f(p) = d\}.$$

Formally, the object type DEPARTMENT is now identified with the above defined collection of disjoint subsets of PROFESSOR determined by f: PROFESSOR → DEPARTMENT. Such a set is called a *quotient set*. A department thus becomes an attribute of a professor. In accordance with the basic relational model, we can take the identifier of the department as an attribute of PROFESSOR to obtain the following representation of partitioning:

```
TYPE Professor  =  RECORD Professor#:    ProfessorId;
                          Name:          String40;
                          Rank:          (assistant, associate, full);
                          Department#:   DepartmentId
            END
```

It should come as no surprise that each particular representation of the considered abstractions has immediate consequences on the action modeling. The relational representation in particular involves due care in maintaining properly referential integrity constraints.

4 Environments

In order to express encapsulation of object attributes and the associated actions in accordance with the objection-action-oriented approach introduced so far, we explore the programming language notion of a *module* as defined in Modula-2. An object type is thus defined as a module with two explicitly separated levels of abstraction in the specification of that object type. In the *definition module* of an object type, attributes of its instances and their types, as well as types of actions on those instances, are specified. Only names and parameters of actions (procedure headings) are defined in the definition module of an object type, since this is what a user of that object must know in order to invoke those actions. So the definition module of an object is an interface to all users of that object and has the following abstract form:

DEFINITION MODULE ObjectName;

> Specification of object attributes;

> Specification of names and
> parameters (procedure headings)
> of the associated actions

END ObjectName.

The other, lower level of abstraction is specified by the creator of the object (type) in the *implementation module* of that object. The implementation module of an object contains the actual representation of the set of objects (e.g., as one or more sets of records) and decomposition of actions associated with the object as (declarations of) procedures that operate on the representation. An implementation module of an object may have the following general form:

IMPLEMENTATION MODULE ObjectName;

   Actual representation of the
      set of objects;

   Decomposition of actions on the
      chosen representation as
      procedure declarations

END ObjectName.

   Users of an object are given access to its definition module only. The creator of an object is responsible for the selection of an appropriate representation (e.g., relational) and for the associated decomposition of actions.

   Users of an object naturally assume correct performance of all actions given in the definition module of that object. Decomposition of actions specified in its implementation module must be performed in such a way that correct performance is guaranteed. This in particular means that the decomposition must be performed so that all integrity constraints that are either associated with the object in the application environment or follow from the chosen representation are maintained. Thus, procedural decomposition of actions must enforce constraints such as uniqueness of (intended) object identifiers, referential integrity constraints, etc.

   Procedures that represent decompositions of actions of an object type (offered or exported to the users of that object type) behave as *transactions*. A transaction is a procedure that is executed successfully as a whole or not at all. In other words, all traces of all possible partial executions of a transaction are erased, either by an explicit abort action if the fatal errors are anticipated and detected by the application programmer (creator of the object) or in a system-determined manner in case of system failure.

   Consider, for example, the following transaction:

FireProfessor: Get professor id;
               Find professor;
               IF found THEN
                   Exclude the professor from the faculty;
                   FOREACH lecture given by the professor
                   DO perform an appropriate replacement;
                       IF   impossible THEN
                           Report error;

Abort transaction
      END
   END
   ELSE Report error
   END

The above transaction is designed in such a way that if it is executed it guarantees the referential integrity constraint associated with the object type LECTURE, or else the FireProfessor action is not performed at all. Of course, it is possible and advisable to apply a different approach in which an attempt is made to perform all the required replacements first and only in the case of success, to perform the required deletion:

Find professor;
Perform all the necessary replacements;
IF successful so far
THEN Exclude professor
ELSE Report failure
END

The problem, however, is that the database objects outlive executions of application programs (they represent persistent data) so that a system failure after some or all replacements have been performed will cause obvious problems. This example hopefully demonstrates the importance of the atomicity of execution of a (transaction) procedure associated with an object. If such a procedure is not successfully completed, the user should at least have an appropriate indication of the effects of its execution and the errors or exceptions that occur during that execution.

Modules open up other possibilities for the representation of the results of conceptual modeling of an application environment. Classification of objects and activities in an application environment of any complexity leads not only to particular object types, but also to collections of object types that often correspond to abstractions suitable to groups of users in that environment. Such an abstraction is called a *submodel,* and a set of actions associated with a submodel reflects the access rights of such groups of users with respect to the common objects in the database.

As a particularly simple example, consider for the purposes of this introduction the subenvironments CourseRegistration and Lecture-Scheduling of a university application environment, where both submodels are based on the aggregation abstraction:

CourseRegistration

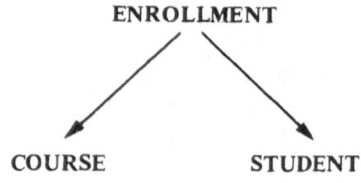

LectureScheduling

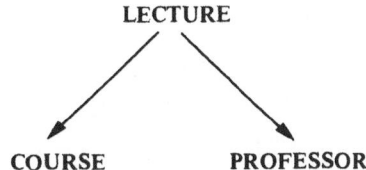

A module can serve to represent a collection of (interrelated) objects and the associated activities (actions). This example shows that sets of objects of two submodels of a model are not, in general, disjoint, and neither are the associated actions.

CHAPTER 1
Data and Actions

1 Simple Types, Records, and Entity Sets

A set E of entities of the same type is characterized by its set of attributes A1,A2,...,An and denoted as E(A1,A2,...,An), where Ai: E→Ti is a function whose codomain Ti is the *type* of the attribute Ai. Given e in E, Ai(ei) in Ti is called the value of the attribute Ai of the entity e. Given an entity type E(A1,A2,...,An), the set of functions A1:E→T1, A2:E→T2,..., An:E → Tn (attributes of that entity type) determine a unique function

$$(A1,A2,...,An): E{\to}T1 \times T2 \times ... \times Tn,$$

where $T1 \times T2 \times ... \times Tn$ denotes the Cartesian product of the sets T1,T2,...Tn (i.e., the set of all n-tuples (t1,t2,...,tn) where ti in Ti for i=1,2,...,n). The function (A1,A2,...,An) is defined as

$$(A1,A2,...,An)(e)=(A1(e),A2(e),...,An(e)),$$

where we require the following condition for the two different entities e1 and e2 of the type E:

$$(A1,A2,...,An)(e1) <> (A1,A2,...,An)(e2).$$

The above condition states that (A1,A2,...,An) is an injective function E→T1 × T2 × ...Tn. This condition will be satisfied if there exists j (j=1,2,...,n) such that

$$Aj(e1) < > Aj(e2).$$

That is, different entities are represented by different tuples. Tuples are different if they have different values of at least one attribute.

A data type is a set of values together with actions that may be performed upon them. In accordance with the relational model of data, we will consider the following attribute types:

(1) Standard Attribute Types

  (i) *Integer*.   A subset of integers MinInt,...,0,..., MaxInt equipped with the following operators:

+ (unary)	identity,
− (unary)	sign inversion,
+	addition,
−	subtraction,
*	multiplication,
DIV	quotient of integer division, and
MOD	remainder of integer division.

  (ii) *Cardinal*. A set of nonnegative integers 0,1,...,MaxCard.

  (iii) *Real*. A subset of real numbers equipped with the following operators:

+ (unary)	identity,
− (unary)	sign inversion,
+	addition,
−	subtraction,
*	multiplication, and
/	real division.

  (iv) *Boolean*. The set whose elements are truth values, denoted false and true, with the following logical operators:

NOT	negation,
OR	disjunction, and
AND	conjunction.

  (v) *Char*. A set of characters whose values are denoted by the characters themselves enclosed within quotes.

  (vi) *String*. This type in fact does not exist per se, but represents a disjoint union of the types actually available:

$$\text{String1, String2,...,StringN,}$$

where

$$\text{StringK}$$

is a set of sequences of characters of length K; this type is in Modula expressed in terms of arrays to be introduced later.

Input and *output actions* associated with standard types are as follows:

ReadCh(x)	WriteLn
ReadString(x)	WriteCh(x)
ReadCard(x)	WriteString(x)
ReadInt(x)	WriteCard(x,n)
ReadReal(x)	WriteInt(x,n)
	WriteReal(x,n)

Each of these actions refers to a standard type that x belongs to. n is of type Cardinal and determines the least number of digits required in the character representation of numeric value x. WriteLn outputs the control character which terminates the current line. All of these actions belong to the abstraction called StandardIO defined later in Chapter 5.

(2) Enumerations

A simple type T may be defined as an enumeration $(c1,c2,...,cn)$ of elements belonging to that type. Elements of this new type are denoted with identifiers ci $(i = 1,2,...,n)$. Examples of enumeration types are

TYPE month = (Jan,Feb,Mar,Apr,May,Jun,Jul,Aug,Sep,Oct,Nov,Dec);
      day   = (Mon,Tue,Wed,Thu,Fri,Sat,Sun)

The ordinal number of a constant ci in the enumeration $(c1,c2,...,cn)$ is obtained by a standard function Ord defined as follows:

$$Ord(ci) = i-1, \quad \text{for } i = 1,2,...,n.$$

The standard type Boolean is also an enumeration type predefined as follows:

$$TYPE \ Boolean = (false, true)$$

(3) Subranges

Given a simple, ordered type (the *base* type) such as Integer, Cardinal, or Char, or an enumeration type, it is possible to define a new type as a range of elements of the base type. A subrange type introduced in such a manner inherits the operators from its base type. Examples of subrange types are

TYPE WorkDays = [Mon..Tue];
      Letter = [" A " .. " Z "];
      Index = [1..256]

The following relational operators are applicable to all of the above types:

=	equality,
< >	inequality,
<	less than,

>   greater than,
< =   less than or equal, and
> =   greater than or equal.

A *record type* is a structured type that has a fixed number of possibly different component types specified in the definition of such a type. Components of a record are called *attributes*. The definition of a record type specifies for each attribute its type and an identifier that denotes it. Its general form is as follows:

TYPE T = RECORD A1: T1;
                    A2: T2;

                   .

                   .

                   .

                    An: Tn
     END

In the above definition, T is the identifier of the record type; T1,T2,...,Tn are types of its components (attributes); and A1,A2,...,An are their respective identifiers. The underlying set of T is

$$T = T1 \times T2 \times ... \times Tn.$$

Given x of type T, its components (projections) are denoted as

$$x.A1, x.A2, ..., x.An.$$

Example

TYPE EmployeeId   = String3;
      DepartmentId = String5;
      EmployeeType = RECORD
                        employee#:   EmployeeId;
                        name: String25;
                        rank: String30;
                        experience: Cardinal;
                        salary: Real;
                        department#: DepartmentId
                 END

The entity-set type is a large set of records whose attributes either are of predefined simple types (Integer, Real, Boolean, Char) or represent strings, enumerations, and subranges. Such a type is introduced in a type definition of the form

TYPE E = ENTITY SET OF R,

where R is the record type whose attributes satisfy the above stated requirement. The underlying set operation is that of the power set $\mathcal{P}(R)$, that is, the set of all subsets of R:

$$E = \mathcal{P}(R).$$

Example

```
TYPE EmployeeId   = String3;
     DepartmentId = String5;

     EmployeeType = RECORD
                        employee#:    EmployeeId;
                        name:         String25;
                        rank:         String30;
                        experience:   Cardinal;
                        salary:       Real;
                        department#:  DepartmentId
                    END;

     DepartmentType = RECORD
                        department#:  DepartmentId;
                        name:         String54;
                        staff:        Cardinal;
                        manager#:     EmployeeId
                    END;

EmployeeSetType   = ENTITY SET OF EmployeeType;
DepartmentSetType = ENTITY SET OF DepartmentType
```

An entity type is equipped with the operators for insertion and deletion of instances of that type, as well as the membership relation, defined as follows:

Insert(e,E) Instance e of the record type T is included in (becomes a member of) the set E of the type ENTITY SET OF T.

Delete(e,E) Instance e of the record T is excluded from the set E of the type ENTITY SET OF T.

Member(e,E) This operator is true if the instance e is a member of the entity set E, and false otherwise.

A particular case occurs when R in the definition of an entity set type

TYPE E = ENTITY SET OF R

has only one attribute. In this case the record notation may be omitted altogether.

2 Variables, Constants, and Expressions

A variable is introduced in its declaration specifying its identifier and type, that is, the set out of which that variable may assume particular values. So the declaration of a variable also determines the operators that may be applied to that variable.

Example

```
VAR found: Boolean;
    ch: Char;
    employee#,manager#: EmployeeId;
    name: String25;
    e: EmployeeType;
    employee: EmployeeSetType
```

A component of a record variable is denoted by the identifier of the record variable followed by the attribute identifier of the component.

Example

```
e.name
e.salary
```

A constant definition introduces an identifier as a synonym for a constant. A constant may be quite general in Modula-2, but for our purposes the most important cases are a number (integer or real), a character constant, or a string.

Example

```
CONST increase = 1.10;
      dot = "." ;
      percentage = 25;
      year = " 1984 " ;
```

Expressions consist of operators and operands. The latter include variables, constants, and function calls. An expression specifies a composition of operations and the order in which these operations are to be performed to obtain the value of that expression. The order in which the operators in an expression are applied to their operands is left to right, unless otherwise dictated by the following list of *priorities of operators:*

NOT	
multiplicative operators	$*$, /, DIV, MOD, AND;
adding operators	$+$, $-$, OR;
relational operators	$=$, $< >$, $<$, $< =$, $>$, $> =$, IN.

The operator NOT has the highest priority, and the relational operators the lowest. Sequences of operators of the same precedence are evaluated from left to right.

The most basic form of expressions are *factors*. They include variables and constants, as well as more complex expressions that become factors when placed in parentheses.

Example

50000
"programmer"
"M.Sc."
employee
e.name
(e.salary > 50000)
(e.department# = d.department#)
NOT found

Terms are built out of factors. They include factors themselves, possibly preceded by the unary operators + and −, as well as all the expressions of the form Term MultiplicativeOperator Term.

Example

salary * 1.1
salary / 12
o.price * l.quantity
(e.job = programmer) AND (e.salary > 50000)

Simple expressions are obtained from terms as operands applying the adding operators. They include all the terms, as well as the expressions of the form SimpleExpression AddingOperator SimpleExpression.

Example

credit - debit
p.price + o.price * l.quantity
(e.degree = MSc) OR (e.degree = PhD)

And, finally, expressions are built from terms as operands applying the relational operators. They contain all simple expressions, as well as the expressions of the form SimpleExpression RelationalOperator Simple-Expression.

Example

e.salary > 50000
e.degree = MSc
e.department# = d.department#

The type of the value of an expression depends on the types of its operands, as well as on the operators and functions that are applied to those operands.

3 Sample Database: Project Management

This section presents a rather typical database for a project-management application. The fundamental entity type in the project-management database is PROJECT. A particularly important attribute is PROJECT#, the project identifier (primary key). We assume that in order to manage a project it is subdivided into a number of tasks (possibly zero) so that a finite set of tasks is associated with each project and each task belongs to one and only one project. This 1 : N relationship between the entity types PROJECT and TASK corresponds to the function

PROJECT

TASK

which partitions the set of tasks into disjoint subsets, one such subset per project.

In the project-management relational schema, this relationship is represented in such a way that the identifier of the entity type PROJECT, denoted as PROJECT#, is regarded as an attribute of the entity type TASK. The task identifier is denoted as TASK#.

We further assume each task is assigned to an organizational unit (a department). So we introduce a new entity type DEPARTMENT, together with its identifier DEPARTMENT#. There exists an 1 : N relationship between the entity types DEPARTMENT and TASK, which means that a finite set of tasks (possibly none) is assigned to each department and a task belongs to one and only one department.

As already indicated, this relationship is represented in the relational schema in such a way that the department identifier DEPARTMENT# is chosen to be an attribute of the entity type TASK:

DEPARTMENT

TASK

In order to perform a task, a set of employees is selected and assigned to the task. This means that we introduce a new entity type EMPLOYEE and its identifying attribute EMPLOYEE# in the project-management relational schema. The relationship among the entity types EMPLOYEE and TASK is assumed to be more complex than the ones introduced so far. It is an M : N relationship, which means that not only a finite set of N employees (possibly zero) is assigned to a task, but also that an employee may be assigned to a finite set (possibly zero) of M tasks. This type of relationship is represented via aggregation, introducing a new entity type, ASSIGNMENT, and two 1 : N relationships corresponding to the projections in the following diagram:

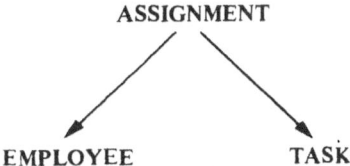

In the project-management relational schema, the above relationship is represented in such a way that the entity type ASSIGNMENT, in addition to its attributes ROLE and DAYS, also contains the identifiers EMPLOYEE# and TASK# as its attributes.

One further, obvious relationship links an employee to the department in which the employee works. We will assume that an employee belongs to one and only one department, and that a department has a finite set (possibly zero) of N employees. So we have the following representation:

This means that in the project-management relational schema the attribute DEPARTMENT# has to be added to the entity type EMPLOYEE. This attribute identifies the department to which an employee belongs.

The overall result of the design phases performed thus far is represented in Figure 1 (next page).

To further develop the project-management relational schema, we introduce three new relationships, the assignment of project leaders, task leaders, and department managers. These relationships are represented in Figure 2.

So a project has a unique leader, but an employee may be the leader

PROJECT MANAGEMENT

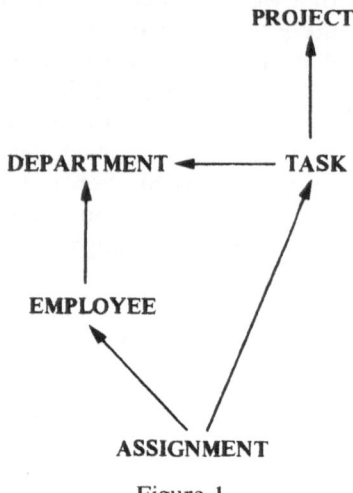

Figure 1

Figure 2

in N projects; and a task has one leader, but an employee may be the leader in N tasks; a department has a unique manager of at most one department. All this implies that in the project-management relational schema the employee identifier will be an attribute of each of the entity types PROJECT, TASK, and DEPARTMENT. In the entity types PROJECT and TASK, this attribute is called LEADER#, and in the entity type DEPARTMENT, it is called MANAGER#. All these three attributes must refer to employees existing in the database.

The result of the overall design procedure is represented in the following programming language notation:

DEFINITION MODULE ProjectManagement;

  EXPORT QUALIFIED
    ProjectId,EmployeeId,TaskId,DepartmentId,

    ProjectType,EmployeeType,TaskType,DepartmentType,
    AssignmentType,

```
        ProjectSetType,TaskSetType,AssignmentSetType,
        EmployeeSetType,DepartmentSetType,

     project, task, assignment, employee, department;

TYPE
   ProjectId      = String6;
   EmployeeId     = String5;
   TaskId         = String6;
   DepartmentId   = String3;

ProjectType = RECORD
                  project#: ProjectId;
                  title:     String25;
                  leader#:   EmployeeId;
                  customer: String20;
                  funds:     Real;
                  start:     Cardinal;
                  finish:    Cardinal
              END;

TaskType = RECORD
                  task#:        TaskId;
                  project#:     ProjectId;
                  department#: DepartmentId;
                  leader#:      EmployeeId;
                  title:        String54;
                  credit:       Real;
                  debit:        Real
              END;

AssignmentType = RECORD
                     task#:       TaskId;
                     employee#:EmployeeId;
                     role:        String12;
                     days:        Cardinal
                 END;

EmployeeType = RECORD
                   employee#:   EmployeeId;
                   name:         String25;
                   degree:       String5;
                   job:          String15;
                   rank:         String30;
                   experience:   Cardinal;
                   salary:       Real;
                   department#:DepartmentId
               END;
```

```
DepartmentType = RECORD
                    department#: DepartmentId;
                    name:        String54;
                    staff:       Cardinal;
                    manager#:    EmployeeId
                 END;

ProjectSetType      = ENTITY SET OF ProjectType;
TaskSetType         = ENTITY SET OF TaskType;
AssignmentSetType   = ENTITY SET OF AssignmentType;
EmployeeSetType     = ENTITY SET OF EmployeeType;
DepartmentSetType   = ENTITY SET OF DepartmentType;

VAR project:    ProjectSetType;
    task:       TaskSetType;
    assignment: AssignmentSetType;
    employee:   EmployeeSetType;
    department: DepartmentSetType;

END ProjectManagement.
```

4 The Relational Model of Data

The relational model of data is based on the observation that entity types are in fact relations in the following precise sense: *R is a relation over the sets T1,T2,...,Tn if and only if*

$$R <= T1 \times T2 \times \dots \times Tn,$$

where <= denotes the subset relation.

The structure of the relation R is described by the notation $R(A1,A2,...,An)$, where $Ai: R \rightarrow Ti$ is an attribute of R, and Ti is its type, for $i = 1,2,...,n$.

A *relational database* is a collection of time-varying relations. A *relational schema* is a description of the structure of relations in a relational database.

The *relational algebra* is a formal relational language consisting of a collection of operations over relations. The operations are chosen in such a way that most well-known types of queries may be expressed by their composition in a rather straightforward manner.

Let $R(A1,A2,...,An)$ be a relation, $X <= \{A1,A2,...,An\}$ and $Y = \{A1,A2,...,An\}/X$. By permuting the attributes of R, we can represent $R(A1,A2,...,An)$ as $R(X,Y)$. The result of the operation of projection of the relation R over the attributes X is denoted as $R[X]$ and defined as

(i) $R[X] = \{x : \text{there exists } y \text{ such that } (x,y) \text{ in } R(X,Y)\}$.

Example. Given a relation

EMPLOYEE(EMPLOYEE#,NAME,JOB,DEPARTMENT#)

the projection

EMPLOYEE[DEPARTMENT#,JOB]

represents a survey of jobs in particular departments.

Let $R(A1,A2,...,An)$ be a relation, and P a logical condition defined on the set $T1 \times T2 \times ... \times Tn$, where Ti is the type of the attribute Ai (for i = 1,2,...,n). The result of restricting the relation R with respect to the condition P is denoted as R[P] and defined as follows:

$$R[P] = \{x : x \text{ in } R \text{ and } P(x) \text{ is true}\}.$$

Example. Given a relation

EMPLOYEE(EMPLOYEE#,NAME,JOB,DEPARTMENT#),

its restriction

EMPLOYEE[JOB = " PROGRAMMER "]

represents a set of those employees who are programmers.

Let $A(A1,A2,...,An)$ and $B(B1,B2,...,Bm)$ be relations, and $X <= \{A1,A2,...,An\}$ and $Y <= \{B1,B2,...,Bm\}$ sets of attributes. Assume that X and Y contain the same number of attributes, and that the corresponding attributes have the same domain.

If $Z = \{A1,A2,...,An\}/X$ and $W = \{B1,B2,...,Bm\}/Y$, then by permuting the order of the attributes the relations A and B may be represented as A(Z,X) and B(Y,W), respectively. The natural join of the relations A and B over the attributes X and Y, respectively, is denoted as A[X = Y]B and defined as

$$A[X = Y]B = \{(z,x,w) : (z,x) \text{ in } A, (y,w) \text{ in } B \text{ and } x = y\}.$$

Observe, first of all, that A[X = Y]B is a relation whose set of attributes is the union of the sets Z,X (or Y) and W. The set A[X = Y]B is obtained by concatenating tuples from A with tuples from B whenever the values of X attributes are equal to the values of Y attributes. In addition, duplicate attributes (X or Y) are eliminated from the concatenated tuples.

Example. Given relations

EMPLOYEE(EMPLOYEE#,NAME,JOB,DEPARTMENT#)
DEPARTMENT(DEPARTMENT#,CITY)

the expression

EMPLOYEE[DEPARTMENT# = DEPARTMENT#]
                                    DEPARTMENT [NAME,CITY]

denotes the composition of two operations: the natural join of the relations
EMPLOYEE and DEPARTMENT over the attributes DEPARTMENT#,
and the projection of the result of the join operation on the attributes
NAME and CITY. The result of the composite operation is a set of employees together with the locations of their departments.

4.1 Functional dependencies and object identifiers

Given a relation $R(A1,A2,...,An)$ and two sets X and Y of its attributes
(i.e., $X <= \{A1,A2,...,An\}$ and $Y <= \{A1,A2,...,An\}$), denote with R[XY]
the projection of the relation R over the attributes $X \cup Y$. A functional
dependency $X \rightarrow Y$ exists in the relation $R(A1,A2,...,An)$ if and only if
R[XY] is in fact a function $R[X] \rightarrow R[Y]$ for every moment of time. If Y
$<= X$, then this condition trivially holds so that such a functional dependency is called *trivial*. This means that, whenever xy and xy' are tuples
of the relation R[XY] then, in fact, $y = y'$ holds. This is precisely the condition that says R[XY] is a function $R[X] \rightarrow R[Y]$. If the functional dependency $X \rightarrow Y$ does not exist, we write $X \nrightarrow Y$. In that case, R[XY] contains at least one pair xy and xy' of tuples where $y < > y'$.

   The property $X \rightarrow Y$ of the relation R is time independent. Although the
set of tuples R changes over time, as does R[XY], R[XY] remains a function for any specific moment of time. The fact that R[XY] viewed as a
set of pairs (x,y), changes over time means that $R[X] \rightarrow R[Y]$ is, in general,
a different function for two different moments of time.

   The above definition of functional dependency allows us to define precisely the notion of a key of a relation: If $R(A1,A2,...,An)$ is a relation
and X a set of its attributes $(X <= \{A1,A2,...,An\})$, then X is a key if and
only if

 (i) X functionally determines all attributes of the relation R; that is, $X \rightarrow Ai$
     for $i = 1,2,...,n$; and
(ii) no proper subset of X has that property; that is, if $X' <= X$, then
     $X' \nrightarrow Aj$ for some j $(j = 1,2,...,n)$.

   Observe that every relation has a key. Indeed, given a relation
$R(A1,A2,...,An)$, we obviously have $A1,A2,...,An \rightarrow A1,A2,...,An$. If
there is no X, $X < \{A1,A2,...,An\}$ such that $X \rightarrow Ai$ for all $i = 1,2,...,n$,
then $A1,A2,...,An$ is a key. Otherwise, X contains a key.

   Among all keys of the relation R, one is chosen to serve as the identifier
of the entity type represented by R. This key is called the *primary key*.
Its intention is that none of its attributes ever obtain an undefined (unknown) value, since otherwise we would not know what entity a tuple
with an undefined value of the primary key represents.

Properties of functional dependencies

 (i) *Reflexivity:* $X \rightarrow X$.

(ii) *Augmentation:* If $X \rightarrow Z$, then $XY \rightarrow Z$.
(iii) *Pseudotransitivity:* If $X \rightarrow Y$ and $YZ \rightarrow W$, then $XZ \rightarrow W$.

The above properties are rather intuitive, but can be checked formally as well. Given f: $X \rightarrow Z$, we obtain g: $XY \rightarrow Z$, defined as $(x,y) \rightarrow f(x)$ (augmentation). Given f: $X \rightarrow Y$ and g: $YZ \rightarrow W$, we obtain k: $XZ \rightarrow W$, defined as $(x,z) \rightarrow (g(f(x),z))$ (pseudotransitivity).

If the above properties are taken as basic (axioms), other important and also quite obvious properties of functional dependencies may be derived from them:

(iv) *Projectivity:* If $X => Y$, then $X \rightarrow Y$.
 (v) *Additivity:* If $X \rightarrow Y$ and $X \rightarrow Z$, then $X \rightarrow YZ$.
(vi) *Transitivity:* If $X \rightarrow Y$ and $Y \rightarrow Z$, then $X \rightarrow Z$.
(vii) *Distributivity:* If $X \rightarrow YZ$, then $X \rightarrow Y$ and $X \rightarrow Z$.
(viii) *Product:* If $X \rightarrow Y$ and $W \rightarrow Z$, then $XW \rightarrow YZ$.

Verification of these properties is left to the reader as an exercise.

The existence of some functional dependencies is an important determination of the behavior of the operations of the relational algebra. Suppose we substitute a relation with a pair of its projections. The question is whether we lost anything in the process—that is, whether it is possible to restore the initial relation applying the natural join operation to its projections. It turns out that the answer is affirmative only if some functional dependencies hold.

Consider a relation R(NAME,ROLE, DEPARTMENT), and suppose the attributes ROLE and DEPARTMENT are not functionally dependent on the attribute NAME (NAME↛ROLE and NAME↛DEPARTMENT). This assumption means that a person may have more than one role in one or more departments. This situation is illustrated by the following table, which represents the relation R(NAME,ROLE,DEPARTMENT) for some moment of time:

NAME	ROLE	DEPARTMENT	
a	r1	d1	
a	r2	d2	R(NAME,ROLE,DEPARTMENT)
b	r3	d1	

The projections R[NAME,ROLE] and R[NAME,DEPARTMENT] of the above relation would for the same moment of time be represented by the following tables:

NAME	ROLE
a	r1
a	r2
b	r3

R[NAME,ROLE]

NAME	DEPARTMENT
a	d1
a	d2
b	d1

R[NAME,DEPARTMENT]

The result of the natural join of the projections R[NAME,ROLE] and R[NAME,DEPARTMENT] is a relation that for the same moment of time is represented by the following table:

NAME	ROLE	DEPARTMENT
a	r1	d1
a	r1	d2
a	r2	d1
a	r2	d2
b	r3	d1

R[NAME,ROLE] [NAME = NAME]
R[NAME,DEPARTMENT]

The problem is now clear: From this last table, we derive the conclusion that there exists a person a who has role r2 in the department d1 and role r1 in the department d2. Both conclusions are wrong. It is easy to see that, if either NAME→ROLE or NAME→DEPARTMENT held, the problem would not have occurred. The relation R[NAME,ROLE] [NAME = NAME] R[NAME,DEPARTMENT] would have been equal to the relation R(NAME,ROLE,DEPARTMENT), precisely as one would expect. This observation may be generalized as follows:

If X→Y or X→Z holds for a relation R(XYZ), where X,Y,Z are sets of attributes, then R(XYZ) = R[XY] [X = X] R[XZ].

In order to prove this property we first observe that R(XYZ) is always a subset of R[XY] [X = X] R[XZ]. Indeed, if xyz in R(XYZ), then xy in R[XY], and xz in R[XZ]. Joining the tuples xy and xz, we obtain the tuple xyz, which means that xyz in R[XY] [X = X] R[XZ]. So every element of the relation R(XYZ) is also an element of the relation R[XY] [X = X] R[XZ].

We still have to prove that given X→Y or X→Z the converse is also true; that is, R[XY] [X = X] R[XZ] is a subset of R(XYZ). Suppose X→Y holds. An element of R[XY] [X = X] R[XZ] must have the form xyz. If xyz in R[XY] [X = X] R[XZ], then there exist y' and z', such that xyz' in R(XYZ) and xy'z in R(XYZ). But then X→Y implies y = y', that is, xyz in R(XYZ). So we have proved that every element of the relation R[XY] [X = X] R[XZ] is at the same time an element of the relation R(XYZ).

R(XYZ)< = R[XY] [X = X] R[XZ]   and   R[XY] [X = X] R[XZ] < = R(XYZ)   imply R(XYZ) = R[XY] [X = X] R[XZ].

4.2 Normal Forms

The basic relational model of data is largely based on the design principle that says that *every entity should be represented by a separate relation.*

This principle applies equally to all entities, including those that are, in fact, relationships. It hardly requires any justification.

In order to apply the above design principle, we need to have criteria that determine what a single entity is. Informal, semantic rules are very important, but often imprecise. *Normal forms* are formal rules for determining whether a relation represents a single entity or not. We already introduced the restrictions required by the first normal form, which simply asks for simple types (including strings) of attributes of relations. We will also present another, much stronger rule that is widely accepted and applies to relations assumed to be in first normal form. The rule is called *third normal form* (3NF).

Suppose that we are given a relation E(EMPLOYEE#, DEPARTMENT#,CITY) and that a triple (x,y,z) belongs to E if and only if the employee x works in department y located in city z. Furthermore, we will assume that an employee may work in only one department and a department is located in only one city. On the other hand, each department has a finite number of employees, and a number of departments may be located in one city. These assumptions are summarized below:

Example

E(EMPLOYEE#,DEPARTMENT#,CITY)
EMPLOYEE# → DEPARTMENT#
DEPARTMENT# ↛ EMPLOYEE#
DEPARTMENT# → CITY
CITY ↛ DEPARTMENT#

The above functional dependencies show that E contains attributes belonging to two different entities. One of these entities is EMPLOYEE, whose attributes are EMPLOYEE# and DEPARTMENT#; the other is DEPARTMENT, with attributes DEPARTMENT# and CITY. The fact that two different entities are represented by a single relation will cause the insertion, deletion, and update anomalies of this relation. In order to illustrate these anomalies, assume the relation E is for some specific moment of time represented by the following table:

EMPLOYEE#	DEPARTMENT#	CITY
a	A	X
b	A	X
c	A	X
d	B	Y
e	B	Y
f	C	X
g	C	X

The relation E(EMPLOYEE#,DEPARTMENT#,CITY) has the insertion anomaly since it is impossible to insert into it the information about the location of a department if it still has no employees. We cannot insert a triple $(-,y,z)$ in E, where $-$ denotes an unknown value, since EMPLOYEE# is the primary key of E and, as such, may never assume an undefined value.

The relation E also has the deletion anomaly. Indeed, if we delete the last employee of a specific department, we loose the information about the location of that department. This may be a quite undesirable side effect. A triple with an undefined value of the attribute EMPLOYEE# and specific values of the attributes DEPARTMENT# and CITY cannot be kept in E since EMPLOYEE# is the primary key of E.

The relation E has the update anomaly as well. It is caused by the fact that the same value of the attribute CITY is repeated for every employee tuple of a specific department. If the location of a department changes, we have to update all employee tuples of that department. Independent updates of the attribute CITY of the relation E are not permitted since they may lead to DEPARTMENT# $\nrightarrow$ CITY, which is contrary to the introduced assumptions.

If we replace the relation E(EMPLOYEE#,DEPARTMENT#,CITY) with its projections E[EMPLOYEE#,DEPARTMENT#], we obtain separate representation of two different entities, an employee and a department, and all the anomalies disappear. The existence of functional dependencies DEPARTMENT# $\rightarrow$ CITY guarantees that application of the natural join operation to E[EMPLOYEE#,DEPARTMENT#] and E[DEPARTMENT#,CITY] produces the original relation E, which can be verified for specific representations in our example.

EMPLOYEE#	DEPARTMENT#
a	A
b	A
c	A
d	B
e	B
f	C
g	C

E[EMPLOYEE#,DEPARTMENT#]

DEPARTMENT#	CITY
A	X
B	Y
C	X

E[DEPARTMENT#,CITY]

Formally, the fact that the relation E represents two different entities is characterized by the statement that the attribute CITY is transitively dependent on the key EMPLOYEE#. The department is an attribute of an employee, and thus EMPLOYEE#$\rightarrow$DEPARTMENT#. The city is an attribute of a department, and thus DEPARTMENT#$\rightarrow$CITY. There-

fore, CITY is not directly, but transitively dependent on EMPLOYEE#.
The notion of transitive dependency may be formally characterized as
follows:

(i) Let X,Y, and Z be distinct sets of attributes of the relation R. We say
that Z is transitively dependent on X if and only if the following conditions
hold:

$$X \rightarrow Y \qquad Y \nrightarrow X \qquad Y \rightarrow Z,$$

where the last functional dependency is not trivial.

Note that from (i) we conclude that $X \rightarrow Z$ and $Z \nrightarrow X$, whereas $Z \rightarrow Y$ is
neither required nor forbidden.

(ii) A relation R is in 3NF if and only if none of its nonkey attributes is
transitively dependent on any key of R.

In a prior example (the relation E(EMPLOYEE#,DEPARTMENT#,
CITY)), we showed that a relation not in 3NF may be substituted
by its projections (E[EMPLOYEE#,DEPARTMENT#] and
E[DEPARTMENT#,CITY]), which are in 3NF. Such a procedure is, in
general, possible.

(iii) If a relation R is not in 3NF, then there exists a decomposition of R
into a set of its projections, which are all in 3NF. Furthermore, this decomposition is such that the original relation may be restored applying
the natural join operation to the projections of R.

The proof of this property is based on the observation that, if $X \rightarrow Y$, $Y \nrightarrow X$,
and $Y \rightarrow Z$ holds for R, then R is first decomposed into its projections
R[XYW] and R[YZ], where W contains all the attributes that are neither
in X, nor in Y, nor in Z. If the above projections are not both in 3NF,
we continue the procedure, which ends in a finite number of steps since
we obtain binary relations in the worst case—and those are certainly in
3NF. Indeed, the existence of transitive dependencies in a binary relation
is obviously impossible.

5 Simple and Composite Actions

Statements denote actions that may be simple or structured. The simplest
kind of simple statement is the empty statement, which consists of no
symbols and performs the identity action. The assignment statement is
also simple. It replaces the current value of a variable by a new value
obtained by evaluating an expression. The syntax is as follows:

$$\text{Variable} := \text{Expression}$$

Generally, the variable and expression must be of the same type.

Example

salary : = salary ∗ 1.1
d.manager# : = e.employee#
d.staff : = d.staff - 1
balance : = credit - debit
p.price : = p.price + o.price ∗ l.quantity

Explicit assignments to the variables of the entity set type are not permitted. The standard operator Copy is used for this purpose.

The simplest kind of action structuring is sequential composition. The component statements are executed in the order in which they are written in a statement sequence:

Statement sequence

Statement1; Statement2; ...; StatementN

Example

e.employee# : = current + 1;
e.name : = f.name;
e.degree : = f.degree;
e.job : = '' programmer '' ;
e.department# : = '' R&D ''

Particular statements in the above sequence act on attributes (components) of the same record variable. Rather than qualifying each particular attribute with the identifier of that record variable, it is possible to use a more concise notation in which the whole statement sequence is qualified by the same identifier. In a statement sequence qualified in such a way, identifiers of record attributes are not prefixed by the identifier of the record variable.

Example

WITH e DO
   employee#: = current + 1;
   name: = f.name;
   degree: = f.degree;
   job: = '' programmer '' ;
   department: = '' R&D ''
END

The above is an example of a WITH statement, which has the following general form:

WITH RecordVariable

DO   StatementSequence
END

As noted above, references of particular attributes of RecordVariable in StatementSequence consist of identifiers of those attributes only.

The conditional composition of actions permits selection of one out of a finite number of actions. It is expressed using the IF statement. Two most frequently occurring forms of the IF statement are

IF Expression THEN
  StatementSequence
END

IF Expression THEN
  StatementSequence1
ELSE StatementSequence2
END

where Expression must be of type Boolean. In the first of the above two forms, Expression is evaluated and StatementSequence executed if this evaluation yields true. In the second form, StatementSequence1 is executed if the Expression is true, and StatementSequence2 if not.

The most general form of the IF statement is as follows:

IF Expression1 THEN StatementSequence1
ELSIF Expression2 THEN StatementSequence2

.
.
.

ELSE StatementSequenceN END

The above statement specifies sequential evaluation of Boolean expressions Expression1, Expression2, ..., ExpressionN. When and if an expression in this sequence yields true, the corresponding statement sequence (the one with the same index) is executed, and the execution of the IF statement completed. If none of the above expressions evaluates to true, the last statement sequence (StatementSequenceN) is executed.

Example

IF degree = PhD THEN job : = ProjectLeader
ELSIF degree = MSc THEN job: = TaskLeader
ELSE job: = TaskMember END

The case statement consists of an expression, called the selector, which must be of simple type, excluding the type Real, and a list of component statement sequences. The component statement sequences are labeled by constants of the type of the selector. The action the case statement specifies is the execution of that component statement sequence whose label equals the current value of the selector. It has the general form

```
CASE Expression OF
Label1: StatementSequence1  |
Label2: StatementSequence2  |
   .
   .
   .
LabelN: StatementSequenceN
ELSE StatementSequence
END
```

where the ELSE clause is optional. The last StatementSequence is executed if Expression $<>$ Labeli for all $i = 1,2,...,N$.

Although the IF statement permits specification of one out of a finite number of actions, it is in fact most frequently used for expressing conditional composition of one, two, and sometimes three component actions. The CASE composition is a more suitable way of expressing selective composition of N actions whose executions are mutually exclusive. The selection is performed in the manner similar to indexing, where the index is a value of simple type.

Example

```
CASE e.job OF
    ProjectLeader: e.salary : = e.salary*1.20  |
    TaskLeader:    e.salary : = e.salary*1.10  |
  ELSE             e.salary : = e.salary*1.05
END
```

Example

```
WriteString(" I)nsert,D)elete,M)odify,Q)uery ");
ReadResponse;
CASE Response OF
   "I": PerformInsertion  |
   "D": PerformDeletion  |
   "M": PerformUpdate  |
   "Q": ExecuteQuery  |
ELSE WrongResponse
END
```

Example

```
TYPE ExceptionType = (None,InvalidMonth,InvalidDay,InvalidYear);

VAR Exception: ExceptionType;
```

```
CASE Exception OF
  None:          WriteString("Correct date entry")  |
  InvalidMonth:  WriteString("Invalid month")  |
  InvalidDay:    WriteString("Invalid day")  |
  InvalidYear:   WriteString("Invalid year")
END
```

The WHILE statement has the following form:

```
WHILE Expression DO
  StatementSequence
END
```

Expression in the above statement must be of type Boolean. While this expression yields the value true, StatementSequence is executed repeatedly. When (if ever) it yields false, the repetition process terminates. If its value is false at the beginning, StatementSequence is not executed at all.

The REPEAT-UNTIL statement has the following form:

```
REPEAT StatementSequence
UNTIL   Expression
```

The sequence of statements between the symbols REPEAT and UNTIL is executed repeatedly until (if ever) the expression evaluates to true. At least one repetition takes place, which is the essential difference in comparison with the WHILE-DO statement.

WHILE-DO and REPEAT-UNTIL repetitive statements are attractive since they clearly exhibit one termination condition at a point that is syntactically obvious. Nevertheless, there exist situations in which it is more appropriate to control the termination of the repetitive statement at one or more points within the repeated statement sequence. Such situations require a generalization of the WHILE-DO and REPEAT-UNTIL statements, called the LOOP statement. It has the following seemingly simple form:

```
LOOP
  StatementSequence
END
```

Termination of repetitions is performed by execution of the Exit statement, as illustrated in the following example:

Example

```
LOOP WriteString("Last candidate? Y/N>");
     ReadCh(Ch);
     CASE Ch OF
```

```
      "Y", "y": LastCandidate: = true;
                  Exit |
      "N","n": LastCandidate: = false;
                  Exit
   ELSE WriteString("Wrong answer!")
   END
END
```

Using the above LOOP statement, we can now produce a more complete example of insertion of a set of candidates. The example contains a composition of LOOP, REPEAT-UNTIL, and CASE statements:

Example

```
TYPE Candidate = RECORD name: String30;
                        score: Cardinal
            END;

VAR Candidates: ENTITY SET OF Candidate;
    c: Candidate;
    Ch: Char;
    LastCandidate: Boolean;
    .
    .

REPEAT WriteString("Enter candidate's name and score");
       ReadString(c.name); ReadString(c.score);
       Insert(c,Candidates);
       LOOP WriteString("Last candidate? Y/N>");
            ReadCh(Ch);
            CASE Ch OF
               "Y", "y": LastCandidate: = true;
                          Exit |
               "N", "n": LastCandidate: = false;
                          Exit
            ELSE WriteString("Wrong answer!")
            END
       END
UNTIL LastCandidate
```

Example

```
FireDepartmentManager;
LOOP SelectReplacement;
     IF ReplacementSelected
     THEN ReplaceManager
          Exit
     END
END
```

The justification for the LOOP statement in this particular case comes from the fact that the loop in the above example is meant to be endless: There is no way to get out of it unless a replacement is selected.

The FOREACH statement has the following syntax:

```
FOREACH RangeList
WHERE    Expression
DO StatementSequence
END
```

The FOREACH statement contains first a range list whose elements are of the form r IN R, where r is a record variable of type T, and R is a variable of type ENTITY SET OF T. The variable r is called the *control variable*, and R is its range within the FOREACH statement, so that r is bound to R within that statement. The FOREACH statement also contains a qualification condition that is a Boolean expression.

The body of the FOREACH statement contains arbitrary statements; in particular, it may contain another FOREACH statement. Nesting FOREACH statements in this way is particularly important since it represents one way of expressing relational joins.

The meaning of the FOREACH statement may be described informally as follows: The body of the FOREACH statement is executed for all tuples (records) of the range relations assigned to the corresponding control variables for which the value of the qualification expression is true.

In what follows, examples of the FOREACH statement are presented in order to illustrate how it can be used in specifying queries as well as data-manipulation actions.

Example. Print the names of all employees who hold an M.Sc. degree and whose salaries are each greater than $50,000:

```
FOREACH e IN employee
WHERE    (e.degree = "M.Sc.")
AND      (e.salary > 50000)
DO       WriteString(e.name);
         WriteLn
END
```

Example. Print the names and salaries of all employees who hold an M.Sc. degree and who manage departments with more than 10 employees:

```
FOREACH e IN employee
WHERE    e.degree = "M.Sc."
DO       FOREACH d IN department
         WHERE (d.manager# = e.employee#)
         AND   (d.staff > 10)
         DO    WriteString(e.name); WriteString(" ");
               WriteReal(e.salary,7); WriteLn
         END
END
```

The above nesting of unary FOREACH statements may be substituted by an explicit binary FOREACH statement as follows:

```
FOREACH e IN employee, d IN department
WHERE     (e.degree  =  " M.Sc. ")
AND       (d.manager# = e.employee#)
AND       (d.staff > 10)
DO        WriteString(e.name); WriteString(" ")
          WriteReal(e.salary,7); WriteLn
END
```

Example. Increase the salaries of all employees who are programmers by 10%.

```
FOREACH e IN employee
WHERE     e.job = " programmer"
DO        e.salary : = e.salary * 1.1
END
```

The above is an example of an update action that is required to be defined on single relations. In other words, an assignment to a control variable is allowed only in the body of a unary FOREACH statement.

Example. The Exit statement is also useful in the statement sequence of the FOREACH statement where it can cause termination by a condition that is not conveniently expressed in the qualification expression. In order to illustrate such a situation, a previously given example of the LOOP statement is now elaborated completely using the LOOP and FOREACH statements, as well as the Exit statement in both of them.

```
FOREACH e IN employee
WHERE     e.employee# = manager#
DO        Delete(e,employee);
          department#: = e.department#
END;
LOOP
  replacement#: = EmptyString;
  FOREACH e IN employee
  WHERE     e.department# = department#
  DO WriteEmployee(e);
     WriteString(" NewManager?Y/N ");
     ReadCh(Ch);
     IF (Ch = " Y ") OR (Ch = " y ") THEN
        replacement#: = e.employee#;
        Exit (*FOREACH*)
     END
  END;
```

```
   IF replacement# < > EmptyString THEN
      FOREACH d IN department
      WHERE d.department# = department#
      DO d.manager#: = replacement#
      END;
      Exit (*LOOP*)
   END
END
```

Example. Print the titles of all projects whose customer is NSF, and whose leader holds Ph.D. degree and is the manager of a department with more than 10 employees.

```
FOREACH p IN project
WHERE     p.customer = "NSF"
DO        FOREACH e IN employee
          WHERE     (p.leader# = e.employee#)
          AND       (e.degree =  "Ph.D.")
          DO        FOREACH   d IN department
                    WHERE (d.manager# = e.employee#)
                    AND     (d.staff > 10)
                    DO        WriteString (p.title); WriteLn
                    END
          END
END
```

An update action is required to be defined on single relations. In other words, an assigment to a control variable is allowed only in the body of a unary FOREACH statement. The same restriction holds for insertion and deletion actions. In spite of this restriction, which is dictated by data-integrity requirements, it is still possible to specify update actions that require relational joins. That is accomplished by nesting the FOREACH statements, as in the following example:

Example. Increase by 10% the salaries of all employees with an M.Sc. degree who are leaders of their projects and whose customer is NSF.

```
FOREACH p IN project
WHERE     p. customer = "NSF"
DO        FOREACH e IN employee
          WHERE     (e.employee# = p.leader#)
          AND       (e.degree = "M.Sc.")
          DO        e. salary := e.salary * 1.1
          END
END
```

6 Arrays

The type definition

TYPE ArrayType = ARRAY SimpleType OF
                       Type

specifies a new type, ArrayType, whose elements are arrays of elements
of Type indexed by elements of SimpleType.

Algebraically, ArrayType is in fact a set

$$[SimpleType \rightarrow Type]$$

of all functions whose domain is SimpleType and whose codomain is Type.
Because elements of ArrayType are functions, the basic action associated with ArrayType is *function evaluation*, or *indexing* since the domain
of these functions is linearly ordered. Given A in ArrayType and *a* in
SimpleType, the result of indexing is denoted as A[a] and, of course, A[a]
in Type.

Since A is an array of elements taken from the set Type, another fundamental action is a sequence of identical actions upon the components
of A, one such action per element of SimpleType. For example, in order
to actually construct a function from the function set [SimpleType →
Type], we need to specify an element of its codomain Type for each element of its domain SimpleType. The required action-composition rule is
called the FOR statement. Its simplest form is as follows:

FOR ControlVariable : = StartingValue TO Limit
DO   StatementSequence
END

The above FOR statement specifies repeated execution of Statement-
Sequence, while ControlVariable assumes values from the range
StartingValue..Limit. StartingValue, Limit, and ControlVariable must be
of (assignment) compatible types. ControlVariable should not be changed
by StatementSequence since in that case the above definition of the semantics of the FOR statement makes no sense.

Example

TYPE Hours = [0..23];

VAR Temperature: ARRAY Hours OF Integer;
       Hour, HotHour: Hours;
       MaxTemperature: Integer;

.
.
.

MaxTemperature : = −999;
FOR Hour : = 0 TO 23 DO
    IF Temperature [Hour] > MaxTemperature
    THEN MaxTemperature : = Temperature [Hour];
          HotHour : = Hour
    END
END

Since we placed no restrictions on the type of the array elements, the following type definition is also quite acceptable:

TYPE A = ARRAY T1 OF
           ARRAY T2 OF T

A is a set of functions whose domain is T1, and whose codomain is a set of functions with domain T2 and codomain T. But then there exists an obvious bijection:

$$[T1{\rightarrow}[T2{\rightarrow}T]] = [T1 \times T2{\rightarrow}T].$$

Indeed given A in [T1→[T2→T]], the corresponding B in [T1 × T2→T] is determined as

$$A[t1][t2] = B[t1,t2],$$

and vice versa.

Because of this the equivalent notation is

TYPE A = ARRAY T1,T2 OF T,

which makes more explicit the fact that we have a two-dimensional array A of elements of type T indexed by pairs of elements [t1,t2], where t1 in T1 and t2 in T2.

In general, the type definition

TYPE A = ARRAY T1,T2,...,Tn OF T

is equivalent to the following:

TYPE A = ARRAY T1 OF
           ARRAY T2 OF

                .
                .
                .

           ARRAY Tn OF T

Example

TYPE Months   = (Jan,Feb,Mar,Apr,May,Jun,Jul,Aug,
                    Sep,Oct,Nov,Dec);
    Hours   = [0..23];
    Days   = [1..31];

```
VAR Temperature: ARRAY Months,Days,Hours OF Integer;
    Hour, HotHour: Hours;
    Day, HotDay: Days;
    Month, HotMonth: Months;
    Max: Integer;
    MonthLength: ARRAY Months OF Days;
    .
    .
    .
Max : =  - 999;
FOR Month : = Jan TO Dec DO
    FOR Day : = 1 TO MonthLength [Month] DO
        FOR Hour : = 0 TO 23 DO
            IF Temperature [Month,Day,Hour] > Max
            THEN Max : = Temperature [Month,Day,Hour];
                    HotHour   : = Hour;
                    HotDay    : = Day;
                    HotMonth : = Month
            END
        END (*Hour*)
    END (*Day*)
END (*Month*)
```

If we attempt to construct the array

MonthLength: ARRAY Months OF Days,

we observe that a more general form of the FOR statement, given below, would in fact be convenient:

```
FOR ControlVariable : = InitialValue TO LimitValue BY Step
DO   StatementSequence
END
```

This is in fact the general form of the FOR statement in which StatementSequence is executed for each value of ControlVariable taken from the range [InitialValue..LimitValue], where the first value is InitialValue, and every subsequent one is determined by the previous one and the value of Step. So if, for example, Step is 2, every second value in the specified range is assigned to ControlVariable, and Statement-Sequence is executed for each such value. This is illustrated in the following example:

```
TYPE Months = (Jan,Feb,Mar,Apr,May,Jun,Jul,Aug,
                  Sep,Oct,Nov,Dec);
     Days    = [0..31];

VAR Month: Months; LeapYear: Boolean;
    MonthLength = ARRAY Months OF Days;
```

.
.
.

```
FOR Month : = Jan TO Jul BY 2 DO
    MonthLength [Month] : = 31
END;
FOR Month : = Aug TO Dec BY 2 DO
    MonthLength [Month] : = 31
END;
FOR Month : = Apr TO Jun BY 2 DO
    MonthLength [Month] : = 30
END;
FOR Month : = Sep TO Nov BY 2 DO
    MonthLength [Month] : = 30
END;
IF LeapYear THEN MonthLength [Feb] : = 29
ELSE MonthLength [Feb] : = 28
END
```

7 Small Set Types

Consider the type definition

```
TYPE Exception = (InvalidYear, InvalidMonth, InvalidDay);
     ExceptionSet = SET OF Exception
```

which is intended to specify the integrity violations that may occur when a date is specified in the usual format as a string Year/Month/Day. The actual violation is a small set of possible exceptions (errors). Those sets are subsets of the set Exception, and the type ExceptionSet is the power set (the set of all subsets) of the set Exception. So the elements (values) of the type ExceptionSet are

{ },

{InvalidYear},{InvalidMonth},{InvalidDay},

{InvalidYear,InvalidMonth},{InvalidYear,InvalidDay},
{InvalidMonth,InvalidDay},

{InvalidYear,InvalidMonth,InvalidDay},

where { } denotes the empty set.

   In general, given a small enumeration or a subrange type T, the type definition

```
TYPE S = SET OF T
```

defines a new type S, which represents the power set $\mathscr{P}(T)$ of T. The type S is equipped with the usual relations and operations. Of course, the fundamental relation is that of membership denoted as

a IN A

where, if A is of type SET OF T, then *a* must be of type T. The Boolean expression a IN A is true if a is an element of the set A, and false otherwise.

The subset relation is denoted as

$$A <= B,$$

where A and B are of the same set type, and the above Boolean expression is true if A is a subset of the set B; that is, whenever *a* IN A, then a IN B. The equality of sets = is also available with the usual meaning:

$$A = B \qquad (A <= B) \text{ AND } (B <= A).$$

A set type is naturally equipped with the standard set operators denoted as follows:

+   set union,
*   set intersection,
−   set difference, and
/   symmetric set difference.

The operands of the above set operators must be of the same set type, which is also the type of the result. The semantics of these operators may easily be defined in terms of the membership relation and the logical operators:

x IN (A + B) <=> (x IN A) OR (x IN B)
x IN (A*B) <=> (x IN A) AND (x IN B)
x IN (A − B) <=> (x IN A) AND NOT (x IN B)
x IN (A/B)   <=> (x IN A) < > (x IN B)

Example. Consider the following set of functional dependencies

Name → Address, AptNum
Address, AptNum → Rent
AptType, Address → Size
Address → LandLord

and their representation in the programming language notation:

```
TYPE Attribute = (Name,Address,AptNum,AptType,Rent,
                   Size,LandLord);
     AttributeSet = SET OF AttributeType;
     Dependency = RECORD Domain: AttributeSet;
                          Codomain: AttributeSet
                   END;
     DependencyArray = ARRAY [1..4] OF Dependency;
```

VAR Fd: DependencyArray;

.

.

.

Fd [1].Domain := AttributeSet{Name};
Fd [1].Codomain := AttributeSet{Address, AptNum};
Fd [2].Domain := AttributeSet{Address, AptNum};
Fd [2].Codomain := AttributeSet{Rent};
Fd [3].Domain := AttributeSet{AptType,Address};
Fd [3].Codomain := AttributeSet{Size};
Fd [4].Domain := AttributeSet{Address};
Fd [4].Codomain := AttributeSet{LandLord}

This example illustrates proper use of the identifier of a small-set type (an enumeration of set elements) that must precede a constant of that type. This requirement does not apply to small sets of cardinals.

Frequently occurring actions of adding and dropping an element from a small set are particular cases of set union $(+)$ and set difference $(-)$, respectively. They may also be expressed more concisely, and more efficiently, using the standard procedures Include and Exclude defined as follows: Suppose $T = $ SET OF E is a small-set type, S a variable of type T, and x a variable or constant of type E. Then, Include(x, S) is equivalent to

$$S := S + T\{x\},$$

and Exclude(x,S) is equivalent to

$$S := S - T\{x\}.$$

Example. In order to illustrate relations and operations associated with small-set types, consider the following basic and derived properties of functional dependencies and their representation in the programming language notation, where X,Y,Z, and W denote sets of attributes of a relation R:

(i)   *Projectivity:*   If $Y <= X$, then $X \rightarrow Y$.
(ii) *Additivity:*   If $X \rightarrow Y$ and $X \rightarrow Z$, then $X \rightarrow YZ$.
(iii) *Transitivity:*   If $X \rightarrow Y$ and $Y \rightarrow Z$, then $X \rightarrow Z$.
(iv) *Distributivity:*   If $X \rightarrow YZ$, then $X \rightarrow Y$ and $X \rightarrow Z$.
(v)   *Product:*   If $X \rightarrow Y$ and $W \rightarrow Z$, then $XW \rightarrow YZ$.
(vi) *Pseudotransitivity:* If $X \rightarrow Y$ and $YZ \rightarrow W$, then $XZ \rightarrow W$.
(vii) *Augmentation:*   If $X \rightarrow Z$, then $XY \rightarrow Z$.

```
TYPE Attributes = EnumerationOfAttributes;
     AttributeSet = SET OF Attributes;
     Dependency = RECORD Domain: AttributeSet;
                         Codomain: AttributeSet
           END;
```

VAR X,Y,Z,W: AttributeSet;
   f,g,k: Dependency

Projectivity

If Y <= X THEN f.Domain := X;
            f.Codomain := Y
   END

Additivity

IF f.Domain = g.Domain THEN
  k.Domain := f.Domain;
  k.Codomain := f.Domain + g.Domain
END

Transitivity

IF f.Codomain = g.Domain THEN
  k.Domain := f.Domain;
  k.Codomain := g.Codomain
END

Distributivity

IF Y <= k.Codomain THEN
  f.Domain := k.Domain;
  f.Codomain := Y;
  g.Domain := k.Domain;
  g. Codomain := k.Domain − Y
END

Product

  k.Domain := f.Domain + g.Domain;
  k.Codomain := f.Codomain + g.Codomain

Pseudotransitivity

IF f.Codomain <= g.Domain THEN
  k.Codomain := g.Codomain;
  k.Domain := g.Domain − f.Codomain + f.Domain
END

Augmentation

  k.Domain := f.Domain + Y;
  k.Codomain := f.Codomain

A particular form of the FOREACH statement is applicable to small sets:

FOREACH x IN S
DO StatementSequence END

In this statement, x is a variable whose type is a small enumeration T so that the type of S is SET OF T.

Examples of use of the FOREACH statement for the specification of actions on small sets appear in the next section, as well as in the section on recursive procedures in the next chapter.

8 Schema Synthesis Algorithms

This section is devoted to the following well-known problem: *Given a set F of functional dependencies of an application environment, synthesize a 3NF relational schema of that environment.* This problem, interesting and important from the formal viewpoint, is chosen as an illustration of algorithms related to formal systems. It also employs a fair amount of the programming language apparatus introduced thus far. The applicability of the presented formal (and algorithmic) approach to data modeling is rather limited. In fact, this book relies on much more subtle, conceptual modeling techniques, introduced in Chapter 3.

A rather obvious, naive algorithm for the above problem is straight-forward:

Naive algorithm

(i) Partition F into groups of functional dependencies in such a way that all functional dependencies belonging to the same group have identical domains. These are candidate keys for the relations synthesized in the next step.

(ii) For each group obtained in step (i), construct a relation that has all the attributes appearing in the domain and codomains of the functional dependencies in that group.

The following example shows that the above simple algorithm is not correct; that is, it does not accomplish the 3NF synthesis task:

Example

$f1: A \rightarrow B$ $f3: B \rightarrow C$
$f2: A \rightarrow C$ $f4: B \rightarrow D$

$f5: D \rightarrow B$ $f6: ABE \rightarrow F$

These functional dependencies have already been partitioned into groups having the same domain side, so that the naive algorithm produces the following relational schema:

R1 (A,B,C)   R2 (B,C,D)
R3 (D,B)   R4 (A,B,E,F)

There are three basic problems exhibited by this example:

(i) The synthesized relations are not in 3NF. Indeed, R1 contains a transitive dependency A → B, B → C; and R4 a transitive dependency AE → A, A → B.

(ii) The common domains of functional dependencies in the same group are not necessarily keys of the synthesized relations. Indeed, ABE in R4 is not a key since A → B, so that B is redundant and the key is *AE*.

(iii) The naive algorithm synthesizes too many relations. The functional dependency D → B must be represented in R2 (in addition to B → C and B → D) in order for the synthesized model to be a model of the application environment described by F. So the relation R3 is formally redundant in that model.

All these problems are caused by redundancies in the given set of functional dependencies that represent the input of the naive synthesis algorithm. Indeed, given f1: A → B, the attribute B is redundant in f6: ABE → F. Given f1: A → B and f3: B → C, f2: A → C is redundant. These redundancies are caused by the fact that given a set of functional dependencies one can derive other functional dependencies using the previously introduced formal properties of functional dependencies. One obvious property used above is transitivity, which establishes f2 given f1 and f2.

Closure of a set of functional dependencies. Given a set F of functional dependencies of an application environment, we can derive formally other functional dependencies valid in that environment using the basic and derived properties of functional dependencies. The set of all functional dependencies derivable from F by repeated applications of those rules is called the *closure* of F and is denoted as F^+.

   Although F^+ is intended to contain all functional dependencies valid in an application environment (i.e., represents a complete description of all functional relationships in that environment), dealing directly with that set is undesirable for semantic and computational reasons. Indeed, even for small sets F of functional dependencies, the set of F^+ is prohibitively large since it contains a large number of redundant functional relationships following obviously from a small subset of F^+. A subset G of F^+ is a covering of F if $G^+ = F^+$. In other words, any set of functional dependencies that generates the same closure F^+ as F is a covering of F. But observe that such a set is not required to be a subset of F. A covering G of F is nonredundant if it contains no proper subset that is also a covering of F. Given these definitions we can be more precise about what we mean by a redundant functional dependency and a redundant attribute in a given set of functional dependencies.

(i) Let f: X → A be a functional dependency. An attribute B is redundant in f, with respect to a given set of functional dependencies F to which f belongs, if B in X and (X-{B}) → A belongs to F^+.

(ii) A functional dependency f is redundant in a set of functional dependencies F if $(F-\{f\})^+ = F^+$.

We are now ready for a synthesis algorithm that actually accomplishes the stated task.

Synthesis algorithm. Let F be a given set of functional dependencies.

  (i) Eliminate all redundant attributes in the domains of functional dependencies in the set F. Denote the set obtained this way as G.
 (ii) Find a nonredundant covering H of G.
(iii) Partition the nonredundant covering H into groups such that all functional dependencies in the same group have the same set of attributes as their domain.
(iv) For each group obtained in the previous step, construct a relation with attributes that appear in the domain and the codomains of the functional dependencies in that group.

It is important to note that the common sets of attributes (domains) of the groups of functional dependencies specified in step (iii) will in fact be keys of the relations constructed in step (iv).

The above algorithm is a simplified version of the algorithm due to Bernstein and Beeri. It synthesizes provably 3NF relations from a given set of functional dependencies. We do not present verification of correctness for this algorithm, but we do mention that it requires a proof that a transitive dependency implies the existence of a redundant functional dependency in a nonredundant covering. Together with elimination of redundant attributes that also takes care of keys, we obtain the desired result.

Now consider the first two steps of the presented algorithm, since the implementation of the remaining steps is much more obvious. In order to determine whether an attribute B is redundant in f: $X \rightarrow A$, we use the following abstract algorithm to reduce X to X', where $X' \rightarrow A$ and X' does not contain redundant attributes:

```
X' := Domain[f];
FOREACH B IN Domain[f]
DO IF ((X' - {B}) →A) IN F
    THEN X' := X' - {B}
    END
END
```

This approach requires an efficient test of membership of a functional dependency ($(X' - \{B\}) \rightarrow A$ in this case) in the closure F^+ of a given set of functional dependencies F.

The implementation for the second step in the synthesis algorithm may be described by the following abstract algorithm, which constructs a subset G of F that is a nonredundant covering of F:

```
G := F;
FOREACH f IN F
```

```
DO IF f IN (G – {f})⁺
     THEN G := G – {f}
     END
END
```

It is straightforward to see that the above algorithm also requires an efficient test of membership of a functional dependency f in the closure of a given set of functional dependencies ((G – {f})⁺ in this particular case).

In order to construct an algorithm for testing membership of a functional dependency f: $X \rightarrow A$ in the closure F^+ of a given set of functional dependencies F, we compute the set Depend of attributes that are functionally dependent on X. Having done this, our test amounts to checking whether the codomain A of the given functional dependency f: $X \rightarrow A$ is contained in Depend. If $A <= $ Depend, then f in F^+.

Now consider the computation of the set Depend. We start with the domain X of f since, by reflexivity, X is dependent on itself. We then repeatedly select a functional dependency f': $Y \rightarrow B$, whose domain Y is contained in X and whose codomain B is not, and include the codomain B in Depend. This step is justified by projectivity and transitivity. Indeed, we have $X \rightarrow$ Depend, Depend $\rightarrow$ Y (since $Y <= $ Depend), and f': $Y \rightarrow$ B, so that the composition of these functional dependencies produces the functional dependency $X \rightarrow B$, indicating that B should be included in Depend.

The above described algorithm is now specified in the programming language notation, where the range of integers [1..m] is used to index (identify) attributes from the set {A1,A2,...,Am}, and the range [1..n] is used to index functional dependencies in the set F = {f1,f2,...,fn}. The functional dependencies are represented as arrays Domain and Codomain of sets of attributes (integers from [1..m]) indexed by functional dependencies (integers from [1..n]). X, A, and Depend are also sets of indexes to attributes.

```
TYPE Attribute = [1..m];
     Dependency = [1..n];
     AttributeSet = SET OF Attribute;
     DependencySet = SET OF Dependency;

VAR  Domain, Codomain: ARRAY Dependency OF AttributeSet;
     X,A,Depend: AttributeSet;
     fd: Dependency; att: Attribute;
     Member, Done: Boolean;

     .
     .
     .
Depend := X;
REPEAT Done := true;
```

```
            FOR fd : = 1 TO n DO
                IF (Domain[fd] < = Depend)
                AND NOT (Codomain[fd] < = Depend)
                THEN Depend : = Depend + Codomain[i];
                       Done: = false
                END
            END
UNTIL Done;
Member : = true;
FOREACH att IN A
DO IF NOT (att IN Depend)
    THEN Member : = false;
       Exit
    END
END
```

An improvement of the presented membership algorithm is based on the following observations:

(i) Once an attribute Ai in Domain[fd] is found to be in Depend (i.e., $X \rightarrow Ai$), that attribute need never be examined again and can be removed from all the domains of functional dependencies in which it appears. Indeed, if we know that $X \rightarrow Ai$, then in order to establish that $X \rightarrow A1,A2,...,Ai,...,Am$ it suffices to show that $X \rightarrow A1,A2,...,Am$.

(ii) Likewise, an attribute Bi in Codomain[fd] need only be examined once, namely, when it has been established that Domain[fd] < = Depend, in which case all Bi in Codomain[fd] should be included in Depend as in the previous algorithm.

While the already presented algorithm iterates over the given set of functional dependencies, the improved algorithm iterates over the set NewDepend of attributes that remain to be considered for inclusion in Depend. Both NewDepend and Depend are initially set to X as in the previous algorithm.

An attribute is selected and removed from NewDepend. Then, only those functional dependencies are considered whose domains contain the selected attribute, which is removed from those domains. If any of those domains remains empty, the corresponding codomain is included in Depend and NewDepend. The process is repeated until NewDepend is reduced to the empty set:

```
Depend : = X; NewDepend : = Depend;
REPEAT NextAtt : = SelectFrom(NewDepend);
        Exclude(NewDepend,NextAtt);
        FOREACH fd of NextAtt DO
          Exclude(NextAtt,Domain[fd]);
          IF Domain[fd] = AttributeSet{ } THEN
```

```
                    Depend : = Depend + Domain[fd];
                    NewDepend : = NewDepend + Domain[fd]
              END
          END
UNTIL NewDepend = AttributeSet{ };
Member : = true;
FOREACH att IN A
DO IF NOT (att IN Depend)
    THEN Member : = false;
            Exit
    END
END
```

In the above algorithm, SelectFrom denotes selection of an arbitrary element from a set.

To avoid scanning of all functional dependencies in each repetition of the above algorithm in order to determine those whose domain contains NextAtt, the array of sets FdsOfAttr whose type is ARRAY[Attribute] OF DependencySet is computed first by a single scan of the given set of functional dependencies:

```
FOR att := 1 TO m DO FdsOfAttr[attr] := { } END;
FOR fd := 1 TO n DO
    FOREACH a IN Domain[fd]
    DO Include(fd,FdsOfAttr[a])
    END
END
```

With the above initialization, the FOREACH loop FOREACH fd of NextAtt DO becomes FOREACH fd IN FdsOfAttr[NextAtt].

Exercises

(1) Repetitive Structures

   (i) Assuming the semantics of the statements

   FOREACH r IN R   IF Q THEN S END
   DO S END

   have been defined, specify the semantics of the following statement:

   FOREACH r IN R
   WHERE Q
   DO S END

(ii) Assuming the semantics of the statements

FOREACH r IN R   FOREACH r IN R
WHERE Q   DO S END
DO S END

have been defined, specify the semantics of the following statement:

FOREACH r1 IN R1, r2 IN R2,..., rn IN Rn
WHERE Q
DO S END

(iii) Express the statements

WHILE B DO S END

REPEAT S UNTIL B END

FOR x: = a TO b BY c
DO S END

using the LOOP statement with one exit.

(2) Arrays and Repetitive Composition

(i) The following data structures are meant to represent the availability of a lecture hall:

TYPE WorkDays = (Mon,Tue,Wed,Thu,Fri);
    WorkHours = [9..16];

VAR HallOccupied = ARRAY [WorkDays,WorkHours] OF
                          Boolean

(ii) Specify decompositions of the following actions:
     Find the first available term and set the variables Day, Time, and Found appropriately.
     Find the next available term where this action is meant to be applied, either after Find first or Find next actions. This action also sets the variables Day, Time, and Found appropriately.
     Free term that tests whether the lecture hall is occupied on a given Day and at a given Time.
     Reserve the term action that for a given Day and Time performs reservation of the lecture hall—only if it is not already occupied of course.
     Clear the schedule action that sets all the terms of the lecture hall free.

(3) Nested Structures

(i) Consider the following hierarchy of object types:

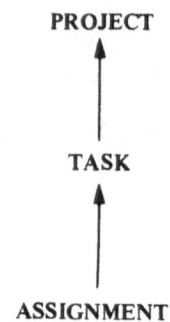

PROJECT

TASK

ASSIGNMENT

The attributes of these object types are specified as in the project management database:

TYPE ProjectType   = RECORD project#: ProjectId;
                                        (* other attributes *)
                     END;

      TaskType   = RECORD task#: TaskId;
                                        project#: ProjectId;
                                        (* other attributes *)
                     END;

      AssignmentType = RECORD task#: TaskId;
                                        (* other attributes *)
                     END

(ii) Specify the following actions:

Insert project   record
Delete project   record
Insert task   record
Delete task   record
Insert assignment record
Delete assignment record

Insertion of a project record requires checking whether the identifier of the project to be inserted already exists in the database. If so, the variable Exception is set appropriately, and the insertion is not performed.

Deletion of a project record with a given project identifier, apart from first checking the existence of such a record, requires deletion of not only the record, but also all the associated task records.

Insertion of a task record requires checking the existence of its associated project record in the database, as well as of the uniqueness of the task identifier. Violation of these conditions sets Exception appropriately and aborts insertion.

Deletion of a task with a given task identifier requires deletion of all its associated assignments.

Insertion of an assignment record requires the existence of the associated task record. To summarize, the basic principle that applies to all the required actions is that the *insertion of an object instance requires the existence of its predecessor in the above hierarchy.*

Deletion of an object instance requires deletion of all its associated (direct or indirect) successors in the above hierarchy.

(iii) Specify the exceptions that may occur during execution of the above actions, and choose the type of the variable Exception as an appropriate enumeration of those exceptions.

(4) Selection and Update

(i) Consider the following two objects from the project management application environment

PROJECT

EMPLOYEE

where the arrow specifies the leader function. The attributes of these two objects are specified as in the project management database.

(ii) Specify decomposition of the action Change leader of the project with a given identifier. Decomposition of the above action requires selection of an appropriate project leader (action Select employee). Assume the new leader is selected among those with the same degree and rank as the old leader (if possible). Candidates for the replacement are displayed to the terminal user (assume the existence of the action WriteEmployee), who selects the desired replacement. Use the Exit statement to terminate the search as soon as the replacement is selected.

(iii) Specify possible exceptions that may occur during the execution of the above actions, and inform the terminal user about them.

(iv) Modify the above decomposition so that it corresponds to the action that performs the replacement of a project leader in all the projects where he performs that role. The replacement should be taken from the department of the old project leader.

(5) Division

  (i) Suppose A(A1,A2,...,An) and B(B1,B2,...,Bm) are entity types such that there exists $Y <= \{A1,A2,...,An\}$ that is of the same type as B, in the sense that Y has m attributes and the corresponding attributes in the sets Y and {B1,B2,...,Bm} are of the same type. Then we can denote entity types A and B as A(X,Y) and B(Z), respectively, where Y and Z are type-compatible in the above defined sense and define the result of division of A(X,Y) with B(Z), denoted A[Y : Z]B, as the maximal subset of the projection A[X] such that its Cartesian product with B(Z) is still contained in A(X,Y). More precisely, the set A[Y : Z]B is defined by the following two conditions:

(a) $A(X,Y) = A[Y :Z] \times B \cup O(X,Y),$

  where A[Y :Z]B is the quotient, and O(X,Y) the remainder of division.

(b) Given $C <= A[X]$ such that $C \times B(Z) <= A(X,Y),\ C <= A[Y : Z]B$ as well.

 (ii) Consider the following two relations:

    TYPE UsageRecord = RECORD department#: DepartmentId;
                               part#: PartId
             END;

        SupplyRecord = RECORD supplier#: SupplierId;
                              part#: PartId
             END;

    VAR Usage: ENTITY SET OF UsageRecord;
         Supply: ENTITY SET OF SupplyRecord

(iii) Observe that the query, *List the identifiers of suppliers that supply all the parts used by a given department*, contains the division operation defined above. Write an algorithm that performs the required division and produces the desired listing.

(6) Boyce–Codd Normal Form (BCNF)

  (i) A stronger and much more elegant definition of a normal form is as follows: *A relation R(A1,A2,...,An) is in BCNF if and only if the existence of a nontrivial functional dependency X→Y, where X and Y are sets of attributes of R, implies the existence of a functional dependency X→Ai for all i=1,2,...,n.* In other words, the domain of each nontrivial functional dependency of a relation in BCNF contains a key of that relation.

 (ii) Give an example of a relation that is in 3NF, but not in BCNF.

(iii) Prove that a relation that is in BCNF is also in 3NF. In other words, demonstrate that transitive dependencies cannot exist in a relation that is in BCNF.

(iv) Specify an abstract algorithm that performs decomposition of a relation that is not in BCNF into a set of its projects that are all in BCNF and whose natural join produces the original relation.

(v) Show that the specified algorithm is correct and terminates in a finite number of steps.

(7) Integrity Constraints

(i) Consider the object types PROJECT and TASK

PROJECT

TASK

with the following attributes:

```
TYPE ProjectType  =  RECORD project#: ProjectId;
                                      funds: Real
                      END;
      TaskType    =  RECORD task#: TaskId;
                                      project#: ProjectId;
                                      funds: Real
                      END
```

(ii) Write up the action that checks the integrity constraint expressed by the following predicate:

Vp(p in Project)
    (p.funds = Σ t.funds | t in Task and
                    t.project# = p.project#)

(iii) Requiring strict equality in the above integrity constraint demands extra attention because the attributes funds are of type Real. Indeed, inherent imprecision associated with the computer representation of this type requires due care since strict equality may not hold, whereas the actual difference may be within the permitted limits. Modify the above action appropriately to allow for these considerations.

(iv) A more complex action that checks more complex integrity constraints is required for the following object relationships

ASSIGNMENT

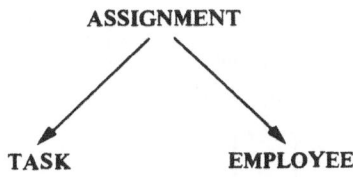

TASK   **EMPLOYEE**

where the relevant attributes for this exercise are specified below:

TYPE AssignmentType = RECORD task#: TaskId;
                                        employee#: EmployeeId;
                                        percentage: Real
                      END;

      TaskType   = RECORD task#: TaskId;
                                        salaries: Real
                      END;

      EmployeeType   = RECORD employee#: EmployeeId;
                                        salary: Real
                      END

The desired action checks whether the attribute salaries of Task equals the sums of all salaries that employees assigned to that task earn, assuming the employees are equally paid on all assignments according to the percentage of their work. The value of the attribute salary for each employee is meant to be equal to the sum of the amounts for particular assignments.

(8) Action Semantics

(i) Semantics of an action S may be expressed in Hoare's style as

$$\{P\}\ S\ \{Q\},$$

where P is the condition (assertion) that is expected to hold before S is performed, and Q the condition (assertion) that holds after S is completed. For example, the semantics of WHILE B DO S END action is defined in that style by the clause

$$\frac{\{P \text{ AND } B\}\ S\ \{P\}}{\{P\}\ \text{WHILE } B \text{ DO } S \text{ END } \{P \text{ AND NOT } B\}}$$

where the horizontal bar denotes implication. The correctness of the above definition follows immediately from the following diagram:

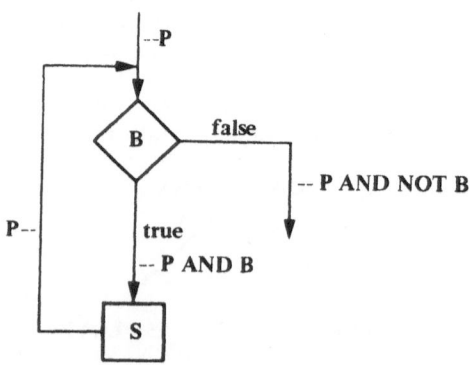

(ii) Define the semantics of the action

REPEAT S UNTIL B END.

(iii) Define the semantics of the following action:

LOOP S1;
      IF B THEN
      Exit END;
      S2
END

(iv) Using the previously described approach and the following two definitions of sequentially and conditionally composed actions

$$\frac{\{P\}\ S1\ \{R\},\ \{R\}\ S2\ \{Q\}}{\{P\}\ S1;\ S2\ \{Q\}}$$

$$\frac{\{P\ AND\ B\}\ S\ \{Q\},\ P\ AND\ B\ =>\ Q}{\{P\}\ IF\ B\ THEN\ S\ END\ \{Q\}}$$,

Specify the semantics of the following conditional composition:

IF B THEN S1 ELSE S2 END

(v) Specify the semantics of the FOR statement of the following form:

FOR x: = a TO b DO S END

(vi) Let P_e^x be the assertion P in which all the occurrences of x are substituted by e (we assume no clashes of bound variables in P). Verify correctness of the following definitions of the semantics of the assignment (update), insert, and delete actions:

$\{P_e^x\}\ x := e\ \{P\}$

$\{P_{E+\{x\}}^E\}\ Insert(x,E)\ \{P\}$

$\{P_{E-\{x\}}^E\}\ Delete(x,E)\ \{P\}$

(vii) Define the semantics of the following action:

FOREACH X IN E
WHERE Q
DO S END

(9) Schema Synthesis Algorithm

(i) Write up a complete specification in the programming language notation of the 3NF schema synthesis algorithm.

(ii) The algorithm presented below is a simplification of an algorithm by Bernstein and Beeri and has the following form:

(1) *Eliminate extraneous attributes.* Let F be a given set of functional dependencies. Eliminate extraneous attributes from the domains of each functional dependency in F producing the set G.

(2) *Find a covering.* Find a nonredundant covering H of G.

(3) *Partition.* Partition H into groups such that all the functional dependencies in the same group have identical domains.

(4) *Merge equivalent keys.* For each pair of groups H1 and H2 with domains X and Y, respectively, merge H1 and H2 together if there is a bijection $X \leftrightarrow Y$ in H^+.

(5) *Construct relations.* For each group construct a relation consisting of all attributes appearing in that group. The domain of the set of functional dependencies in each group is a key of the relation constructed from that group.

What is the purpose of step (4) in the above algorithm? Does this algorithm always produce a 3NF relational schema? In order to answer this last question, consider the following set of functional dependencies:

$$
\begin{aligned}
&\text{f1: } X1X2 \rightarrow AD \\
&\text{f2: } CD \quad \rightarrow X1X2 \\
&\text{f3: } AX1 \quad \rightarrow B \\
&\text{f4: } BX2 \quad \rightarrow C \\
&\text{f5: } C \quad\;\; \rightarrow A
\end{aligned}
$$

Derive the dependency $X1X2 \rightarrow CD$, and construct the relational schema according to the above algorithm. Then check whether the constructed schema is in 3NF.

(iii) The final form of Bernstein and Beeri's algorithm is as follows:

(1) *Eliminate extraneous attributes.* Let F be the given set of functional dependencies. Eliminate extraneous attributes from the domain of each functional dependency in F producing the set G.

(2) *Find a covering.* Find a nonredundant covering H of G.

(3) *Partition.* Partition H into groups such that all the functional dependencies in each group have identical domains.

(4) *Merge equivalent keys.* Let J = { }. For each pair of groups Hi and Hj with domains X and Y, respectively, merge Hi and Hj together if there is a bijection $X \leftrightarrow Y$ in H^+. For each such bijection, add $X \rightarrow Y$ and $Y \rightarrow X$ to J. For each A in Y, if $X \rightarrow A$ is in H, then delete it from H. Do the same for each $Y \rightarrow B$ in H with B in X.

(5) *Eliminate transitive dependencies.* Find an $H' <= H$ such that $(H' + J)^+ = (H + J)^+$ and no proper subset of H' has this property. Add each functional dependency of J into its corresponding group of H'.

(6) *Construct relations.* For each group construct a relation consisting of all attributes appearing in that group. Each set of attributes appearing as the domain of any functional dependency in the group is a key of the relation. Construct the relational schema for the set of functional dependencies given in (ii) and make appropriate conclu-

sions about the algorithm (iii). Write up the algorithm (iii) in the programming language notation.

Bibliographical Notes

The basic references on simple and composite data types and actions as defined in Modula-2 are (Wirth, 1983a) and (Wirth, 1983b). The presented approach, however, is based mainly on (Alagić and Arbib, 1978). Relational extensions of Pascal by Schmidt (1977) and Alagić (1981) contain some of the database-oriented language constructs appearing in this chapter. Two other approaches to database extensions of Modula, quite different from the approach presented in this book are by Rowe and Shones (1979) and Mall, Reimer, and Schmidt (1984). The section on the relational model of data is derived from (Alagić, 1986). Two classical references are (Codd, 1971a) and (Codd, 1971b). The section on schema synthesis algorithms is entirely based on (Bernstein, 1976) and (Beeri and Bernstein, 1979), and so is Exercise (9). The approach to action semantics presented in Exercise (8) is due to Hoare. It is elaborated in detail by Alagić and Arbib (1978). Among the classical references, we mention Hoare and Wirth, (1973). Further reading relating to Exercises (5) and (6) is by Alagić (1986). The example in the section on arrays is based on (Knepley and Platt, 1985).

CHAPTER 2
Procedures and Modules

1 Procedure Declaration and Procedure Call

Actions associated with an object (entity type) appear simple to the users of that object, but are, in fact, usually quite complex. Their specification is performed by the creator of the object in terms of primitive actions and action-composition rules. This decomposition is of no concern to the user of the object, whose viewpoint is that all that matters is what an action accomplishes and how it is invoked in order to perform its task. The details of how exactly that action performs its task are not and should not be of any concern to its user. The user expects the action to behave according to its specifications. The essential parts of such specifications are (pre-) conditions required (expected to hold) before an action is invoked and the effects that action accomplishes. The latter may often be expressed as conditions that are guaranteed to hold upon correct invocation of that action.

The creator of an object and all the actions associated with that object works at a quite different (much lower) level of abstraction. Given the external specification of an action (as seen by its users), the creator of that action is concerned with its decomposition into simpler actions all the way down to either primitive or already defined actions, and in doing so, relies on the available action-composition rules, performing the decomposition in such a way that the action behaves according to its specifications. This in particular means that the decomposition is performed so that all the integrity constraints associated with an object are maintained, including those specifing the relationships of that object with other objects in the database. These integrity constraints (in addition to others) appear as both preconditions and postconditions of all actions associated with an object.

This clear distinction of two semantic levels associated with a composite action is reflected in the programming language notions of *procedure declaration* and *procedure call*. Procedure declaration is the definition of an action in terms of simpler actions and action-composition rules. Such a decomposition is associated with the action (procedure) identifier. That identifier is then used to invoke the action at the place where its effect is desired. As an example, consider the object PROJECT, together with three typical actions associated with that object:

(i) When a new project is established, the action InsertProject is invoked in order to place data about the new project in the database.
(ii) When a project is abolished, its data may be kept in the database for a while, but after some expiration date, DeleteProject action may be appropriate in order to erase its data from the database.
(iii) If additional funds are allocated to the project, IncreaseProjectFunds action is invoked in order to reflect this change in the application environment in the database.

Syntactically, InsertProject, DeleteProject, and IncreaseProjectFunds are procedure calls. A procedure call in its simplest form consists of an identifier of the invoked action (procedure) only. The procedure declarations corresponding to these three calls are given below:

PROCEDURE InsertProject;

BEGIN Get project;
       IF acceptable project
       THEN insert project;
           InsertTasks
       ELSE Error
       END
END InsertProject;

PROCEDURE DeleteProject;

BEGIN Get project identifier;
       IF project exists
       THEN delete project;
           DeleteTasks
       ELSE Error
       END
END DeleteProject;

PROCEDURE UpdateProjectFunds;

BEGIN Get project identifier;
      Get new funds; (* if acceptable *)
      Find project;
      IF found THEN update funds
      ELSE Error
      END
END UpdateProjectFunds

Insert action requests project data from the user of that action and checks whether the data are acceptable. If so, a new instance of the entity (object) type PROJECT is inserted in the database, followed by insertion of all tasks of that project. This last action is specified by the action InsertTasks. DeleteProject action requests the identifier of the action to be deleted, checks if it exists in the database, and, if so, excludes that instance of the entity type PROJECT together with all instances of the entity type TASK associated with the deleted project instance.

IncreaseProjectFunds action requests from its user the project identifier and the new funds. It then finds the instance of the entity type PROJECT with the given identifier (if it exists) and updates its funds.

Note that the above decomposition of actions InsertProject, Delete-Project, and IncreaseProjectFunds is still abstract: It contains actions that are assumed to be defined and appear at this level of abstraction as procedure calls. Unless these actions are primitive, the corresponding procedure declarations, will be developed further in the decomposition process.

In order to invoke an action specified as a procedure, a user of that action is required to supply certain parameters specific to the circumstances of an invocation. For example, in order to insert an object, an instance of its type must be supplied. In addition, a set of instances (of that type) into which the given instance should be included must also be determined. When these parameters are supplied to the insertion action, the action may then perform its task. Likewise, deletion requires the identifier of the object to be deleted, as well as the specification of the set from which that object should be excluded. Update of the value of an attribute of an object requires an identifier of the object, specification of the set of entities where it belongs, and the value of the new attribute. These observations are summarized below:

Typical actions	*Parameters*
insert an object:	object; set of objects of the same type;
delete an object:	object identifier; set of objects of the same type;
update an attribute of an object:	object identifier; set of objects of the same type; new attribute value.

If an object of a given type belongs to a uniquely determined set of objects (in the database), that set may be a global object of the above procedures, so that we have the following:

Actions	*Global variables*	*Parameters*
insert an object:	set of objects;	object;
delete an object:	set of objects;	object identifier;
update an attribute of an object:	set of objects;	object identifier, new attribute value.

Global objects are not specified when a procedure is invoked. Rather, they are unambiguously assumed in the environment of the procedure and referred to by their identifiers in the corresponding declarations of those procedures. For example, global objects for the procedures InsertProject, DeleteProject, and IncreaseProjectFunds may be specified as follows:

```
TYPE ProjectId = String6 ;
     TaskId    = String6 ;
     ProjectType = RECORD project#:    ProjectId;
                          title:       String25;
                          funds:       Real;
                          start,finish: String10
                   END;

     TaskType  = RECORD task#:      TaskId;
                        project#:   ProjectId;
                        title:      String45;
                        credit,debit: Real
                   END;
     ProjectSetType = ENTITY SET OF ProjectType;
     TaskSetType    = ENTITY SET OF TaskType;

VAR  project: ProjectSetType;
     task:    TaskSetType
```

Given the above specification of the global objects for the procedures InsertProject, DeleteProject, and IncreaseProjectFunds, we present below the first refinement of their abstract declarations in the programming language notation:

```
PROCEDURE InsertProject(p: ProjectType);

BEGIN IF ProjectExists(p.project#) THEN Error
      ELSE Insert(p,project);
            InsertTasks(p.project#)
      END
END InsertProject;

PROCEDURE DeleteProject(project#: ProjectId);
```

```
BEGIN IF ProjectExists(project#) THEN
         PerformDelete(project#);
         DeleteTasks(project#)
      ELSE Error
      END
END DeleteProject;
```

```
PROCEDURE UpdateProjectFunds(project#: ProjectId;
                                    newfunds: Real);
```

```
BEGIN FindProject(project#);
       IF found THEN Update(newfunds)
       ELSE Error
END UpdateProjectFunds
```

In the above procedure declarations, identifiers that stand for their parameters are introduced, and the type of these parameters is specified. Parameters as they appear in a procedure declaration are *formal*. The *actual* parameters are specified in each particular procedure call in the order in which their corresponding formal parameters appear in the heading of the procedure declaration. The type of an actual parameter must be the same as the type of its corresponding formal parameter.

A procedure declaration consists of a *procedure heading* and *procedure body*. A procedure heading starts with the key identifier PROCEDURE, which is followed by the identifier of the declared procedure and a list of its parameters placed in parentheses. Each parameter in this list is specified by its formal identifier and its type. A procedure body contains a composition of actions that are placed between BEGIN and END brackets, and the end of the overall declaration is denoted by the procedure identifier.

In the bodies of the above procedure declarations, calls of other procedures are composed using the required action-composition rules. Among them are calls of standard procedures insert and delete that are applicable to all entity types. Other procedure calls such as InsertTasks, DeleteTasks, FindProject, ProjectExists, UpdateProjectFunds, and Error are still to be defined in the further development of our three global procedures associated with the entity type PROJECT.

For example, consider the refinement of the Boolean expression (predicate) ProjectExists, which appears as primitive in the declaration of the procedure InsertProject. On the lower level of abstraction, this predicate is elaborated as a function procedure whose declaration is given below:

```
PROCEDURE ProjectExists(project#: ProjectId): Boolean;
```

```
VAR p: ProjectType;
```

```
BEGIN FOREACH p IN project
        WHERE    p.project# = project#
```

```
        DO              Return(true) END;
        Return(false)
END ProjectExists
```

The heading of the declaration of a function procedure requires specification of the type of the result of that procedure, which is Boolean for
the procedure ProjectExists. Consequently, a call of a function procedure
is not an action but an expression of the type specified in the declaration
of that procedure (Boolean in this case). In the body of such a procedure,
one or more Return statements specify the value of the result in the form
of an expression of the result type. At least one Return statement had
better be executed during the execution of a function procedure or else
the value of its result is undefined. The Return statement may also appear
in the procedure declaration, in which case the Return statement is not
followed by an expression and denotes an exceptional termination of procedure execution.

The declaration of the procedure ProjectExists makes it clear that in
order to check whether a project with a given identifier exists we need
a control variable p of type ProjectType. Its range specified in the
FOREACH statement in the body of the procedure ProjectExists is the
set of instances of that type. This set (represented as the value of the
variable Project) and its type are both global to the procedure Project-
Exists. The variable p is local to this procedure. Its scope of validity is
the body of the procedure ProjectExists, and has no meaning or value
outside of that scope. Consequently, the declaration of this variable is
given inside the procedure ProjectExists. Since this variable performs its
temporary role within the procedure ProjectExists, its existence is limited
to the execution of a call of ProjectExists. Upon such a call, the local
variable p is created, and when that call is completed, p does not exist
anymore. If we decompose the action IncreaseProjectFunds, we discover
that such a decomposition also requires local, temporary variables p and
found:

```
PROCEDURE UpdateProjectFunds(project#: ProjectId;
                             newfunds: Real);

  VAR p: ProjectType; found: Boolean;

BEGIN found: = false;
        FOREACH p IN project
        WHERE     p.project# = project#
        DO found: = true;
            p.funds: = newfunds
        END;
        IF NOT found THEN
           WriteString(" No such project ");
           WriteLn
        END
```

END   UpdateProjectFunds

Local variables: p,found

Global types: ProjectType, ProjectId

Global variable: project

2 Scopes: Local and Global Objects

The concept of locality does not only apply to variables, but to all objects
that are defined or declared: types, constants, variables, and procedures
themselves. This last case is of particular interest, and to illustrate it,
consider the following refinement of the procedure InsertTasks whose
call appears in the procedure InsertProject:

PROCEDURE InsertTasks(project#: ProjectId);

VAR t: TaskType;

```
PROCEDURE LastTask( ): Boolean;
  VAR ch: Char;
BEGIN WriteString(" Last task? Y/N > ");
      ReadCh(ch);
      IF (ch = " Y ") OR (ch = " y ") THEN
      Return(true) ELSE Return(false)
      END
END LastTask;
```

PROCEDURE InsertTask(t: TaskType); (* still unspecified *)

```
BEGIN WHILE NOT LastTask ( )
      DO ReadTask (t);
        IF t.project# = project#
        THEN InsertTask(t)
        ELSE WriteString(" Wrong project identifier ");
            WriteLn
        END
      END
END InsertTasks
```

Local variable: t

Global type: TaskType, ProjectId

Global variable: task

Global procedure: ReadTask

Local procedure: InsertTask

Local function procedure: LastTask

Local procedure to InsertTasks: InsertTask

```
PROCEDURE InsertTask(t: TaskType);

  VAR x: TaskType;
      found: Boolean;

BEGIN found: = false;
      FOREACH x IN task
      WHERE     x.task# = t.task#
      DO found: = true
      END;
      IF found THEN
        WriteString ("Duplicate task");
        WriteLn
      ELSE Insert(t,task)
      END
END InsertTask
```

Following the same approach, we can further develop the procedure DeleteProject, providing declarations of procedures DeleteTasks and Delete whose calls appear in the body of this procedure. These declarations are given below:

Local procedure to DeleteProject: DeleteTasks

```
PROCEDURE DeleteTasks(project#: ProjectId);

  VAR t: TaskType;

BEGIN FOREACH t IN task
      WHERE     t.project# = project#
      DO        Delete(t,task)
      END
END DeleteTasks
```

Global type: TaskType

Global variable: task

Local procedure to DeleteProject: PerformDelete

```
PROCEDURE PerformDelete(project#: ProjectId);

  VAR p: ProjectType;

BEGIN FOREACH p IN project
      WHERE     p.project# = project#
      DO        Delete(p,project)
      END
END PerformDelete
```

This completes our decomposition of the actions InsertProject, DeleteProject, and IncreaseProjectFunds associated with the entity type Project. The result of our development is presented below and exhibits nested procedure structure of the developed actions. Our development also shows that the action ProjectExists is required on the same level of abstraction as the above three actions for two reasons: It is used by both InsertProject and DeleteProject procedures, and is obviously a useful primitive action for a user of the object Project.

```
PROCEDURE ProjectExists(project#: ProjectId): Boolean;

    VAR p: ProjectType;
BEGIN FOREACH p IN project
        WHERE    p.project# = project#
        DO       Return(true) END;
        Return(false)
END ProjectExists;


PROCEDURE InsertProject(p: ProjectType);

PROCEDURE InsertTasks(project#: ProjectId);

    VAR t: TaskType;

PROCEDURE LastTask( ): Boolean;
    VAR ch: Char;
BEGIN WriteString(" Last task? Y/N > ");
        ReadCh(ch);
        IF (ch = " Y ") OR (ch = " y ") THEN
        Return(true) ELSE Return(false)
        END
END LastTask;

PROCEDURE InsertTask(t: TaskType);

    VAR x: TaskType;
        found: Boolean;

BEGIN found: = false;
        FOREACH x IN task
        WHERE    x.task# = t.task#
        DO found : = true
        END;
        IF found THEN
            WriteString(" Duplicate task ");
            WriteLn
        ELSE Insert(t,task)
        END
END InsertTask;
```

```
BEGIN WHILE NOT LastTask( )
      DO ReadTask(t);
          IF t.project# = project#
          THEN InsertTask(t)
          ELSE WriteString(" Wrong project identifier ");
                 WriteLn
          END
      END
END InsertTasks;

BEGIN IF ProjectExists(p.project#) THEN
          WriteString(" Duplicate project identifier ");
          WriteLn
      ELSE Insert(p,project);
             InsertTasks(p.project#)
      END
END InsertProject;

PROCEDURE DeleteProject(project#: ProjectId);

PROCEDURE PerformDelete(project#: ProjectId);

   VAR p: ProjectType;
BEGIN FOREACH p IN project
      WHERE     p.project# = project#
      DO        Delete(p,project)
      END
END PerformDelete;

PROCEDURE DeleteTasks(project#: ProjectId);

   VAR t: TaskType;

BEGIN FOREACH t IN task
      WHERE     t.project# = project#
      DO        Delete(t,task)
      END
END DeleteTasks;

BEGIN IF NOT ProjectExists(project#)
      THEN WriteString(" No such project ");
             WriteLn
      ELSE PerformDelete(project#);
             DeleteTasks(p.project#)
      END
END DeleteProject;


PROCEDURE UpdateProjectFunds(project#: ProjectId;
                                     newfunds: Real);
```

```
        VAR p: ProductType;
BEGIN FOREACH p IN project
        WHERE    p.project# = project#
        DO       p.funds: = newfunds
        END
END UpdateProjectFunds
```

The nested structure of the procedures InsertProject and DeleteProject reflects the semantics of the application environment for which we assumed a task can exist as long as its project exists. However, the procedures InsertTask and DeleteTask are also required on the same level of abstraction as InsertProject and DeleteProject in spite of the fact that a task is existent dependent on its project. Indeed, there is also an obvious need to insert a new task or delete a task of an existing project.

```
PROCEDURE TaskExists(task#: TaskId): Boolean;

    VAR t: TaskType;

BEGIN FOREACH t IN task
        WHERE    t.task# = task#
        DO       Return(true) END;
        Return(false)
END TaskExists;


PROCEDURE InsertTask(t: TaskType);

PROCEDURE AcceptableTask(t: TaskType): Boolean;

BEGIN IF ProjectExists(t.project#) THEN
          IF TaskExists(t.task#) THEN
              WriteString(" Duplicate task identifier" );
              WriteLn; Return(false)
          ELSE Return(true)
          END
      ELSE WriteString(" Project does not exist" );
          WriteLn; Return(false)
      END
END AcceptableTask;

BEGIN IF AcceptableTask(t) THEN
          Insert(t,task)
      END
END InsertTask;

PROCEDURE DeleteTask(task#: TaskId);

    VAR t: TaskType;
        found: Boolean;
```

```
BEGIN found: = false;
      FOREACH t IN task
      WHERE      t.task# = task#
      DO found: = true;
          Delete(t,task)
      END;
      IF NOT found THEN
         WriteString(" No such Task ");
         WriteLn
      END
END DeleteTask
```

Note that the scope rules of identifiers guarantee that no ambiguity will arise because of the same identifiers of procedures InsertTask and DeleteTask that appear on the same level of abstraction as procedures InsertProject and DeleteProject, and the local procedures InsertTask and DeleteTask that are declared within the procedures InsertProject and DeleteProject.

3 Variable and Value Parameters

Value parameters of a procedure serve to supply input values to that procedure from the environment of its call. *Variable parameters* serve to transmit the effects of procedure execution to the environment of its call. The distinction may be easily appreciated from the following procedure declaration:

```
PROCEDURE ComputeSalary(e: EmployeeType;
                        increase: Real;
                        VAR newsalary: Real);

BEGIN newsalary: = e.salary + e.salary*increase/100.0
END ComputeSalary
```

Value parameters: e,increase

Variable parameter: newsalary

The actual value parameters (i.e., those supplied in a procedure call) are, in general, expressions. The values of those expressions are evaluated in the environment of the procedure call and supplied to the procedure (substituted for their corresponding formal parameters) before its execution is initiated. An actual variable parameter must be a particularly simple sort of an expression—a variable. This variable is almost literally substituted for its corresponding formal parameter in such a way that the formal variable parameter refers to the actual variable parameter during the execution of the procedure occurring upon its call. This means that assignments to the formal variable parameter are in fact assignments to the corresponding actual parameter, and this is how a procedure call affects the environment in which it occurs.

For example, in the environment (a procedure) in which the call

ComputeSalary(emp,a∗b,salary)

occurs, emp must be of type EmployeeType, a∗b must be a real expression, and salary must be a real variable. The effect of the call is to assign a new real value to the variable salary.

Although emp is in fact a variable (a more complex expression of type EmployeeType is not permitted anyhow), we could not affect its value by a call of the procedure ComputeSalary. Indeed, since it is a value parameter, all that is transmitted in the parameter substitution process is the value of the variable emp and not the variable itself.

In fact, a value parameter behaves as a local variable whose value is initialized by the value of the corresponding actual parameter. This should be taken into account when the selection of the appropriate parameter substitution (value or variable) is considered. As an example, consider the following procedure declaration:

PROCEDURE ComputeAverage(employee: EmployeeSetType;
                         VAR average: Real);

```
   VAR e: EmployeeType;
       count: Cardinal; sum: Real;
BEGIN count: = 0; sum: = 0.0;
       FOREACH e IN employee
       DO count: = count + 1;
          sum: = sum + e.salary
       END;
       IF count = 0 THEN average: = 0.0
       ELSE average: = sum/Float(count)
       END
END ComputeAverage
```

Although employee is correctly specified as a value parameter on the grounds that it represents the input to the procedure ComputeAverage, which is consequently inspected in read-only mode, this has some undesirable effects in terms of (unexpected) memory requirements and efficiency of execution. Indeed, a local variable that corresponds to employee will be allocated, and the whole (possibly huge) entity set that represents the corresponding actual parameter will be copied to this local variable, which doubles the effort required to compute the average salary. Hence, contrary to the reasons we used for the distinction between variable

and value parameters, we propose the following change in the declaration
of the procedure ComputeSalary:

PROCEDURE Average(VAR employee: EmployeeSetType): Real;

```
    VAR e: EmployeeType;
        count: Cardinal; sum: Real;
BEGIN count: = 0; sum: = 0.0;
        FOREACH e IN employee
        DO count: = count + 1;
            sum: = sum + e.salary
        END;
        IF count = 0 THEN Return(0.0)
        ELSE Return(sum/Float(count))
        END
END Average
```

We conclude that, although value substitution may be appropriate for
the role a parameter plays, if the size of that parameter is large, variable
substitution is recommended on the grounds of economy of storage and
efficiency of execution. But here is an example in which the described
behavior of a value parameter is used appropriately in spite of its size.
Producing an alphabetical listing of employees is certainly not permitted
to affect the set of employees whose alphabetical listing is produced, and
hence, it is performed by a call of the following procedure ListEmployees:

PROCEDURE ListEmployees(Employee: EmployeeSetType);

```
    VAR e: EmployeeType;

BEGIN Sort(Employee,Employee,name);
        FOREACH e IN Employee
        DO WriteEmployee(e)
        END
END ListEmployees
```

The effect of the above procedure is the same as that of the following
procedure:

PROCEDURE ListEmployees(Employee: EmployeeSetType);

```
    VAR e: EmployeeType;
        LocalSet: EmployeeSetType;

BEGIN Copy(Employee,LocalSet);
        Sort(LocalSet,LocalSet,name);
        FOREACH e IN LocalSet
        DO WriteEmployee(e)
        END
END ListEmployees
```

If we assume the sort procedure does not affect the input set, this last procedure is then equivalent to the following:

```
PROCEDURE ListEmployees(VAR Employee: EmployeeSetType);

   VAR e: EmployeeType;
       LocalSet: EmployeeSetType;

BEGIN Sort(Employee,LocalSet,name);
      FOREACH e IN LocalSet
      DO WriteEmployee(e)
      END
END ListEmployees
```

We conclude our discussion of value and variable parameters with declarations of three procedures performing typical actions associated with an entity type: insertion, deletion, and update. Since the intent of each of those actions is to affect the entity set that is supplied as the actual parameter of those procedures, the parameter is necessarily a variable parameter. The new instance inserted into that set is a value parameter (procedure InsertEmployee) and thus is the identifier of the instance that is to be deleted from that set (procedure DeleteEmployee). Similarly, the new value of an attribute is a value parameter of an update action (procedure UpdateEmployeeSalary).

```
PROCEDURE UpdateEmployeeSalary(VAR employee:
                                EmployeeSetType; increase: Real);

   VAR e: EmployeeType;

BEGIN FOREACH e IN employee
      DO e.salary: = e.salary +
                     e.salary*increase/100.0
      END
END UpdateEmployeeSalary;

PROCEDURE DeleteEmployee(VAR employee: EmployeeSetType;
                         employee#: EmployeeId);

   VAR e: EmployeeType;

BEGIN FOREACH e IN employee
      WHERE    e. employee# = employee#
      DO       Delete(e,employee)
      END
END DeleteEmployee;

PROCEDURE InsertEmployee(VAR employee: EmployeeSetType;
                         e: EmployeeType);
```

```
   VAR x: EmployeeType;
          found: Boolean;

BEGIN found: = false;
          FOREACH x IN employee
          WHERE     x.employee# = e.employee#
          DO found: = true
          END;
          IF NOT found THEN
              Insert(e,employee)
          END
END InsertEmployee
```

If the type of a formal parameter is an array, then its corresponding actual parameter must be an array of the same type. This means that not only the elements of those two arrays must be of the same type, but their index types must be identical as well. This severe restriction is well known to Pascal programmers. It is relaxed in Modula-2 by introducing open array parameters in which index ranges of formal parameters are left unspecified (open). The types of elements of a formal parameter and its corresponding actual parameter must of course be the same, but now it is possible to declare more flexible, general procedures that act on arrays of the same type but whose sizes are different.

The type of an array (formal) parameter is specified as

ARRAY OF T

and the implication is that an array of any size whose elements are of type T may be substituted for such a formal parameter.

Example

```
PROCEDURE Concatenate(s1,s2: ARRAY OF Char;
                      VAR result: ARRAY OF Char)
```

The heading of the procedure Concatenate makes the advantages of open array parameters obvious. This procedure can now be used to concatenate any two strings irrespective of their actual size. Of course, the size of the actual result had better be large enough. Also note that the notation ARRAY OF Char is equivalent to String.

The lower bound of the index range of a formal open array parameter is always 0. The upper bound is computed using the standard function High. High(A) equals the number of elements of the array A minus 1.

Exercise (5) toward the end of this chapter contains a collection of procedures for variable-length string handling. Parameters of these procedures are specified as open arrays of characters.

4 Procedures Types and Parameters

Our approach to conceptual modeling of application environments requires specification of objects in that environment together with actions associated with those objects. Objects are classified into sets of objects of the same type. The question is whether we can apply this classification abstraction to actions as well, regarding actions themselves as objects. If we accept this sort of semantic relativism, it leads us to *action types*. An action type is a set of actions sharing the same properties. But what are those properties? Well, the most essential property of all the actions of the same type is the type of objects upon which those actions may be performed.

This line of thinking may seem unusual, but actually has a sound mathematical interpretation. It is based on the fact that given sets of objects A and B we may consider the set of all functions whose domain is A and codomain is B. This set is usually denoted as $[A \rightarrow B]$, and its particular case is the set of all actions $[O \rightarrow O]$ applicable to the set of objects O.

Action types are introduced into programming languages as procedure types. The definition of a procedure type specifies the types of parameters of the procedures of that type and the type of their result if those procedures are functions. Thus, we obtain procedure types that are in a way orthogonal to data types.

This sort of generality may be carried out very far, but is not necessarily practical. We restrict ourselves to the observation that procedure types allow declaration of procedures having other procedures as their parameters. This permits specification of generalized actions associated with an entity type, as illustrated by the following general pattern:

```
TYPE ObjectType = RECORD {object attributes}
                  END;

     ObjectSetType = ENTITY SET OF ObjectType;

     SelectorType = PROCEDURE(o: ObjectType): Boolean;

     ActionType = PROCEDURE(VAR o: ObjectType);

PROCEDURE GeneralAction(VAR ObjectSet: ObjectSetType;
                            qualification: SelectorType;
                            action: ActionType);
VAR x: ObjectType;

BEGIN FOREACH x IN ObjectSet
       WHERE    qualification(x)
       DO       action(x)
       END
END GeneralAction
```

What the above generality indicates in the case of a particular entity type is illustrated for the employee object. Two particular function procedures that are instances of the procedure type SelectorType are declared for that entity type: SelectProgrammers and SelectExperienced. Likewise, two procedures are declared that are instances of the procedure type ActionType: UpdateSalaryOfQualified and UpdateSalaryOfLeaders:

```
TYPE EmployeeId = String5;
     DepartmentId = String3;

EmployeeType = RECORD employee#: EmployeeId;
                      name:       String25;
                      degree:     String5;
                      job:        String15;
                      rank:       String3;
                      experience: Cardinal;
                      salary:     Real;
                      department: DepartmentId
              END

EmployeeSetType = ENTITY SET OF EmployeeType;

SelectorType = PROCEDURE(o: EmployeeType): Boolean;

ActionType = PROCEDURE(VAR o: EmployeeType);

PROCEDURE UpdateEmployee(VAR EmployeeSet: EmployeeSetType;
                         qualification: SelectorType;
                         action: ActionType);
   VAR e: EmployeeType;

BEGIN FOREACH e IN EmployeeSet
        WHERE    qualification(e)
        DO       action(e)
        END
END UpdateEmployee;

PROCEDURE SelectProgrammers(e: EmployeeType): Boolean;

BEGIN IF e.job = "programmer"
        THEN Return(true)
        ELSE Return(false)
        END
END SelectProgrammers;

PROCEDURE SelectExperienced(e: EmployeeType): Boolean;

BEGIN IF e.experience > 10
        THEN Return(true)
        ELSE Return(false) END
END SelectExperienced;
```

```
PROCEDURE UpdateSalaryOfQualified(VAR e: EmployeeType);
BEGIN
  CASE e.degree OF
    "B.Sc.": e.salary := e.salary*1.10 |
    "M.Sc.": e.salary := e.salary*1.15 |
    "Ph.D.": e.salary := e.salary*1.20
  END
END UpdateSalaryOfQualified;

PROCEDURE UpdateSalaryOfLeaders (VAR e: EmployeeType);
BEGIN
  CASE e.job OF
    "projectleader":e.salary := e.salary*1.20 |
    "taskleader":   e.salary := e.salary*1.15 |
    "taskmember":   e.salary := e.salary*1.10
  END
END UpdateSalaryOfLeaders
```

Another example is a general procedure for computing the average salary of selected employees, where the qualification condition is specified as a function procedure:

```
PROCEDURE AverageSalary(VAR EmployeeSet: EmployeeSetType;
                        qualification: SelectorType): Real;

  VAR e: EmployeeType; count: Cardinal;
      sum: Real;

BEGIN
  sum:= 0.0; count:= 0;
  FOREACH e IN EmployeeSet
  WHERE qualification(e)
  DO sum:= sum + e.salary;
     count:= count + 1
  END;
  IF count = 0 THEN Return(0.0)
  ELSE Return(sum/Float(count))
  END

END AverageSalary
```

It is certainly interesting to explore various possibilities that this sort of generality offers in conceptual modeling of application environments. Nevertheless, it is also important to observe some restrictions that are obviously recommended as sound programming practice. One such restriction is that procedures, instances of a procedure type, should communicate with their environment through parameters only. Indeed, if they perform direct assignments to global variables rather than via variable parameters, the notion of a procedure type hardly makes any sense.

5 Recursive Procedures

Many common application environments contain objects whose precise definitions are naturally recursive. In such a definition, an object is defined not only in terms of references to other already defined objects, but also in terms of references to itself. For example, consider the following recursive definition of the product object:

Product Object
    with Attributes

    Product identifier
    Product name
    Unit of measure
    Measure
    Quantity
    Price
    Set of parts each of which is

    Product Object

When an object (entity type) is defined recursively, the actions associated with that object type are naturally defined using recursive composition of actions. Three typical recursively defined actions are illustrated below for the recursively defined object Product:

InsertProduct: Get product attributes;
                Insert product;
                For each of its subproducts
                    InsertProduct

DeleteProduct: Get product identifier;
                Delete product;
                For each of its subproducts
                    DeleteProduct

DisplayProductStructure: Get product identifier;
                        Display product attributes;
                        For each of its subproducts
                            DisplayProductStructure

Although the presented definitions of the object type Product and its associated actions are attractive, their interpretation causes some well-known problems or anomalies. If a set of parts, or *subproducts*, is an attribute of a product, then those sets are generally not disjoint for two different products. Indeed, a product may participate as a part in a number of products. This means that we would have repeated instances of the same object in the database, which may cause inconsistencies if all those instances are not changed in the same way by product update actions. Although possible, this makes the update actions quite complex, in addition to the already observed undesirable multiplication of storage requirements. This explains the reasons for introducing the first-normal-form discipline.

In order to solve this problem, instead of taking the set of immediate subproducts we take the set of references to those subproducts to be an attribute of the entity type product. The relational model suggests those references should be product identifiers so that we obtain the following recursive definition of the entity type PRODUCT expressed in the programming language notation:

```
TYPE ProductId = [1..126];
     ProductType = RECORD product#:       ProductId;
                          name:           String30;
                          unit:           Char;
                          quantity,price: Real;
                          parts:          SET OF ProductId
            END;
     ProductSetType = ENTITY SET OF ProductType;

VAR product: ProductSetType
```

The motivation for this representation comes from a rather standard approach in programming languages with pointer types (references) and from the relational model of data where those references are object identifiers. However, the above model is not a normalized relational model in any way since the type of the attribute parts is not simple. It is not an arbitrary (entity) set type, but rather a small set type whose elements are simple—which makes a big difference. Because of the problems outlined above, we will refrain from the representation of entity types whose attributes are other entity types. Rather, we will restrict the types of such attributes to small set types.

With the adopted recursive definition of the entity type PRODUCT, we are now in the position to define recursively the actions associated with that entity type. Recursive composition of actions is achieved by *recursive procedures*. A procedure is recursive if its declaration contains calls of that very procedure. There is nothing in our definitions of the notions of procedure declarations and procedure calls that prevents such recursive calls. Consequently, we specify the action DisplayProduct-Structure in terms of a recursive procedure Descent as follows:

```
PROCEDURE DisplayProductStructure(product#: ProductId);

PROCEDURE Descent(product#: ProductId;
                  level: Cardinal);
```

```
        VAR  p: ProductType; x: ProductId;
             i: Integer;

BEGIN  FOREACH p IN product
       WHERE     p.product# = product#
       DO        FOR i: = 1 TO level DO WriteCh(" > ") END;
                 WriteString(p.product#); WriteCh("  ");
                 WriteString(p.name); WriteLn;
                 FOREACH x IN p.parts DO
                    Descent(x,level + 1)
                 END
       END
END Descent;

BEGIN  Descent(product#,0)
END DisplayProductStructure
```

DisplayProductStructure displays a hierarchical product structure in terms of its immediate (direct) subproducts (parts), their immediate subproducts, and so on. Recall that a local variable is created upon every call of the procedure in which it is declared and deleted upon completion of execution of that call. This general rule applies to all procedure calls, including the recursive ones. Entering a new hierarchical (sub-) level by a recursive call of the procedure Descent causes creation of new instances of variables p, x, and i, which are private variables of that particular call and have nothing to do with instances of these variables that correspond to other hierarchical levels (calls of the procedure Descent). Not only does this follow from our definitions given so far, but also represents obvious requirements for correct performance of the specified recursive algorithm.

Following the same approach, we specify actions InsertProduct and DeleteProduct using recursive procedure calls. Note the subtle difference between the definitions of these procedures and their previously given abstract counterparts. Insertion of a product is performed only if that product is not already a member of the set product. The same applies to its subproducts. In other words, if a subproduct already exists in the set product, only a reference to that subproduct is included in the set parts. Symmetrically, deletion of a product is followed by deletion of all its direct or indirect subproducts. Their identifiers are accumulated in the set DeletedProducts. This hierarchical deletion may or may not be appropriate depending on the actual application environment. But, if the hierarchical deletion as specified in the procedure DeleteProduct is appropriate, then our representation of the recursive definition of the object PRODUCT requires deletion of all references to the deleted products, since otherwise we would have products whose attribute parts refers to nonexistent products. This demonstrates a rather critical problem that our representation of recursive definition of an object type in terms of references to itself has: These references had better be maintained properly by representations of actions associated with such an entity type.

```
PROCEDURE InsertProduct(p: ProductType);

  PROCEDURE InsertParts(product#: ProductId);

    VAR p,new: ProductType;

      PROCEDURE LastPart( ): Boolean;
        VAR Ch: Char;
      BEGIN WriteString("Last part? Y/N>");
            ReadCh(Ch);
            IF (Ch = "Y") OR (Ch = "y")
            THEN Return(true)
            ELSE Return(false) END
      END LastPart;

  BEGIN WHILE NOT LastPart( ) DO
            WriteString("Enter part of product:");
            WriteString(product#); WriteLn;
            ReadProduct(new);
            IF NOT Member(new,product) THEN
              InsertProduct(new);
            END;
            FOREACH p IN product
            WHERE    p.product# = product#
            DO       Include(new.product#,p.parts)
            END
        END
  END InsertParts;

BEGIN
  Insert(p,product);
  InsertParts(p.product#)
END InsertProduct;

PROCEDURE DeleteProduct(product#: ProductId);

  VAR DeletedProducts: SET OF ProductId;
      x: ProductId; p: ProductType;

PROCEDURE Descent(product#: ProductId);

  VAR p: ProductType; x: ProductId;

BEGIN
  FOREACH p IN product
  WHERE    p.product# = product#
```

```
    DO Delete(p,product);
       Include(product#,DeletedProducts);
       FOREACH x IN p.parts
       DO Descent(x)
       END
    END
END Descent;

BEGIN Descent(product#);
       FOREACH p IN product
       DO FOREACH x IN p.parts
          DO IF x IN DeletedProducts
             THEN Exclude(x,p.parts)
             END
          END
       END
END DeleteProduct
```

6 Modules: Definition and Implementation of Objects

To specify the type of an object together with the types of actions applicable to that object, we use the concepts of the definition and implementation modules as defined in Modula-2. The *definition module* of an object specifies the type of that object. It also specifies actions applicable to the object as *procedure headings*. As such, it is an interface to all users of the object. The details of an implementation of the object are hidden in its *implementation module*. In particular, the implementation module of an object contains complete declarations of procedures whose headings appear in its definition module. These procedures are specified by the creator of that object in such a way that integrity constraints related to the object are maintained when actions upon it are performed.

The implementation module is hidden from all users who have access to the module's definition part only. Two important goals are achieved by this: (1) A user of an object is forced to use a predefined set of actions upon that object that perform correctly, and their internals are protected from the outside access so that their correctness can be guaranteed; and (2) the internals may be changed (within some limits) without affecting the users' importing modules so that, in particular, their recompilation is not necessary—this is particularly valuable when the application environment activities (procedures) are changed.

A module contains a number of IMPORT clauses and an EXPORT clause. The former specify all identifiers of objects that are declared outside the module and used within that module so that they have to be imported.

The EXPORT clause specifies all identifiers defined within the module and used outside it. So a module constitutes a wall around an object whose transparency is strictly under the control of its designer (creator). All identifiers declared in a definition module are automatically imported into its associated implementation module (i.e., they do not have to be listed in its IMPORT clauses).

The programming language notation for the definition and implementation modules of an object is illustrated below for the entity type STUDENT:

DEFINITION MODULE Student;

EXPORT QUALIFIED StudentType, StudentId, LevelType,
                 FindStudent, EnrollStudent, DropStudent,
                 ChangeLevel, ChangeAddress, ChangePhone,
                 ReadStudent, WriteStudent,
                 StudentExceptionType, StudentException;

```
TYPE StudentId   = String5;
     LevelType   = (undergraduate, graduate);
     StudentType = RECORD student#: StudentId;
                          name:     String30;
                          level:    LevelType;
                          address:  String30;
                          phone:    String7
          END;
```

StudentExceptionType = (None, DuplicateStudentId,
                        NonexistentStudent, ReadException,
                        WriteException);

VAR StudentException: StudentExceptionType;

PROCEDURE ReadStudent(VAR student: StudentType);

PROCEDURE WriteStudent(student: StudentType);

PROCEDURE EnrollStudent(student: StudentType);

PROCEDURE DropStudent(student#: StudentId);

PROCEDURE FindStudent(name: String30;
                      VAR student#: StudentId);

PROCEDURE ChangeAddress(student#: StudentId;
                        address: String30);

PROCEDURE ChangePhone(student#: StudentId;
                      phone: String7);

PROCEDURE ChangeLevel(student#: StudentId);

END Student.

The above definition module used as an interface to all users of objects of type STUDENT clarifies what the properties (and their types) of those objects are, as well as what actions users of objects of type STUDENT may perform upon them and how those actions are to be invoked.

Indeed, actions are specified as procedure headings whose identifiers make clear their general effect or intention. In addition, parameter sections of the procedure headings specify what actual parameters users of objects of type STUDENT are required to supply when invoking actions upon those objects. So, in order to enroll (EnrollStudent) or display a student (WriteStudent), an instance of the entity type STUDENT must be supplied. In order to drop a student, it suffices to specify its identifier. That identifier is also required when various types of update actions are performed (ChangeAddress, ChangePhone, ChangeLevel), together with the new value of the attribute that is being updated.

Of course, users of STUDENT objects are not always expected to know identifiers of those objects. Selection of the desired student, given a more meaningful property of that student as its name, is performed by the action FindStudent whose result (variable parameter) is the identifier of the desired student. Actions performing selection of the desired instance of the entity type STUDENT, given the values of its other attributes (one or more), may be specified in the same fashion.

Even if a user of an object correctly invoked an action upon that object and, in particular, supplied the required parameters of the appropriate type, it is still possible that during the action execution various conditions occur that prevent its successful completion. Such conditions are generally called exceptional or error conditions. It is certainly of utmost importance for the user who invoked an action to know whether that action has been performed effectively and, if not, what the reasons for its failure are. The exported variable StudentException in the definition module STUDENT serves that purpose. For reasons of simplicity, its type contains identifiers of only two exceptional situations (duplicate student identifier and non-existent student) together with the identifier of the successful action (no exception).

Now consider the implementation module of the entity type STUDENT. The actual set of instances of this entity type is represented as the value of the variable StudentSet. This variable is not exported. It is accessible only within this implementation module via procedures whose declarations are specified in the module in such a way that actions associated with the entity type STUDENT in its definition module accomplish their desired effect (i.e., perform correctly).

Apart from the specification of the entity type STUDENT as a set of its instances, the most essential aspect of the implementation of the STUDENT object is the decomposition of its associated actions given in the corresponding procedure declarations. In order to illustrate what a correct performance of an action means, consider the declaration of the EnrollStudent procedure. This action is responsible for maintaining uniqueness of values of the attribute student# in the entity set StudentSet. In other words, this is the only action whose incorrect performance may violate the integrity constraint expressed in the form of the functional dependency

$$\text{student\#} \rightarrow \text{name, level, address, phone,}$$

since other actions associated with StudentType do not affect this integrity constraint in any way. Consequently, the action EnrollStudent is in its procedure declaration decomposed in such a way that insertion of a new instance of the entity type StudentType is not performed if this integrity constraint is violated. When this happens the appropriate exception is indicated. The same approach would be applied for checking whether the value of the attribute student# is null. Only by checking both of these conditions would we guarantee that student# does indeed behave as the identifier of entity type STUDENT.

Possible exceptions and how they are handled are introduced here only to a limited degree. One frequently occurring exceptional situation preventing correct performance of an action is the attempt to delete or update an instance of an entity type STUDENT that does not exist. Such an action cannot be performed correctly, and this requires appropriate indication of an exception.

Note that we do not assume any other method of checking integrity constraints associated with an object other than that embedded in the procedure declarations of the object's implementation module. This means that no matter what the integrity constraints are the insertion or deletion of an instance of that object type is not permitted by the corresponding procedures if that instance violates the constraints. Likewise, procedure declarations of update actions must be specified so that the integrity constraints are maintained, or else updates are not performed.

IMPLEMENTATION MODULE Student;

FROM StandardIO IMPORT ReadCh, ReadString,
                       WriteLn, WriteString, WriteCh;

TYPE StudentSetType = ENTITY SET OF StudentType;

VAR StudentSet: StudentSetType;

PROCEDURE EnrollStudent(student: StudentType);

   PROCEDURE DuplicateId(student#: StudentId): Boolean;
     VAR s: StudentType;
   BEGIN FOREACH s IN StudentSet
           WHERE   s.student# = student#
           DO Return(true) END;
           Return(false)
   END DuplicateId;

```
BEGIN IF DuplicateId(student.student#) THEN
        StudentException := DuplicateStudentId
        ELSE Insert(student, StudentSet);
                StudentException: = None
        END
END EnrollStudent;

PROCEDURE DropStudent(student#: StudentId);
  VAR s: StudentType;
BEGIN StudentException := NonexistentStudent;
        FOREACH s IN StudentSet
        WHERE    s.student# = student#
        DO StudentException := None;
           Delete(s,StudentSet)
        END
END DropStudent;

PROCEDURE ChangeLevel(student#: StudentId);
  VAR s: StudentType;
BEGIN StudentException := NonexistentStudent;
        FOREACH s IN StudentSet
        WHERE    s.student# = student#
        DO StudentException := None;
          CASE s.level OF
            undergraduate: s.level := graduate  |
            graduate:      s.level := undergraduate
          END
        END
END ChangeLevel;

PROCEDURE ChangeAddress(student#: StudentId;
                        address:  String30);
  VAR s: StudentType;
BEGIN StudentException := NonexistentStudent;
        FOREACH s IN StudentSet
        WHERE    s.student# = student#
        DO StudentException := None;
           s.address := address
        END
END ChangeAddress;

PROCEDURE ChangePhone(student#: StudentId;
                      phone:   String7);
  VAR s: StudentType;
BEGIN StudentException := NonexistentStudent;
        FOREACH s IN StudentSet
        WHERE    s.student# = student#
```

```
        DO StudentException : = None;
            s.phone : = phone
        END
END ChangePhone;

PROCEDURE FindStudent(name: String30;
                        VAR student#: StudentId);

PROCEDURE Selected ( ): Boolean;
  VAR ch: Char;
BEGIN WriteString("Desired student? Y/N");
      ReadCh(ch);
      IF (ch = "Y") OR (ch = "y")
      THEN Return(true)
      ELSE Return(false)
      END
END Selected;

VAR s: StudentType;

BEGIN student# : = EmptyString;
      StudentException : = NonexistentStudent;
      FOREACH s IN StudentSet
      WHERE    s.name = name
      DO WriteStudent(s);
          IF Selected( ) THEN
            student# : = s.student#;
            StudentException : = None;
            Exit
          END
      END
END FindStudent;

PROCEDURE ReadStudent(VAR s: StudentType); (* block *)

PROCEDURE WriteStudent(s: StudentType); (* block *)

BEGIN Exception : = None
END Student.
```

Now consider some examples of clients, that is, users of the Student module. Such a module typically imports StudentType and those procedures declared in the module Student that the module needs in order to accomplish its task. To find out what the actual effects accomplished by those procedures are, as opposed to the intended effects, a user module requires import of StudentException. Other import lists are also typically included, for example, import of procedures declared in the module StandardIO in order to communicate with the terminal user (the one who activated a user module). An example of such a module that is also a program module (i.e., a program, a compilation unit) is given below:

```
MODULE EnrollStudents;

    FROM Student IMPORT StudentType, ReadStudent, EnrollStudent,
                        StudentExceptionType, StudentException;

    FROM StandardIO IMPORT WriteString, WriteLn;

    VAR s: StudentType;

BEGIN ReadStudent(s);
        WHILE NOT(StudentException = ReadException) DO
          EnrollStudent(s);
          IF StudentException = DuplicateStudentId THEN
            WriteString(" Duplicate student id ");
            WriteString(s.student#); WriteLn
          END;
          ReadStudent(s)
        END
END EnrollStudents.
```

Further examples are modules performing deletion and update of students using the only possible way: via procedures declared in the module
Student.

```
MODULE DeleteStudents;

    FROM Student IMPORT StudentType, DropStudent,
                        StudentExceptionType, StudentException;

    FROM StandardIO IMPORT ReadString,
                        WriteString, WriteLn,
                        IOException;

    VAR Student#: StudentId;

BEGIN ReadString(Student#);
        WHILE NOT IOException DO
          DropStudent(Student#);
          IF StudentException = NonexistentStudent THEN
            WriteString(" Nonexistent student id ");
            WriteString(Student#); WriteLn
          END;
          ReadString(Student#)
        END
END DeleteStudents.

MODULE UpdateAddresses;

    FROM Student IMPORT StudentType, ChangeAddress,
                        StudentExceptionType, StudentException;
```

```
  FROM StandardIO IMPORT ReadString,
                         WriteString, WriteLn,
                         IOException;

VAR Student#:StudentId;
    Address:  String30;

BEGIN ReadString(Student#);
      WHILE NOT IOException DO
        ReadString(Address);
        IF IOException THEN
          WriteString(" Student id not followed by address ");
          WriteLn
        ELSE
          ChangeAddress(Student#, Address);
          IF StudentException = NonexistentStudent
          THEN WriteString(" Nonexistent student id ");
               WriteString(Student#); WriteLn
        END
      END;
      ReadString(Student#)
      END

END UpdateAddresses.
```

7 Levels of Object-Type Safety

The examples presented thus far illustrate a *strict object-action-oriented approach* expressed in terms of modules. Its major advantage is strict control of actions performed by users of an object defined as a module. Only those actions (procedures) exported from the definition module of that object may be performed upon that object, and absolutely nothing else. Even queries are restricted to those specified by the exported procedures. Not only does this guarantee correctness of users' actions with respect to various types of integrity constraints associated with an object, but it also represents a mechanism for enforcing access rights to an object. Users of an object are allowed to see and change only those properties of an object accessible via exported procedures.

This strict approach to object-type safety is often too restricted. For example, consider the situation in which we allow users to perform arbitrary queries upon a particular object, but restrict their data-manipulation actions to those specified in the definition module of that object. The justification for this approach is that it is not realistic to expect that all queries that users of an object may wish to ask can be anticipated and specified as procedures exported from the definition module of an object. As in the relational approach, we often have to allow for unanticipated users' queries. Furthermore, database systems are equipped with stand-alone query languages for easy specification of such unanticipated queries. Note that object-type safety, as far as the integrity constraints associated with the object are concerned, is still guaranteed.

This approach is illustrated by the following definition of the object type Student:

```
DEFINITION MODULE Student;

    EXPORT QUALIFIED StudentType, StudentId,
                     StudentSetType,
                     StudentSet,(* READONLY *)
                     ReadStudent, WriteStudent,
                     EnrollStudent, DropStudent,
                     UpdateStudent,
                     StudentExceptionType, StudentException;

    TYPE StudentId = String7;
         LevelType = (undergraduate, graduate);
         StudentType = RECORD student#:StudentId;
                              name:    String30;
                              address: String30;
                              phone:   String7;
                              level:   LevelType;
                              gradeaverage: Real
                       END;
         StudentSetType = ENTITY SET OF StudentType;

         StudentExceptionType = (None,
                                 DuplicateStudentId,
                                 NonexistentStudent,
                                 ReadException,
                                 WriteException);

    VAR StudentSet: StudentSetType;
        StudentException: StudentExceptionType;

    PROCEDURE EnrollStudent(student: StudentType);
    PROCEDURE DropStudent(student#: StudentId);
    PROCEDURE UpdateStudent(student: StudentType);
    PROCEDURE ReadStudent(VAR student: StudentType);
    PROCEDURE WriteStudent(student: StudentType);
END Student.
```

In the above definition module, the entity set variable StudentSet is exported in read-only mode so that arbitrary queries of this set are permitted by the modules that import StudentSet, as in the following example:

```
MODULE DisplayExcellentGraduates;

   FROM Student IMPORT StudentType, LevelType,
                         StudentSetType, StudentSet,
                         WriteStudent;

   VAR s: StudentType;

BEGIN FOREACH s IN StudentSet
         WHERE   (s.level = graduate)
         AND     (s.gradeaverage > 4.5)
         DO      WriteStudent(s)
         END
END DisplayExcellentGraduates.
```

Another example is a module that computes the cumulative average grade of all undergraduate students:

```
MODULE UndergraduateAverage;

   FROM Student IMPORT StudentType, LevelType,
                         StudentSetType, StudentSet;

   FROM StandardIO IMPORT WriteString, WriteReal,
                            WriteLn;

   VAR s: StudentType;
       Sum, Average: Real; Count: Cardinal;

BEGIN Sum := 0.0; Count := 0;
      FOREACH s IN StudentSet
      WHERE    s.level = undergraduate
      DO Sum := Sum + s.average;
         Count := Count + 1
      END;
      IF Count < > 0 THEN
         Average := Sum/Float(Count)
      END;
      WriteString(" Undergraduate cumulative average: ");
      WriteReal(Average,3); WriteLn

END UndergraduateAverage.
```

Actions that actually affect the set StudentSet are possible as long as procedures exported from the module Student are used, as in the following example:

```
MODULE MoveGraduates;

   FROM Student IMPORT StudentType, LevelType,
                         StudentSetType, StudentSet,
                         UpdateStudent;
```

```
FROM StandardIO IMPORT ReadString, WriteString;

VAR s: StudentType;
    newaddress: String30;

PROCEDURE ReadAddress;

BEGIN WriteString("Enter new address of student:");
      WriteString(s.name);
      WriteString(s.address);
      ReadString(newaddress)
END ReadAddress;

BEGIN FOREACH s IN StudentSet
      WHERE     s.level = graduate
      DO ReadAddress;
         s.address := newaddress;
         UpdateStudent(s)
      END
END MoveGraduates.
```

Note that the assignment s.address := newaddress has no effect on the variable StudentSet, which is necessarily imported in read-only mode. It is the execution of the procedure call UpdateStudent that in fact affects StudentSet.

We now consider unrestricted export of an entity set variable so that we obtain the situation that corresponds to unified relational query and manipulation languages. These languages permit specification of queries, insertions, deletions, and updates in a unified, relational manner. In order to obtain such a situation in our framework, no insert, delete, or update actions are associated with an object in its definition module. Appropriate specification of such actions is thus left to the users of that module. We emphasize, however, that this is only an illustration. Entity set (and all other) variables are in our approach always exported in read-only mode, and the only way to affect those variables is by invoking procedures exported from the definition modules in which those variables are declared.

```
DEFINITION MODULE Student;

EXPORT QUALIFIED StudentType, StudentId, LevelType,
                 StudentSetType, StudentSet,
                 ReadStudent, WriteStudent,
                 StudentExceptionType, StudentException;

TYPE StudentId = String7;
     LevelType = (undergraduate,graduate);

     StudentType = RECORD student#: StudentId;
                          name:     String30;
```

```
                                    address:   String30;
                                    phone:     String7;
                                    level:     LevelType;
                                    gradeaverage: Real
                  END;
        StudentSetType = ENTITY SET OF StudentType;

        StudentExceptionType = (None,
                                ReadException,
                                WriteException);

VAR StudentSet: StudentSetType;
    StudentException: StudentExceptionType;

PROCEDURE ReadStudent(VAR student: StudentType);
PROCEDURE WriteStudent(student: StudentType);

END Student.
```

For the above definition module, we present two examples of its users: modules that import StudentType and StudentSet, and perform some actions on the latter. Since no actions on StudentSet are defined in the module Student, its user modules necessarily specify those actions entirely by itself (ReadStudent and WriteStudent are terminal input/output actions, and obviously do not affect StudentSet in any way). The module DropPoorGraduates, given below, performs a query, interrogates the terminal user, and performs deletion if it is confirmed:

```
MODULE DropPoorGraduates;

    FROM Student IMPORT StudentType, LevelType,
                        StudentSetType, StudentSet,
                        WriteStudent;

    FROM StandardIO IMPORT ReadCh, ReadString,
                           WriteString;

    VAR s: StudentType;

    PROCEDURE DeletionConfirmed( ): Boolean;
      VAR ch: Char;
    BEGIN WriteString("Confirm deletion: Y/N >");
          ReadCh(ch);
          IF (ch = "Y") OR (ch = "y") THEN
          Return(true) ELSE Return(false) END
    END DeletionConfirmed;

BEGIN FOREACH s IN StudentSet
        WHERE     (s.level = graduate)
        AND       (s.gradeaverage < 3.5)
```

```
      DO WriteStudent(s);
          IF DeletionConfirmed( ) THEN
              Delete(s, StudentSet)
          END
      END
```

END DropPoorGraduates.

The module InsertStudents performs insertion of a set of students and then handles the problem of uniqueness of student identifiers in StudentSet. In reality, end users of an object are not expected to check violation of integrity constraints in advance. Rather, the violations are detected by a database system and are not accepted. Specification of integrity constraints associated with an object type is performed in a nonprocedural, query-like language. We do not deal with such languages and related matters in this book, since it is entirely devoted to the programming language level where such features are difficult to introduce in a nice, simple, and consistent manner (with respect to other programming language concepts).

MODULE InsertStudents;

```
    FROM Student IMPORT StudentType, StudentId,
                        StudentSetType, StudentSet,
                        StudentExceptionType, StudentException;

    FROM StandardIO IMPORT WriteString, WriteLn;

    VAR s: StudentType;

    PROCEDURE UniqueStudentId(student#: StudentId): Boolean;
      VAR s: StudentType;
    BEGIN FOREACH s IN StudentSet
          WHERE     s.student#  = student#
          DO Return(false) END;
          Return(true)
    END UniqueStudentId;

BEGIN ReadStudent(s);
      WHILE NOT StudentException = ReadException
      DO
        IF UniqueStudentId(s.student#) THEN
           Insert(s,StudentSet)
        ELSE
           WriteString(" Duplicate student id " );
           WriteString(s.student#); WriteLn
        END
      END
```

END InsertStudents.

At the other extreme, it is possible to hide completely StudentType in the Student implementation module, so that the object type Student appears to its clients as a collection of actions applicable to the instances of that object type. Only those properties (attributes) of Student that are specified in the selector (projection) actions exported from its definition module are visible to its users. A particular instance of Student that is acted upon by a procedure exported from its definition module is determined by its identifier. So, in order to perform such an action, it is necessary to know that identifier. All of this is illustrated by the following Student definition module:

DEFINITION MODULE Student;

EXPORT QUALIFIED StudentId, SelectName,
                 SelectAddress, SelectPhone,
                 ChangeAddress, ChangePhone,
                 StudentExceptionType, StudentException;

TYPE StudentId = String7;
     StudentExceptionType = (None,
                               NonexistentStudent);
VAR StudentException: StudentExceptionType;

PROCEDURE SelectName(student#: StudentId;
                     VAR name: String30);
PROCEDURE SelectAddress(student#: StudentId;
                        VAR address: String30);
PROCEDURE SelectPhone(student#: StudentId;
                      VAR phone: String30);
PROCEDURE ChangeAddress(student#: StudentId;
                          newaddress: String30);
PROCEDURE ChangePhone(student#: StudentId;
                        newphone: String7);
END Student.

The above module is an illustration of what is called an *abstract data type* in programming languages. The actual representation of its instances is completely hidden from the users of that type. As far as the users are concerned, that type is defined entirely in terms of actions applicable to its instances. Introducing this type of abstraction prevents users from directly manipulating object instances. Why this is important is easily seen by the following module defining the abstraction called *output stream:*

DEFINITION MODULE OutputStream;

EXPORT QUALIFIED Exception, OpenOutput,
                 CloseOutput, WriteCh, WriteLn;
     VAR Exception: Boolean;

```
PROCEDURE OpenOutput(s: String);
PROCEDURE CloseOutput(s: String);
PROCEDURE WriteCh(ch: Char);
PROCEDURE WriteLn;
```

END OutputStream.

The output-stream abstraction hides from its users all the differences and peculiarities of various types of output devices (terminal screen, disk or tape file, printer). It recognizes only the structure of the output stream as a sequence of characters structured into lines, and provides actions for writing (appending) new characters to that sequence (WriteCh) and for controlling its line structure (WriteLn). Output is by default directed to the user terminal. OpenOutput action redirects output to a file, and CloseOutput back to the terminal.

8 Export-Import Rules

We now summarize briefly the main features of modules and clarify the rules governing export and import of identifiers.

   (i) We have introduced three types of modules: main (program) modules, definition modules, and implementation modules. Each is a compilation unit, that is, a program text that may be submitted for separate compilation.
  (ii) A main module is in fact a main program. It behaves as a transaction. It consists of a collection of declarations and a sequence of statements enclosed in brackets MODULE and END. Its heading contains the module identifier, and it may contain a number of import lists. An import list contains identifiers of objects declared in another, separately compiled module. A program module is not permitted to export objects (i.e., its heading cannot contain an export list).
 (iii) A definition module contains a collection of constant, type, and variable declarations, and specifications of procedure headings. It may contain a number of import lists and an export list. The export list contains identifiers of objects declared in the module that may be used by the clients (i.e., users) of that module.
 (iv) Definition modules require QUALIFIED export of identifiers, which means that those identifiers must be prefixed by the definition module identifier in all importing modules. Qualified export avoids clashes of identical identifiers exported from different modules and presumably denoting different objects. If such clashes do not occur, the FROM clause, which indicates the source of import, is used in an importing module, in which case imported identifiers are used directly, without the prefix required by qualified export.

  (v) Standard identifiers are always imported automatically into all mod-
       ules. If a module name is imported, all identifiers in the export list
       of that module are imported. However, they must be prefixed (qual-
       ified) by the module identifier when used in the importing module.
       If a module identifier is exported, then all identifiers in the export
       list of that module are exported.
 (vi) If a record type is exported, all identifiers of its attributes are ex-
       ported as well. If an enumeration type is exported, then all identifiers
       of its elements are also exported.
(vii) An implementation module contains a collection of declarations of
       constants, types, variables, and procedures, and a sequence of state-
       ments (the latter is called a *module body*).
(viii) Definition and implementation modules exist in pairs. Both may
       contain import lists, but an implementation module cannot contain
       an export list. All identifiers of objects declared in a definition module
       are automatically imported into its corresponding implementation
       module. The implementation module must contain complete dec-
       larations of procedures whose headings appear in its corresponding
       definition module. It also contains other declarations of objects that
       are not exported from the corresponding definition module; that is,
       that are not relevant to the users of that module, but rather, pertinent
       to its implementation.

To illustrate some of these rules, consider the following example of a
clash of variables:

MODULE DeleteStudents;

  FROM NewStudent IMPORT Id, Drop,
                                ExceptionType, Exception;

  FROM StandardIO IMPORT ReadString,
                         WriteLn, WriteString,
                         Exception;

  VAR Student#: Id;

BEGIN ReadString(Student#);
          WHILE NOT Exception DO
            Drop(Student#);
            IF Exception = Nonexistent THEN
              WriteString(" Nonexistent student id ");
              WriteString(Student#); WriteLn
            END;
            ReadString(Student#)
          END
END DeleteStudents.

There are several ways to avoid this problem. Two are presented below:

```
MODULE DeleteStudents;

   FROM Student IMPORT StudentId, DropStudent,
                        StudentExceptionType, StudentException;

   FROM StandardIO IMPORT ReadString,
                          WriteString,WriteLn,
                          IOException;

   VAR Student#: StudentId;

BEGIN ReadString(Student#);
         WHILE NOT IOException DO
            DropStudent(Student#);
            IF StudentException = NonexistentStudent THEN
               WriteString("Nonexistent student id");
               WriteString(Student#); WriteLn
            END;
            ReadString(Student#)
         END

END DeleteStudents.

MODULE DeleteStudents;
   IMPORT NewStudent;
   IMPORT StandardIO;

VAR Student#: NewStudent.Id;

BEGIN StandardIO.ReadString(Student#);
         WHILE NOT StandardIO.Exception DO
            NewStudent.Drop(Student#);
            IF NewStudent.Exception =
               NewStudent.Nonexistent THEN
               StandardIO.WriteString(Student#);
               StandardIO.WriteLn
            END;
            StandardIO.ReadString(Student#)
         END

END DeleteStudents.
```

Exercises

(1) Traversal Recursion (see Dayal et al. (1985))

   (i) Consider the following representation of a road map:

```
TYPE Road    = RECORD SourceCity:       String20;
                      DestinationCity:  String20;
                      RoadLength:       Real
             END;
     RoadSet = ENTITY SET OF Road;

VAR RoadNetwork: RoadSet
```

(ii) Write a recursive procedure that prints out the names of all cities that may be reached by strings of roads starting from a given city (the parameter of the desired procedure).

(iii) Write a recursive procedure that prints out the names of all cities within a given distance of a given city (parameter of the desired procedure).

(iv) Write a recursive procedure that computes the shortest path (string of roads) from a given source city to a given destination city (parameters of the desired procedure).

(v) Observe that the above road network contains cycles that should be treated appropriately in the design of the above procedures.

(2) Train Timetable

(i) Suppose a train timetable is defined as follows:

```
TYPE ClassType = (business, first, second, third);

     Connection = RECORD Connection#:        String7;
                         SourceStation:      String20;
                         DestinationStation: String20;
                         Distance:           Real;
                         LengthOfTravel:     Real;
                         AvailableClasses:   SET OF ClassType
                  END;

VAR Timetable: ENTITY SET OF Connection;

PROCEDURE Fare(Distance: Real;
               Class: ClassType): Real;
(* block *)
```

(ii) Write an application procedure that is triggered by a terminal user who provides the source station, the destination station, and a set of acceptable classes, and obtains as a response a schedule of train connections with a minimum total time of the journey.

(iii) Modify the above application procedure so that the output is the cheapest required connection (i.e., so that acceptable classes is not an input any more)

(3) Integrity Constraints

(i) Suppose the object types Department and Employee have the following attributes:

```
TYPE DepartmentRecord  = RECORD department#: DepartmentId;
                                 name:       String30;
                                 manager#:   EmployeeId
                         END;
TYPE EmployeeRecord    = RECORD employee#:  EmployeeId;
                                 name:       String30;
                                 salary:     Real;
                                 department#: DepartmentId
                         END
```

(ii) Write up a complete specification of the definition modules for the above two object types.

(iii) Write an implementation module of the object type Employee with the condition that actions InsertEmployee and UpdateSalary associated with this object type maintain the integrity constraint that each employee earns less than his or her manager. Observe that this requires the action SelectManager associated with the object type Department that returns the manager identifier given the department identifier.

(iv) Observe that this integrity constraint may also be affected by the actions ChangeManager (of a department) and ChangeDepartment (of an employee). Write up the declarations of these two procedures with the condition that the above integrity constraint is satisfied. Add the appropriate actions to the definition modules of the object types Employee and Department, if necessary.

(v) Consider some possible exceptions to the stated integrity constraint. For example,
(a) an employee works overtime and thus has an exceptionally high salary;
(b) a manager is a part-time employee and, consequently, has an exceptionally low salary; and
(c) an employee is only temporarily appointed to the manager position, and thus, subordinates (employees) may have higher salaries.
(vi) Revise the specified definition and implementation modules of the object types Department and Employee to take into account the above possible violations of the specified integrity constraint.

(4) Computed Attribute Values

(i) Consider the following action-oriented definition of the object type Department:

```
DEFINITION MODULE Department;

EXPORT QUALIFIED DepartmentId, SelectDepartment,
                 Address, NumberOfEmployees,
                 AverageSalary;

TYPE DepartmentId = String7;

PROCEDURE SelectDepartment(name: String20;
                 VAR department#:
                 DepartmentId);

PROCEDURE NumberOfEmployees(department#:
                 DepartmentId): Cardinal;

PROCEDURE AverageSalary(department#: DepartmentId): Real;

PROCEDURE Address(department#: DepartmentId;
                 VAR address: String7);

TYPE ExceptionType = (None,NonExistentDepartment);
VAR Exception: ExceptionType;

END Department.
```

Note that the object type Department, in addition to the ordinary attributes such as department#, name, and address, also has attributes whose values are meant to be computed from values of attributes of the corresponding instances of object type Employee.

(ii) Specify an implementation module of the object type Department and the requirements of that implementation with respect to the module Employee.

(iii) Analyze other possible representations of the object types Department and Employee in view of the requirement for the existence of NumberOfEmployees and AverageSalary attributes of the object type Department.

(5) String Handling and Open Arrays (see Logitech Modula-2/86)

(i) Consider the following definition of a variable character string handler:

```
DEFINITION MODULE Strings;

EXPORT QUALIFIED AssignString, CopyString,
                 InsertString, DeleteString,
                 StringPosition, StringLength,
                 ConcatenateStrings, CompareStrings;

PROCEDURE AssignString(VAR source, destination: ARRAY OF
                 Char);
```

```
        PROCEDURE InsertString(substr: ARRAY OF Char;
                               VAR str: ARRAY OF Char;
                               index: Cardinal);

        PROCEDURE DeleteString(VAR str: ARRAY OF Char;
                               index: Cardinal;
                               length: Cardinal);

        PROCEDURE StringPosition(substr, str: ARRAY OF Char):
                                                        Cardinal;

        PROCEDURE CopyString(str: ARRAY OF Char;
                             index: Cardinal;
                             VAR result: ARRAY OF Char);

        PROCEDURE ConcatenateString(s1,s2: ARRAY OF Char;
                                    VAR result: ARRAY OF Char);

        PROCEDURE StringLength(VAR str: ARRAY OF Char):
                                                        Cardinal;

        PROCEDURE CompareStrings(s1,s2: ARRAY OF Char): Integer;

        END Strings.
```

(ii) The procedures in the above definition module perform the following actions:

    assignment of the value of the string variable source into the string variable destination;

    insertion of the string substr into the string variable str starting at the position determined by index;

    deletion of length characters from the string variable str starting at the position determined by index;

    computation of the position (index) in the string variable string of the first occurrence of the string substr;

    copying of at most length characters from the string str into the string variable result starting at the position index;

    concatenation of strings s1 and s2, where s1 is the left string and s2 the right string in the result;

    computation of the number of characters in a string; and

    comparison of strings s1 and s2, with the result being an integer value, according to the following convention:

      -1 if s1 is less than s2,

       0 if s1 equals s2, and

       1 if s1 is greater than s2.

(iii) Extend the above definition module with appropriate indication of exceptions that may occur during execution of the above described actions. Examples of such exceptions are when an assigment is performed, the destination is not large enough to accept the source;

when an insertion is performed, index is greater than the length of the destination string (StringLength(str));

likewise for deletion; and also, when deletion is performed, there are no length characters to delete;

when determining the position of a substring, the substring does not occur in the given string (str);

when copying is performed, the length of the string to be copied is larger than the destination;

when concatenating strings s1 and s2, the sum of their lengths (StringLength(s1) + StringLength(s2)) is larger than the resultant string (StringLength(result))

(iv) Propose an appropriate extension of the definitions of string-handling actions that takes into account possible exceptions. Propose an exception-handling technique.

(6) Budget Breakdown

(i) Budget breakdown is an example of a hierarchical, acyclic structure. Its relational representation is given below:

```
TYPE ItemId = String5;
        BudgetItem = RECORD Item#:     ItemId;
                            allocation: Real;
                            priority:   Integer
                     END;
        BreakDownItem = RECORD Item#:      ItemId;
                               SubItem#: ItemId
                        END;

    VAR Budget:    ENTITY SET OF BudgetItem;
        BreakDown: ENTITY SET OF BreakDownItem;
```

(ii) Write a procedure

```
PROCEDURE Predecessor(item#: ItemId;
                      VAR pred#: ItemId);
```

that computes the immediate predecessor of a budget item in the budget breakdown.

(iii) Write a recursive function procedure

```
PROCEDURE PercentOfTotal(item#: ItemId): Real;
```

that computes the percentage of the total budget allocated to a particular budget item.

(iv) The budget breakdown abstraction may be viewed in the object-oriented approach as follows:

DEFINITION MODULE Budget;

  EXPORT QUALIFIED ItemId, BudgetItem,
                              InsertItem, DeleteItem,
                              ChangeAllocation, ChangePriority,
                              PercentageOfTotal, Predecessor,
                              DisplayItem, DisplaySubItems,
                              ExceptionType, Exception;

  TYPE ItemId   = String8;
       BudgetItem = RECORD Item#:   ItemId;
                              allocation: Real;
                              priority: Cardinal
                    END;
       ExceptionType = (None,DuplicateItemId,
                              NonexistentItem);
  VAR Exception: ExceptionType;

  PROCEDURE InsertItem(item: BudgetItem);
  PROCEDURE DeleteItem(item#: ItemId);
  PROCEDURE ChangeAllocation(item#: ItemId;
                                   newallocation: Real);
  PROCEDURE ChangePriority(item#: ItemId;
                                   newpriority: Cardinal);
  PROCEDURE PercentageOfTotal(item#: ItemId): Real;
  PROCEDURE DisplayItem(item#: ItemId);
  PROCEDURE DisplaySubItems(item#: ItemId);
  PROCEDURE Predecessor(item#: ItemId;
                                   VAR pred#: ItemId);
  PROCEDURE AddSubItem(item#, subitem#: ItemId);
  PROCEDURE DropSubItem(item#, subitem#: ItemId);

END Budget.

Observe that the above representation indicates that the actual relational representation of the budget breakdown is hidden in the implementation module. Write up the implementation module Budget.

(7) Circuit Design

(i) Separation of two levels of abstraction in the definition of an object type, its external specification, and its implementation is of fundamental importance in circuit design (see (Batory and Kim, 1986)). The interface of a circuit specifies its inputs and outputs, and the function that relates the two. An implementation of a circuit is usually defined as a composition of less complex circuits based on the given interface specifications of those components. Each of those components again has its implementation guaranteeing correctness of its external (interface) specification, and so on. This hierarchical decomposition, down to the level of primitive components, is perhaps the only way of coping with the immense complexity of the design of complex circuits.

(ii) An example is a circuit of a 4-bit adder. Its interface specification contains a pair (X, Y) of 4-bit input numbers and a 5-bit output number Z representing their sum and a carry:

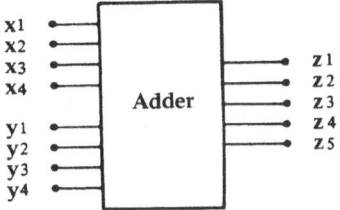

(iii) To what extent is the definition module suitable for the interface specification of the adder object type? Write up such a definition module.

(iv) One possible implementation of an adder is a so-called ripple-carry through the required number of adder-slice circuits. For example, an implementation of a 4-bit adder may be specified in terms of four adder-slice circuits as follows:

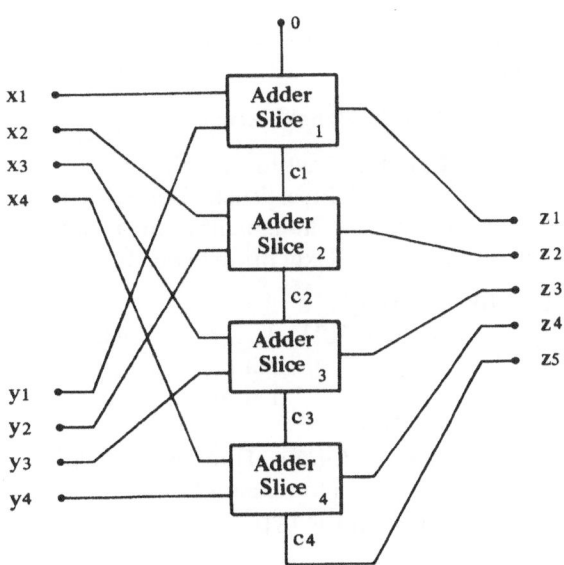

 (v) Specify the interface of the adder-slice object.

 (vi) Given specifications of the interfaces of the adder and adder slice objects, specify the implementation of the adder object according to the diagram presented in (iv).

 (vii) Make an appropriate conclusion about the suitability of the definition and implementation modules for the interface and implementation specification of a circuit object.

(8) Task network (see (Dayal et al., 1985))

 (i) The following diagram is an example of a task network:

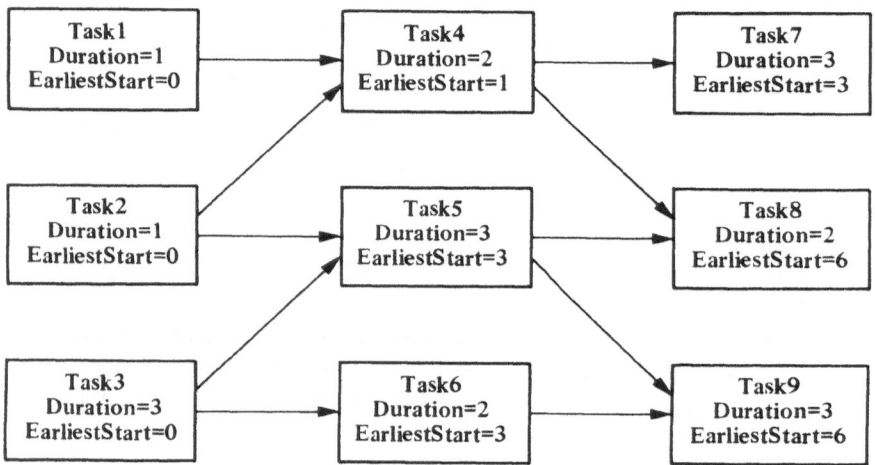

 (ii) Consider the following object-oriented specification of the task network abstraction:

DEFINITION MODULE TaskNetwork;

    EXPORT QUALIFIED TaskId, TaskType,
                     InsertTask, DeleteTask,
                     ChangeDuration, DisplayPredecessors,
                     ExceptionType, Exception;

    TYPE TaskId = String8;
         TaskType = RECORD Task#:   TaskId;
                           Name: String;
                           Duration: Real
                   END;
         ExceptionType = (None, DuplicateTaskId,
                          NonexistentTask);
    VAR Exception: ExceptionType;

```
      PROCEDURE InsertTask(task: TaskType);
      PROCEDURE DeleteTask(task#: TaskId);
      PROCEDURE ChangeDuration(task#: TaskId;
                                      NewDuration: Real);
      PROCEDURE ConnectTask(task#: TaskId;
                                  predecessor#: TaskId);
      PROCEDURE DisconnectTask(task#: TaskId;
                                  predecessor#: TaskId);
      PROCEDURE EarliestStart(task#: TaskId): Real;
      PROCEDURE DisplayTask(task#: TaskId);
      PROCEDURE DisplayPredecessors(task#: TaskId);

   END TaskNetwork.
```

Observe that the task attribute EarliestStart is specified as a function that computes the value of that attribute for the current values of the duration attribute of the task's predecessors. Furthermore, the actual implementation of interconnections among tasks in the network is hidden in the implementation module of the task network abstraction.

(iii) Specify the implementation module TaskNetwork using the relational (cartesian, aggregation) representation for the network, and recursion for the function EarliestStart.

(iv) Observe that procedure types permit the following representation of the task network abstraction:

```
   DEFINITION MODULE TaskNetwork;

   EXPORT QUALIFIED TaskId, EarliestStart, TaskType,
                        .
                        .
                        .
   TYPE TaskId = String8;

      EarliestStart = PROCEDURE(TaskId): Real;

      TaskType = RECORD Task#:    TaskId;
                        Name:     String;
                        Duration: Real;
                        Start:    EarliestStart
         END;
      .
      .
      .
   END TaskNetwork.
```

(v) Analyze the advantages and problems associated with the above representation, and write up its implementation module.

(9) Integrity Constraints

(i) Consider the following definition module of the object type Employee:

DEFINITION MODULE Employee;

EXPORT QUALIFIED EmployeeType, EmployeeId, JobType,
                 EmployeeSetType, EmployeeSet;

TYPE EmployeeId = String10;
     JobType = (programmer, analyst, technician);

     EmployeeType = RECORD employee#: EmployeeId;
                           name: String30;
                           job: JobType;
                           salary: Real;
                           department: String20
                    END;
     EmployeeSetType = ENTITY SET OF EmployeeType;

VAR EmployeeSet: EmployeeSetType;
TYPE ExceptionType = (None,NonExistentEmployee,
                      DuplicateEmployeeId, HighSalary);
VAR Exception: ExceptionType;

PROCEDURE InsertEmployee(employee: EmployeeType);

PROCEDURE DeleteEmployee(employee#: EmployeeId);

PROCEDURE ChangeJob(employee#: EmployeeId;
                    NewJob: JobType);

CONST SalaryLimit = 100000.00;

PROCEDURE UpdateSalary(employee#: EmployeeId;
                       increase: Real);

END Employee.

(ii) The purpose of the above example is to illustrate a rather typical integrity constraint that is specified as a permitted range of values of
an attribute. But, in this particular case, the type of the attribute is
Real, so that subranges of Modula-2 are not applicable. Write up the
implementation module of the above definition module.

(10) Precomputed Views

(i) The project-management model does not contain an explicit association
of employees and projects. The module Participants presented below
constructs the association in its implementation module:

DEFINITION MODULE Participants;

FROM ProjectManagement IMPORT ProjectId, EmployeeId;

```
EXPORT QUALIFIED Participant, ParticipantSet,
                 EmployeesOnProjects;

TYPE Participant = RECORD employee#: EmployeeId;
                          project#:   ProjectId
                 END;
     ParticipantSet = ENTITY SET OF Participant;

VAR EmployeesOnProjects: ENTITY SET OF Participant;

END.

IMPLEMENTATION MODULE Participants;

FROM ProjectManagement IMPORT TaskType, TaskSetType, Task,
                              AssignmentType,
                              AssignmentSetType,
                              Assignment;

VAR t: TaskType; a: AssignmentType;
    p: Participant;

BEGIN Empty(EmployeesOnProjects);
      FOREACH t IN Task, a IN Assignment
      WHERE    t.task# = a.task#
      DO p.employee# := a.employee#;
         p.project# := t.project#;
         Insert(p, EmployeesOnProjects)
      END
END Participants.
```

(ii) Give examples of clients of the module Participants.

(11) View Definition and Update

(i) One way of constructing views is by restriction and projection. For example, given the set of employees specified in exercise (9), we can construct a view consisting of those employees who are programmers. Furthermore, we can also decide that the relevant attributes of the view are only employee#, name, and salary (the attribute job is redundant in the view). The definition module presented below is one possible approach of expressing the described view:

```
DEFINITION MODULE Programmers;

FROM Employee IMPORT EmployeeId;

EXPORT QUALIFIED ProgrammerType, ProgrammerSetType,
                 ProgrammerSet,
                 ExceptionType, Exception;
```

```
TYPE ProgrammerType = RECORD employee#: EmployeeId;
                             name:        String30;
                             salary:      Real
          END;
     ProgrammerSetType = ENTITY SET OF ProgrammerType;

     ExceptionType = (None, NonExistentProgrammer,
          HighSalary);

PROCEDURE SelectProgrammers(VAR programmers:
                                    ProgrammerSetType);

PROCEDURE UpdateSalary(employee#: EmployeeId;
                       increase: Real);
END Programmers.
```

(ii) Assuming the object type Employee is defined in exercise (9), write up the implementation module Programmers.

(iii) Explore other possibilities and limitations of modules in terms of appropriate representations of views.

Bibliographical Notes

The basic references on procedures and modules as defined in Modula-2 are (Wirth, 1983a) and (Wirth, 1983b). The object-oriented approach to database management and database programming languages based on modules is the original contribution developed in this book. For a relational-oriented extension of Modula-2 see (Mall, Reimer, and Schmidt, 1984) and (Reimer, 1984). Yet another approach based on Modula (a predecessor of Modula-2) is (Rowe and Shones, 1979). Exercises (1), (2), (6), and (8) are based on examples in (Dayal et al., 1985). Exercise (5) is based on Logitech Modula-2/86, and exercise (7) on (Batory and Kim, 1985).

CHAPTER 3
Design Methodology

1 Abstraction, Localization, Refinement, and Incremental Design

The term *conceptual modeling* in this book refers to the specification of structural properties of entities and their relationships, and the associated actions upon them that preserve all those properties—the integrity constraints, in particular.

Structure modeling at the conceptual level involves classification of entities into entity types and specification of the associated integrity constraints. Furthermore, it requires application of data abstraction techniques such as aggregation, generalization, and covering to compose/decompose entity types. Each such application within the relational framework requires specification of the associated referential integrity constraints.

Conceptual action modeling consists of specification of abstract actions upon each entity type that preserve all the properties of such a type, particularly the integrity constraints. Such an action is specified using action-composition rules (sequential, conditional, selective, and foreach composition) starting from the primitive actions associated with the classification (insert, delete, and update instance of an entity type).

The design methodology presented in this section relies on a number of techniques, all of which are in one way or another based on some form of *abstraction*, a technique in which some properties of an application environment are suppressed at a particular design phase in order to emphasize other properties considered to be more relevant for that phase. This, in particular, means that after the final design phase the developed model contains only those properties abstracted from the application environment that are considered to be relevant.

This technique is used for both structure and action modeling. Classification, aggregation, generalization, and covering are data abstractions used in structure modeling. They have corresponding abstractions that are used for action modeling (parallel or sequential, selective, and foreach composition).

Actions associated with an object type in fact correspond to activities in the application environment involving objects of that type. This means our approach to conceptual modeling presented so far has to be refined in a crucial way. An application environment is still viewed as a collection of object types, but the essential part of specification of such a type is a set of actions upon instances of that type that correspond to the actual activities involving those objects in the application environment. For example, conceptual representation of the object type STUDENT would now be completed in the following manner:
it by the above data-abstraction techniques.

Thus, localization permits *incremental design,* which reduces the complexity of each design phase. Furthermore, since every entity type can simultaneously have component-of, is-a, and member-of relationships with other entity types, if the incremental-design methodology is used it is possible to introduce those relationships gradually, one at a time, each time redefining the appropriate abstract actions.

Refinement is a technique in which global design is performed first in order to produce a global model consisting of global data and action specification. In subsequent phases this global model is gradually decomposed into a hierarchy of more detailed specifications of both structure and actions. This technique of top-down design in which the amount of detail is carefully controlled in each step of the refinement process is a well-known programming methodology. However, a complementary bottom-up approach is also required for both structure and action modeling.

Using the top-down approach, entities are decomposed into their components (aggregation), subtypes (generalization), and member types (covering). This decomposition of structure is accompanied with the decomposition of abstract actions using sequential, conditional, selective, repetitive, and foreach composition rules. Using the bottom-up approach, higher level entities are derived from the already defined ones using the above data-abstraction techniques. These higher level entities are accompanied with higher level actions that are composed using the abstract actions upon the previously defined entities.

Having briefly introduced the conceptual modeling techniques, we will illustrate most of them on a particular example. We assume that the flight-reservation activity is abstracted from an application environment and our task is data modeling of that particular application. Since this application can be very complex, we will adopt some further simplifications along the way again using the abstraction technique. Hence, only three types of abstraction—aggregation, partitioning, and covering—will be used for data modeling. Consequently, sequential and foreach composition will be used for the specification of abstract actions.

The top-down design methodology will be applied in such a way that the most fundamental entity type (which is obviously FLIGHT) will be introduced first, together with its associated abstract actions. Further development of the model will proceed incrementally, introducing at each step one relationship of a previously defined entity with another entity that is either introduced at that step or already defined in one of the previous steps. Whenever such a relationship is introduced, all the relevant actions are either specified or redefined so that the referential integrity constraints are satisfied.

Localization is used frequently, particularly in the way abstract actions are specified for each entity type. Each such action is defined for only one entity type. In addition to that entity type, the action refers only to those entity types immediately related to that entity via aggregation and covering. Consequently, whenever a new relationship is introduced, only actions upon the related entities must be reconsidered for the refinement, and this would maintain the referential integrity constraints.

A particularly simple use of abstraction occurs in the presented design example. Initially, out of all possibly relevant attributes only the identifiers of entities are introduced. Specification of other attributes of the introduced entities is suppressed until the design phase in which all entities and their relationships, as well as all the actions upon them that maintain those relationships, are specified.

(i) *FLIGHT*. In the first design phase, we introduce the most fundamental entity type FLIGHT and its identifier FLIGHT#. Specification of other attributes of the entity type FLIGHT is postponed for some later design phase. We also specify three actions associated with this entity type: Insert a flight, Delete a flight, and Select a flight. The action Get that appears in these three composite actions associated with the entity type FLIGHT is used to obtain the values of the attributes specified in that action. Those values are either requested from the terminal or, in the case of entity identifiers, may be generated in some other, possibly system-determined manner.

FLIGHT

Select: Get flight attributes;
        Display flights with the given attributes;
        Select one and return its identifier

Insert: Get flight identifier;
        Get other flight attributes;
        Insert flight

Delete: Get flight identifier;
    Delete flight

FLIGHT(FLIGHT#, OTHER_ATTRIBUTES)

(ii) *DEPARTURE.* In the second design phase, we observe an obvious fact that each particular flight (an instance of the entity type FLIGHT) has its set of departures, where a departure is associated with a particular date. Departures are instances of an entity type DEPARTURE. Furthermore, there exists a functional dependency

DEPARTURE → FLIGHT,

which maps a departure into its flight. Indeed, a departure belongs to one and only one flight, and thus, the set of departures is partitioned into disjoint subsets, one such subset per instance of the entity type FLIGHT. A departure cannot exist without a flight, which means that the function DEPARTURE → FLIGHT is total.

To represent this sort of decomposition of entities of type FLIGHT into disjoint sets of entities of type DEPARTURE, we introduce two attributes of the latter entity type: its identifier DEPARTURE#, and the identifier of the flight FLIGHT# to which an instance of the entity type DEPARTURE belongs. But then this sort of representation requires careful maintenance of the referential integrity constraint, which requires that a departure must belong to an existing flight:

DEPARTURE[FLIGHT#] <= FLIGHT[FLIGHT#]

This means that the specification of insert and update actions associated with the entity type DEPARTURE must be performed in such a way that this integrity constraint is maintained.

Three basic actions—Insert, Delete, and Select—are specified below for the entity type DEPARTURE:

DEPARTURE

Select: Get departure attributes;
    Display departures with the given attributes;
    Select one and return its identifier

Insert: Get flight identifier;
    Get departure identifier;
    Get other departure attributes;
    Insert departure

Delete: Get departure identifier;
    Delete departure

Since we in fact redefined FLIGHT as the quotient type of the earlier introduced entity type DEPARTURE, however, we have to redefine the actions associated with the former entity type. Insertion of an instance of the entity type FLIGHT is followed by insertion of its associated set of instances (its associated partition, possibly empty) of the entity type DEPARTURE, and deletion of such an instance is followed by deletion of all its associated DEPARTURE instances. The reasons were explained above.

FLIGHT

DEPARTURE

FLIGHT(FLIGHT#, OTHER_ATTRIBUTES)
DEPARTURE(DEPARTURE#, FLIGHT#, OTHER_ATTRIBUTES)
DEPARTURE[FLIGHT#] < = FLIGHT[FLIGHT#]

FLIGHT

Insert: Get flight identifier;
       Check if it exists;
       Get other flight attributes;
       Insert flight;
       Insert the set of flight departures

Delete: Get flight identifier;
       Delete flight;
       Delete the set of flight departures

(iii) *PASSENGER*. Further decomposition of our model of the flight-reservation application is based on the observation that in order to make a reservation we have to specify a flight, its departure, and a passenger. Since each departure has its associated set of passengers, we could say that DEPARTURE is the cover type of the entity type PASSENGER. But note that a passenger may be booked to a (nonempty) set of departures, just as a departure has a set (possibly empty) of passengers. So a set of passengers is a property of a departure and a set of departures is a property of a passenger, as indicated in the following diagram:

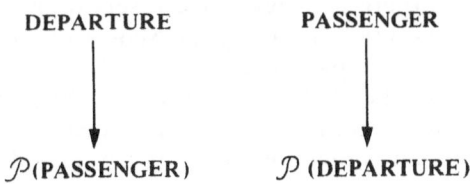

     DEPARTURE   PASSENGER

    $\mathcal{P}$(PASSENGER) $\mathcal{P}$ (DEPARTURE)

(iv) *RESERVATION*. Immediate representation of the above fact is per-haps appealing from the semantic viewpoint, but its implementation causes some well-known problems, which we discussed in the section on nor-malized models. In addition, we can naturally use the bottom-up approach at this design phase and compose entity types DEPARTURE and PAS-SENGER using the aggregation abstraction to obtain a new entity type, which is obviously the entity type RESERVATION. This approach is well suited to the relational model. Indeed, the relationship between entity types DEPARTURE and PASSENGER is not of the functional nature; it is, in fact, a relation, and thus, it is natural to represent it as such. Perhaps more important is that it corresponds to the entity type RES-ERVATION whose semantics is quite clear in this example. In accordance with the aggregation abstraction, we can take identifiers of the entity types DEPARTURE and PASSENGER as the attributes of the entity type RESERVATION to obtain a data model conforming to the requirements of the relational approach:

PASSENGER(PASSENGER#, OTHER_ATTRIBUTES)
DEPARTURE(DEPARTURE#, OTHER_ATTRIBUTES)
RESERVATION(RESERVATION#, DEPARTURE#,
                    PASSENGER#, OTHER_ATTRIBUTES)

With the above relational design decision, two referential integrity con-straints must be observed. They require that a reservation must refer to an existing departure and to an existing passenger. Formally, we must have

RESERVATION[DEPARTURE#] < = DEPARTURE[DEPARTURE#]
RESERVATION[PASSENGER#] < = PASSENGER[PASSENGER#]

at any moment of time. These conditions impose some constraints on the specification of actions associated with the entity type RESERVATION. When a new reservation is inserted, the values of its attributes DEPAR-TURE# and PASSENGER# must be identifiers of an existing departure and existing passenger, respectively. Update actions such as change de-parture or change passenger of a reservation must also ensure the same condition is satisfied. It is natural to assume a passenger exists in the database as long as there is at least one reservation for that passenger. So deletion of a reservation or change passenger of a reservation actions may imply deletion of the passenger.

Deletion actions of the DEPARTURE and PASSENGER entity types must now be redefined so that deletion of an instance of either of these two entity types requires deletion of all its associated RESERVATION instances.

PASSENGER

Select: Get passenger attributes;
   Display passengers with the given attributes;
   Select one and return passenger identifier

Insert: Get passenger identifier;
   Get other passenger attributes;
   Insert passenger;
   Insert the set of passenger's reservations

Delete: Get passenger identifier;
   Delete passenger;
   For each reservation of the given passenger,
    Delete reservation

RESERVATION

Insert: Get reservation identifier;
   Get passenger identifier;
   Get departure identifier;
   Get other reservation attributes;
   Insert reservation

Delete: Get reservation identifier;
   Find the reservation with the given identifier and get its
    passenger identifier;
   If last reservation of the passenger, then
    Delete passenger;
   Delete reservation

DEPARTURE

Delete: Get departure identifier;
   For each reservation of the departure,
    Delete reservation;
   Delete departure

(v) *Graphical representation*

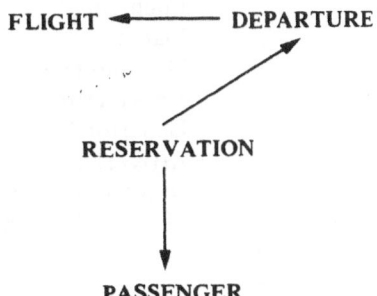

(vi) *Relational schema*

FLIGHT(FLIGHT#, SOURCE, DESTINATION, DAYS)
PASSENGER(PASSENGER#, NAME, ADDRESS, PHONE, SEX,
        NUMRESERVATIONS)
DEPARTURE(DEPARTURE#, FLIGHT#, PLANE,
        DEPARTUREDATE, ARRIVALDATE,
        DEPARTURETIME, ARRIVALTIME,
        NUMOFPASSENGER, MAXNUMPASSENGER)
RESERVATION(RESERVATION#, PASSENGER#,
        DEPARTURE#, STATUS, EXPDATE)

The above schema is now presented in the programming language notation:

DEFINITION MODULE Booking;

EXPORT QUALIFIED FlightType, DepartureType,
                 ReservationType, PassengerType,

                 FlightId, DepartureId,
                 ReservationId, PassengerId,
                 DayType,

                 FlightSetType, DepartureSetType,
                 ReservationSetType, PassengerSetType,

                 Flight, Departure, Reservation, Passenger;

```
TYPE DayType        = (Mon,Tue,Wed,Thu,Fri,Sat,Sun);
     FlightId       = String7;
     DepartureId    = String8;
     ReservationId  = String9;
     PassengerId    = String12;

     FlightType      = RECORD Flight#:              FlightId;
                              Source,Destination: String3;
                              Days:                SET OF DayType
                       END;

     DepartureType   = RECORD Departure#:           DepartureId;
                              Flight#:              FlightId;
                              Plane:                String5;
                              DepatureDate,
                              ArrivalDate:          String8;
                              DepartureTime,
                              ArrivalTime:          String5;
                              NumOfPassenger:       Cardinal;
                              MaxNumPassenger: Cardinal
                       END;
```

```
ReservationType  = RECORD Reservation#:      ReservationId;
                          Passenger#:        PassengerId;
                          Departure#:        DepartureId;
                          Status:            String2;
                          ExpDate:           String8
                   END;

PassengerType    = RECORD Passenger#:        PassengerId;
                          Name:              String30;
                          Sex:               Char;
                          Phone:             String8;
                          Address:           String30;
                          NumReservations:   [1..20]
                   END;

FlightSetType       = ENTITY SET OF FlightType;
DepartureSetType    = ENTITY SET OF DepartureType;
ReservationSetType  = ENTITY SET OF ReservationType;
PassengerSetType    = ENTITY SET OF PassengerType;

VAR Flight:       FlightSetType;
    Departure:    DepartureSetType;
    Reservation:  ReservationSetType;
    Passenger:    PassengerSetType;

END Booking.
```

Complex actions (*transactions*) refer to a collection of related objects. Such actions are in the object-oriented approach specified in a modular fashion as compositions of simpler actions associated with particular, (but related) objects. As an example, consider the following abstract decompositions of four complex actions that refer to object types RESERVATION, DEPARTURE, and PASSENGER. The actions are

(i) select a reservation of a given passenger for a given departure,
(ii) insert a reservation of a given passenger for a given departure,
(iii) delete a reservation of a given passenger for a given departure, and
(iv) update a reservation of a given passenger for a given departure.

The abstract decompositions of the above four actions are presented below and specified in terms of basic actions associated with the particular objects involved. Furthermore, all the above actions are associated with the entity type RESERVATION, and their abstract decompositions refer only to the immediately related entity types DEPARTURE and PASSENGER, as in the following diagram:

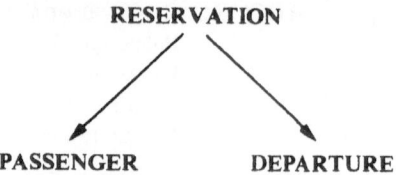

However, the action Select departure requires flight attributes, since it is decomposed according to the relationship expressed in the following diagram:

This means that the aforementioned four abstract actions in fact refer to all four entity types introduced thus far. When further refined and specified as procedures, attributes and actions associated with those entities will appear as their parameters. For example, insertion of a reservation will require as parameters source and destination of a flight, date of a departure, name of a passenger, etc.

RESERVATION

Insert: Select departure;
          If departure booked then Select reservation that expired;
          Select passenger;
          If it does not exist, then
              Insert passenger;
          If no exceptions then
              Insert reservation

Select: Select departure;
          Select passenger;
          Select reservation (given passenger and departure)

Update: Select reservations;
          If last reservation of the passenger, then
              Delete passenger;
          Select (new) passenger;
          Change passenger identifier of the selected reservation

Delete: Select reservation;
          Delete it;
          Decrease the number of passengers of the departure;

If last reservation of the passenger, then
Delete passenger

2 Sample Object-Oriented Top-Down Design: Project Management

(i) *Introducing projects*. In the first design phase, we introduce the most fundamental entity type PROJECT, and its identifier PROJECT#, as the only attribute postponing the specification of its other attributes for some later design phase. We also specify two actions associated with the entity type PROJECT—Insert and Delete—using sequential composition. The primitive action Request is used to obtain the values of the attributes quoted in the action. Those values may be requested interactively from the user or, in case of entity identifiers, generated in some system-determined manner, as was proposed for the exended relational model. Data abstraction techniques used thus far are classification and aggregation.

PROJECT   PROJECT(PROJECT#)

PROJECT

Insert: Request project identifier;
        Request project attributes;
        Insert project

Delete: Request project identifier;
        Delete project

(ii) *Subdividing projects into tasks*. To manage a project, we subdivide it into a number of tasks. Thus, a set of tasks is associated with each project in such a way that it partitions the set of entities of the newly introduced entity type TASK into disjoint subsets, and hence, two attributes of the entity type TASK are introduced: its entity identifier TASK#, and the identifier PROJECT# of the project to which it belongs. This representation of partitioning within the basic relational framework requires specification of the appropriate referential integrity constraint stating that a task must refer to an existing project.

PROJECT

TASK

PROJECT(PROJECT#)
TASK(TASK#, PROJECT#)

TASK[PROJECT#] < = PROJECT[PROJECT#]

PROJECT

INSERT: Request project identifier;
           Request project attributes;
           Insert project;
           For each task of the project, insert task

Delete: Request project identifier;
           Delete project;
           For each task of the project, delete task

TASK

Insert: Request task identifier;
           Request project identifier;
           Request task attributes;
           Insert task

Delete: Request task identifier;
           Delete task

Two actions—Insert and Delete—are introduced at this phase, specified for the entity type TASK in the same way as they are specified for the entity type PROJECT in the previous design phase. However, since PROJECT has been redefined as the quotient type of the newly introduced entity type TASK, we need to redefine the Insert and Delete actions associated with that entity type. Insertion of a project is refined so that it requires insertion of all its tasks. Deletion of a project requires deletion of all its tasks in accordance with the requirement that a task can exist in the database only if the project to which it belongs also exists in the database. Note that this action in fact specifies an important property of the chosen application environment.

The refinement of Insert and Delete actions is performed by applying the localization technique, considering only the relationships of the entity type PROJECT with the entity type TASK, which is immediately related to it by the partitioning abstraction. Consequently, in the refinement of the above actions, the foreach composition rule is used.

(iii) *Assignment of tasks to departments.* In the further development of our conceptual model, we assume the application environment has the property that each task is assigned to an organizational unit such as a department; thus, a new entity type DEPARTMENT and its identifying attribute DEPARTMENT# are introduced. The entity types DEPARTMENT and TASK are immediately related by the partitioning abstraction. In other words, a task belongs to one and only one department, and so we refine its specification by introducing a new attribute DEPART-

MENT#, which identifies the department of a task. As in design phase (ii), we introduce the appropriate referential integrity constraint stating that a task must refer to an existing department.

DEPARTMENT

TASK

TASK(TASK#, PROJECT#, DEPARTMENT#)
DEPARTMENT(DEPARTMENT#)
TASK[DEPARTMENT#] <= DEPARTMENT[DEPARTMENT#]

DEPARTMENT

Insert:	Requst department identifier; Request department attributes; Insert department
Delete:	Request department identifier; Delete department; For each task of the department, change its department identifier

TASK

Insert:	Request task identifier; Request project identifier; Request task attributes; Select department; Insert task
Change department:	Request task identifier; Request new department; Select task and change its department identifier

Specification of the insert action of the entity type DEPARTMENT does not introduce anything new. However, specification of the Delete action requires update of the department identifier of each task assigned to the deleted department. Consequently, the new update action Change department is associated with the entity type TASK. Insertion of a task now requires specification of an existing department, and thus, the action is redefined appropriately. Note once again that specification of actions captures some important properties of the application environment without which our conceptual model would have been incomplete.

(iv) *Assignment of employees to tasks.* In order to perform a task, a set of employees is assigned to that task. Thus, a new entity type EMPLOYEE is introduced and related immediately to the TASK entity type via covering abstraction; in other words, an employee may be assigned to a number of tasks. Note that this is a property of the application environment. To represent this property within the relational framework, we introduce a nonentity aggregation ASSIGNMENT of the entity types TASK and EM-PLOYEE whose only attributes are for the time being identifiers of the task TASK# and the employee EMPLOYEE# participating in an instance of that association. An instance of the entity ASSIGNMENT is permitted to exist in the database as long as the instances of the entity types EM-PLOYEE and TASK participating in the association exist in the database. This referential integrity constraint is introduced together with the entity type ASSIGNMENT, and the actions specified in this design phase are defined so that this newly introduced integrity constraint is maintained.

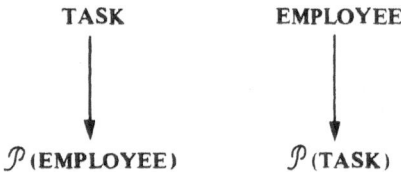

TASK(TASK#, PROJECT#, DEPARTMENT#)
EMPLOYEE(EMPLOYEE#)
ASSIGNMENT(EMPLOYEE#, TASK#)

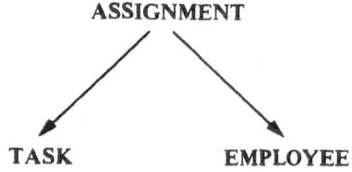

ASSIGNMENT[TASK#] <= TASK[TASK#]
ASSIGNMENT[EMPLOYEE#] <= EMPLOYEE[EMPLOYEE#]

EMPLOYEE

Insert: Request employee identifier;
                   Request employee attributes;
                   Insert employee

Delete: Request employee identifier;
                   Delete employee;
                   For each assignment of the employee, change the
                        employee identifier

TASK

Insert:	Request project identifier; Request task identifier; Request task attributes; Select department; Insert task; Select employees for the task; For each selected employee, insert its assignment to the task
Delete:	Request task identifier; Delete task; For each assignment of the task, delete assignment

ASSIGNMENT

Insert:	Request task identifier; Request employee identifier; Request assignment attributes; Insert assignment
Delete:	Request task identifier; Request employee identifier; Delete assignment
Change employee:	Request task identifier; Request employee identifier; Request new employee identifier; Select assignment and change its employee identifier

Specification of actions associated with the newly introduced entity type is performed in such a way that, whenever an employee is deleted, each of its assignments is updated (i.e., its employee identifier is changed). An alternative would be to delete all of them. This alternative is adopted when the delete action of that entity type is also further refined so that it refers to its relationship with the newly introduced and immediately related entity type EMPLOYEE. In view of how this immediate conceptual relationship is represented within the relational framework, insertion of a task calls for selection of the employees to be assigned to the task and insertion of an assignment of each selected employee to the task. Specification of the Insert, Delete, and Update actions of the entity type AS-SIGNMENT is straightforward.

(v) *Assignment of employees to departments.* We do not introduce anything new with the further development of the conceptual model. Further relationships of the entity types introduced thus far are modeled using the same design methodology. The assignment of employees to departments is represented, and afterwards the assignment of projects, task leaders, and department managers. Whenever a new relationship is introduced, further refinement of the already specified actions or specification of new ones is performed, but always locally.

DEPARTMENT

EMPLOYEE

DEPARTMENT(DEPARTMENT#)
EMPLOYEE(EMPLOYEE#, DEPARTMENT#)
EMPLOYEE[DEPARTMENT#] <=
  DEPARTMENT[DEPARTMENT#]

EMPLOYEE

Insert: Request employee identifier;
                       Request employee attributes;
                       Select department;
                       Insert employee

DEPARTMENT

Delete: Request department identifier;
                       Delete department;
                       For each employee of the department, change its
                           department

EMPLOYEE

Change department: Request employee identifier;
                       Request new department identifier;
                       Select employee and change its department
                           identifier

(vi) *Assignment of project leaders*

EMPLOYEE

PROJECT

PROJECT(PROJECT#, LEADER#)
PROJECT[LEADER#] <= EMPLOYEE[EMPLOYEE#]

PROJECT

Insert: Request project identifier;
                    Request project attributes;
                    Select project leader;
                    Insert project;
                    For each task of the project, insert task

Change leader: Request project identifier;
                    Request/Select new leader;
                    Select project and change its leader identifier

EMPLOYEE

Delete: Request employee identifier;
                    Delete employee;
                    For each assignment of the employee, change its
                        employee identifier;
                    For each project where the employee is the leader,
                        change the leader identifier of the project

(vii) *Assignment of task leaders*

EMPLOYEE

TASK

EMPLOYEE(EMPLOYEE#, DEPARTMENT#)
TASK(TASK#, PROJECT#, DEPARTMENT#, LEADER#)
TASK[LEADER#] <= EMPLOYEE[EMPLOYEE#]

TASK

Insert: Request/Select project identifier;
                    Request task identifier;
                    Request task attributes;
                    Select department;
                    Select employees;
                    Select leader;
                    Insert task;
                    For each selected employee, insert its assignment to
                        the task

Change leader: Request task identifier;
              Select new leader;
              Change the leader of the task

EMPLOYEE

Delete: Request employee identifier;
               Delete employee;
               For each assignment of the employee, change its
                   employee identifier;
               For each project where the employee is the leader,
                   change the leader identifier;
               For each task where the employee is the leader,
                   change its leader identifier

(viii) *Assignment of department managers*

DEPARTMENT

EMPLOYEE

EMPLOYEE(EMPLOYEE#, DEPARTMENT#)
DEPARTMENT(DEPARTMENT#,MANAGER#)
DEPARTMENT[MANAGER#] <= EMPLOYEE[EMPLOYEE#]

DEPARTMENT

Insert: Request department identifier;
               Request department attributes;
               Select/Insert manager;
               Insert department

Change manager: Request department identifier;
                Select new manager;
                Change department manager

EMPLOYEE

Delete: Request employee identifier;
               Delete employee;
               For each assignment of the employee, change its
                   employee identifier;
               For each task where the employee is the leader,
                   change its leader identifier;
               For each project where the employee is the leader,
                   change the leader identifier;
               For each department where the employee is the
                   manager, change the department identifier

Relational schema. Having developed our conceptual model of the project-management application to the level of detail at which all the entity types are introduced, their relationships are established, and actions upon them that properly maintain those relationships are defined, we consider other attributes of those entities and relationships, as well as other update actions these new attributes may require. Further development of the conceptual model along those lines is left to the reader. However, we do present a relational schema of the possible outcome of such further development:

```
EMPLOYEE(EMPLOYEE#, NAME, JOB, EXPERIENCE,
          SALARY, DEPARTMENT#)
DEPARTMENT(DEPARTMENT#, NAME, MANAGER#)
PROJECT(PROJECT#, NAME, LEADER#, CUSTOMER, FUNDS,
          BALANCE, STARTDATE, DEADLINE)
TASK(TASK#, PROJECT#, DEPARTMENT#, LEADER#, NAME,
          FUNDS, BALANCE)
ASSIGNMENT(TASK#, EMPLOYEE#, ROLE, PERCENTAGE)
```

```
DEFINITION MODULE ProjectManagement;

EXPORT QUALIFIED
   ProjectId, EmployeeId, TaskId, DepartmentId,

   ProjectType, EmployeeType, TaskType, AssignmentType,
   DepartmentType,

   ProjectSetType, EmployeeSetType, TaskSetType,
   AssignmentSetType, DepartmentSetType,

   Project, Employee, Task, Assignment, Department;

TYPE ProjectId      = String6;
     TaskId         = String6;
     EmployeeId     = String3;
     DepartmentId   = String5;

ProjectType         = RECORD
                        project#      ProjectId;
                        title:        String25;
                        leader#:      EmployeeId;
                        customer:     String20;
                        funds:        Real;
                        start:        Cardinal;
                        finish:       Cardinal
                      END;

TaskType            = RECORD
                        task#:        TaskId;
```

```
                    project#:      ProjectId;
                    department#:DepartmentId;
                    leader#:       EmployeeId;
                    title:         String54;
                    credit:        Real;
                    debit:         Real
                END;

AssignmentType  = RECORD
                    task#:         TaskId;
                    employee#:     EmployeeId;
                    role:          String14;
                    days:          Cardinal
                END;

EmployeeType    = RECORD
                    employee#:     EmployeeId;
                    name:          String25;
                    degree:        String5;
                    job:           String15;
                    rank:          String30;
                    experience:    Cardinal;
                    salary:        Real;
                    department#:DepartmentId
                END;

DepartmentType  = RECORD
                    department#:DepartmentId;
                    name:          String54;
                    staff:         Cardinal;
                    manager#:      EmployeeId
                END

ProjectSetType      = ENTITY SET OF ProjectType;
TaskSetType         = ENTITY SET OF TaskType;
AssignmentSetType   = ENTITY SET OF AssignmentType;
EmployeeSetType     = ENTITY SET OF EmployeeType;
DepartmentSetType   = ENTITY SET OF DepartmentType;

VAR Project:     ProjectSetType;
    Task:        TaskSetType;
    Assignment: AssignmentSetType;
    Employee:   EmployeeSetType;
    Department: DepartmentSetType;

END ProjectManagement.
```

3 Action and Transaction Development

Our goal now is to proceed from the conceptual level of abstraction to the lower level, which requires complete specification of actions as procedure declarations. This in fact, is the major effort in the design of the implementation module of an object. A procedure that implements an abstract action is generally structured according to the levels of abstraction introduced during the conceptual design phase. This means that, in order to reduce the complexity of each development step, we consider only immediate relationships of an object with other objects and design its associated actions accordingly.

This principle of localization determines almost precisely the steps constituting the incremental design process. It also directly determines the structure of the developed procedures. We will first illustrate the overall approach with the development of procedures that implement Insert and Delete actions associated with the object types PROJECT and EMPLOYEE of the project-management conceptual model.

The entity type PROJECT participates in two immediate relationships represented by the following diagram:

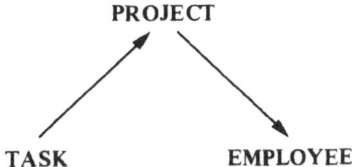

The leader-of relationship affects the development of the chosen actions in a very simple manner: When a project is inserted, we must check whether its LEADER# attribute refers to an existing employee. The task-of-a-project relationship, however, affects the development of the required actions in a much more complex manner, which is obvious from the following abstract algorithms of the desired actions:

InsertProject: Get project identifier;
               Check if unique;
               Get project leader;
               Check if it exists;
               Get other project attributes;
               Insert project;
               For each task of the project, InsertTask

DeleteProject: Get project identifier;
               Check if it exists;

```
                    Delete project;
                    For each task of the project, DeleteTask

PROJECT

PROCEDURE InsertProject(p:ProjectType);

   PROCEDURE InsertTasks(project#:ProjectId);
     VAR t: TaskType;
     PROCEDURE LastTask( ): Boolean;
     (* interrogate terminal user *)

   BEGIN WHILE NOT LastTask ( ) DO
                    t.project# : = project#;
                    ReadString(t.task#);
                    InsertTask(t)
          END
   END InsertTasks;

BEGIN IF NOT ProjectExists(p.project#)
        AND EmployeeExists(p.leader#)
        THEN Insert(p,Project);
                InsertTasks(p.project#)
        END
END    InsertProject;

PROCEDURE DeleteProject(project#: ProjectId);
   VAR p: ProjectType;

PROCEDURE DeleteTasks(project#: ProjectId);
   VAR t: TaskType;
BEGIN FOREACH t IN Task
        WHERE    t.project# = project#
        DO       DeleteTask(t.task#)
        END
END    DeleteTasks;

BEGIN FOREACH p IN Project
        WHERE    p.project# = project#
        DO       Delete(p,Project);
                 DeleteTasks(p.project#)
        END
END    DeleteProject
```

In addition to the procedures associated with the entity type PROJECT
(ProjectIdExists) in accordance with the localization principle, the above
two procedures contain only references (*procedure calls*) to those actions
that are associated with entity types TASK (InsertTask, DeleteTask) and

EMPLOYEE (EmployeeIdExists) that are immediately related to PROJ-ECT.

We now apply the same principle to those actions. Consider the development of the actions InsertTask and DeleteTask associated with the entity type TASK. The immediate relationships of that entity type with other entity types are represented in the following diagram:

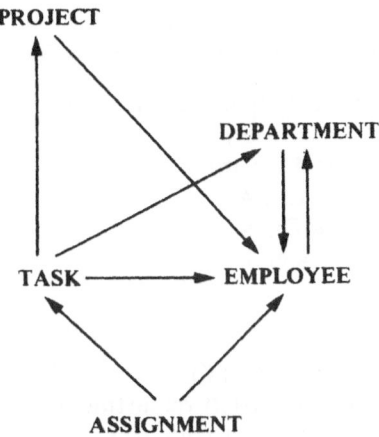

The abstract algorithms for the desired actions given below are specified taking precisely those immediate relationships into account:

InsertTask: Get task identifier;
          Check if unique;
          Get project identifier;
          Check if it exists;
          Get leader identifier;
          Check if it exists;
          Get department identifier;
          Check if it exists;
          Get other task attributes;
          Insert task;
          For each assignment of the task, insert assignment

DeleteTask: Get task identifier;
          Check if it exists;
          Delete task;
          For each assignment of the task, delete assignment

We are now ready for the specification of the above abstract algorithms in the programming language notation:

TASK

```
PROCEDURE InsertTask(t: TaskType);

  PROCEDURE InsertAssignments(task#: TaskId;
                                      department#: DepartmentId);
    VAR Members: IdSetType;
        m: EmployeeId;
        a: AssignmentType;
    PROCEDURE GetRoleAndDays; (* block *)

  BEGIN SelectEmployees(department#, Members);
        FOREACH m IN Members
        DO a.employee# := m;
           a.task# := task#;
           GetRoleAndDays;
           Insert(a, Assignment)
        END
  END InsertAssignments;

BEGIN IF ProjectExists(t.project#)
      AND   DepartmentExists(t.department#)
      AND   EmployeeExists(t.leader#)
      AND   NOT TaskExists(t.task#)
      THEN Insert(t,Task);
           InsertAssignments(t.task#, t.department#)
      END
END InsertTask;

PROCEDURE DeleteTask(task#: TaskId);
   VAR t: TaskType;

  PROCEDURE DeleteAssignments(task#: TaskId);
   VAR a: AssignmentType;
  BEGIN FOREACH a IN Assignment
        WHERE    a.task# = task#
        DO       Delete(a, Assignment)
        END
  END DeleteAssignments;

BEGIN FOREACH t IN Task;
      WHERE    t.task# = task#
      DO       Delete(t,Task);
               DeleteAssignments(task#)
      END
END DeleteTask
```

Selection of a set of task members from a specified department is a rather straightforward action associated with the entity type EMPLOYEE, as specified below:

EMPLOYEE

```
PROCEDURE SelectEmployees(department#: DepartmentId;
                          VAR Employees: IdSetType);
   VAR e: EmployeeType;

   PROCEDURE Selected ( ): Boolean;
   (* Interrogate terminal user *)

BEGIN Empty(Employees);
      FOREACH e IN Employee
      WHERE   e.department# = department#
      DO WriteEmployee(e);
         IF Selected ( ) THEN
            Insert(e.employee#, Employees)
         END
      END
END SelectEmployees
```

Insert and Delete actions associated with the entity type EMPLOYEE are developed using the same incremental development methodology. The refinement steps are determined by the immediate relationship of the entity type EMPLOYEE with entity types PROJECT, TASK, ASSIGNMENT, and DEPARTMENT. Those relationships and abstract algorithms for the desired actions are given first:

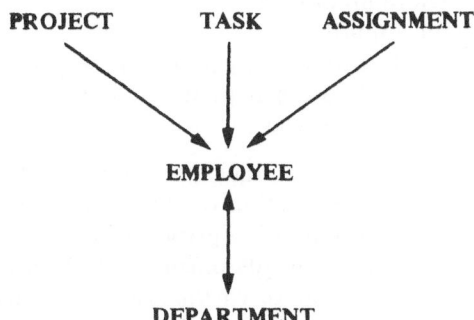

The above relationships are represented below in the programming language notation:

```
ProjectType      = RECORD project#:    ProjectId;
                          leader#:     EmployeeId;
                          (* other attributes *)
                   END;
TaskType         = RECORD task#:       TaskId;
                          project#:    ProjectId;
```

```
                                department#: DepartmentId;
                                leader#:       EmployeeId;
                                (* other attributes *)
                      END;
  AssignmentType  = RECORD task#:         TaskId;
                                employee#:   EmployeeId;
                                (* other attributes *)
                      END;
  EmployeeType    = RECORD employee#:   EmployeeId;
                                department#: DepartmentId;
                                (* other attributes *)
                      END;
  DepartmentType  = RECORD department#: DepartmentId;
                                (* other attributes *)
                      END;
```

```
DeleteEmployee:  Get employee identifier;
                 Check if it exists;
                 For each assignment of the employee, change its em-
                    ployee identifier;
                 For each project where the employee is the leader,
                    change project leader;
                 For each task where the employee is the leader, change
                    task leader;
                 For each department where the employee is the man-
                    ager, change department manager;
                 Delete employee
InsertEmployee:  Get employee;
                 Check if its employee identifier is unique;
                 Check if its department exists;
                 Insert employee
```

As is clear from the above abstract algorithms, the major problem in the development of the Delete action of the entity type EMPLOYEE is proper maintenance of referential integrity constraints. This is precisely the reason why we have chosen this particular action as an illustration. In order to simplify the selection of various replacements that deletion of an employee requires, we assume the replacements are selected from the employee's department. This assumption also makes selection of replacements a much more efficient procedure since it is performed from a set much smaller than the set of all employees.

With this assumption, DeleteEmployee is specified in the following procedure declaration:

EMPLOYEE

```
PROCEDURE DeleteEmployee(employee#: EmployeeId);
  VAR e: EmployeeType;
```

```
BEGIN FOREACH e IN Employee
       WHERE    e.employee# = employee#
       DO ChangeAssignments(e.employee#, e.department#);
          ChangeProjectLeaders(e.employee#, e.department#);
          ChangeTaskLeaders(e.employee#, e.department#);
          ChangeDepartmentManager(e.employee#, e.department#);
          Delete(e, Employee)
       END
END DeleteEmployee
```

The actions in the above procedure declaration are associated with entity types immediately related to the entity type EMPLOYEE. Their decomposition is given in the next development step:

ASSIGNMENT

```
PROCEDURE ChangeAssignments(employee#: EmployeeId;
                                       department#: DepartmentId);

   VAR a: AssignmentType;
       replacement#: EmployeeId;

BEGIN FOREACH a IN Assignment
       WHERE    a.employee# = employee#
       DO WriteAssignment(a);
          WriteString("Select replacement");
          SelectEmployee(employee#, department#, replacement#);
          a.employee# := replacement#
       END
END ChangeAssignments
```

PROJECT

```
PROCEDURE ChangeProjectLeaders(employee#: EmployeeId;
                                       department#: DepartmentId);

   VAR p: ProjectType;
       replacement#: EmployeeId;

BEGIN FOREACH p IN Project
       WHERE    p.leader# = employee#
       DO WriteProject(p);
          WriteString("Select new leader");
          SelectEmployee(employee#, department#, replacement#);
          p.leader# := replacement#
       END
END ChangeProjectLeaders
```

TASK

```
PROCEDURE ChangeTaskLeaders(employee#: EmployeeId;
                                       department#: DepartmentId);
```

```
    VAR t: TaskType;
         replacement#: EmployeeId;

BEGIN FOREACH t IN Task
         WHERE    t.leader# = employee#
         DO WriteTask(t);
             WriteString(" Select new leader" );
             SelectEmployee(employee#, department#, replacement#);
             t.leader# := replacement#
         END
END ChangeTaskLeaders
```

DEPARTMENT

```
PROCEDURE ChangeDepartmentManager(employee#: EmployeeId;
                                            department#: DepartmentId);
    VAR d: DepartmentType;
         replacement#: EmployeeId;

BEGIN FOREACH d IN Department
         WHERE    (d.department# = department#)
         AND      (d.manager#    = employee#)
         DO WriteDepartment(d);
             WriteString(" Select new manager" );
             SelectEmployee(employee#, department#, replacement#);
             d.manager# := replacement#
         END
END ChangeDepartmentManager
```

All of the above four actions associated with respective entity types
ASSIGNMENT, PROJECT, TASK, and DEPARTMENT refer back to
the entity type EMPLOYEE via the action SelectEmployee that selects
an appropriate replacement.

```
PROCEDURE SelectEmployee(employee#: EmployeeId;
                             department#: DepartmentId;
                             VAR replacement#: EmployeeId);

    VAR e: EmployeeType; ReplacementSelected: Boolean;

PROCEDURE Selected ( ): Boolean;
(* Interrogate terminal user *)

BEGIN ReplacementSelected := false;
         LOOP
             FOREACH e IN Employee
             WHERE    (e.department# = department#)
             AND      (e.employee# < > employee#)
```

```
          DO WriteEmployee(e);
              IF Selected ( ) THEN
                 replacement# : = e.employee#;
                 ReplacementSelected : = true;
                 Exit
              END
          END;
          IF ReplacementSelected THEN Exit
          ELSE WriteString(" Select replacement!!!")
          END
      END
END SelectEmployee
```

Unfortunately, the above development does not properly handle some special cases that illustrate a general, but very important problem. The only way to terminate the loop in the action SelectEmployee is by selecting a replacement for the employee to be deleted. This replacement, however, is impossible if the employee is the last one in the given department. A revision of the presented algorithms that handles this special case properly is left to the reader, who is also advised to study exercise (6).

PROCEDURE InsertEmployee(e: EmployeeType);

```
BEGIN IF NOT EmployeeExists(e.employee#)
          AND DepartmentExists(e.department#)
          THEN Insert(e, Employee)
          END
END InsertEmployee
```

Note that in the last presentation of the referential integrity constraints in the project-management relational model, one of the integrity constraints is omitted. Indeed, the attribute manager# of the object Department creates a very serious problem associated with the action InsertEmployee if the object-oriented approach is applied. This problem is elaborated in detail in exercise (6).

4 Object-Oriented versus Relational-Oriented Procedures

In the object-oriented design methodology, an action associated with an entity type E that is related to other entity types E1,E2,...,En is expressed in terms of actions on E and actions on E1,E2,...,En. This design discipline, which is based on localization, leads to procedures that exhibit a specific structure quite different from the structure obtained if the relational design methodology is applied. For example, an action SelectFlight is expressed in terms of an action SelectDeparture associated with a related entity type DEPARTMENT:

```
PROCEDURE SelectFlight(Source, Destination: String3;
                                day: DayType;
                                VAR flight#: FlightId);
    VAR f: FlightType; departure#: DepartureId;

BEGIN flight# : = EmptyString;
      FOREACH f IN Flight
      WHERE      (f.Source = Source)
      AND        (f.Destination = Destination)
      AND        (day IN f.Days)
      DO         SelectDeparture (f.Flight#, departure#);
                 IF departure# < > EmptyString
                 THEN flight# : = f.Flight#;
                          Exit
                 END
      END
END SelectFlight;

PROCEDURE SelectDeparture(flight#: FlightId;
                                VAR departure#: DepartureId);
    VAR d: DepartureType;

BEGIN departure# : = EmptyString;
      FOREACH d IN Departure
      WHERE      d.Flight# = flight#
      DO WriteDeparture(d);
          IF Selected( ) THEN
             departure# : = d.Departure#;
             Exit
          END
      END
END SelectDeparture
```

In the relational design methodology, a database is viewed as a flat structure of entity types related by entity identifiers. A complex action (*transaction*) is then designed accordingly using relational joins to express the desired relationships. The result is a procedure that is not necessarily structured into levels of abstraction where each such level is associated with one entity type. For example, the action SelectFlight may have the following implementation:

```
PROCEDURE SelectFlight(Source, Destination: String3;
                                day: DayType;
                                VAR flight#: FlightId);
```

```
VAR f:  FlightType;
    d:  DepartureType;

BEGIN flight# := EmptyString;
      FOREACH f IN Flight
      WHERE     (f.Source = Source)
      AND       (f.Destination = Destination)
      AND       (day IN f.Days)
      DO FOREACH d IN Departure
          WHERE     d.Flight# = f.Flight#
          DO   WriteDeparture(d);
               IF Selected( ) THEN
                  flight# := f.Flight#;
                  Exit
               END
          END
      END
END SelectFlight
```

The above embedded structure of unary FOREACH statements that operate on particular objects still to some extent isolates actions associated with particular objects. However, strictly following the relational approach, we would use an explicit form of a natural join expressed by a binary FOREACH statement to obtain the following structure:

```
FOREACH f IN Flight, d IN Departure
WHERE (f.Source = Source)
AND      (f.Destination = Destination)
AND      (day IN f.Days)
AND      (f.Flight# = d.Flight#)
DO    WriteDeparture(d);
      IF    Selected( ) THEN
            flight# := f.Flight#;
            Exit
      END
END
```

It is a crucial observation that, in spite of all generality of the FOREACH statement, there is hardly ever any need for its binary and higher order forms in the object-oriented design methodology that leads to joins expressed in terms of procedure calls. There is hardly any question about which approach produces a more satisfactory procedure structure. But, given a classical relational system where efficient execution of joins is a major system-design issue, the relational form of actions is bound to be more efficient in most cases. This, of course, is also a very important design consideration.

To further illustrate this important point, consider the following complex action (transaction), which is expressed first in the relational style using embedded unary FOREACH statement, where each such statement acts on one entity type:

```
PROCEDURE FindReservation(Source, Destination: String3;
                          day:  DayType;
                          date: String8;
                          name: String30);
  VAR f: FlightType;
      d: DepartureType;
      r: ReservationType;
      p: PassengerType;
BEGIN FOREACH f IN Flight
      WHERE    (f.Source = Source)
      AND      (f.Destination = Destination)
      AND      (day IN f.Days)
      DO FOREACH  d IN Departure
          WHERE    (d.Flight# = f.Flight#)
          AND      (d.Date = date)
          DO FOREACH r IN Reservation
              WHERE    r.Departure# = d.Departure#
              DO       FOREACH p IN Passenger
                       WHERE    (p.Passenger# = d.Passenger#)
                       AND      (d.Name = name)
                       DO       WritePassenger(p);
                                IF Selected( ) THEN
                                   WriteReservation(r);
                                   Exit
                                END
                       END
              END
          END
      END
END FindReservation
```

If we strictly follow the object-oriented approach, the action Find-Reservation will be defined on the entity type Reservation, where references to the immediately related entity types DEPARTURE and PASSENGER will be expressed as calls of actions (procedures) associated with those entity types.

The embedded structure of the FOREACH statements in the above complex action reflects the hierarchical structure of functionally related entity types shown in Figure 3.

In the object-oriented approach, we would first consider the object type RESERVATION and its immediately related object types DEPARTURE and PASSENGER, according to Figure 4.

The procedure FindReservation will then be expressed in terms of procedure calls that represent actions associated with the entity types DEPARTURE and PASSENGER.

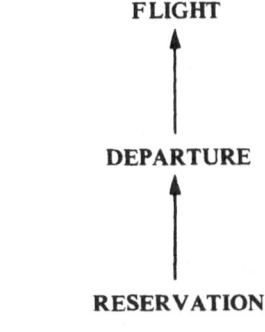

Figure 3

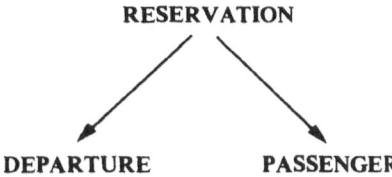

Figure 4

```
TYPE PassengerIdSet = ENTITY SET OF PassengerId;
     FlightIdSet    = ENTITY SET OF FlightId;
     DepartureIdSet = ENTITY SET OF DepartureId;

PROCEDURE FindReservation(Source, Destination: String3;
                          day: DayType;
                          date: String8;
                          PassengerName: String30);

  VAR r: ReservationType;

      SelectedDepartures: DepartureIdSet;
      SelectedPassengers: PassengerIdSet;

BEGIN SelectDepartures (Source,Destination,
                        day,date,
                        SelectedDepartures);
      SelectPassengers(PassengerName,SelectedPassengers);

      FOREACH r IN Reservation
      WHERE     Member(r.Departure#,SelectedDepartures)
      AND       Member(r.Passenger#,SelectedPassengers)
      DO        WriteReservation(r)
      END

END   SelectReservation
```

PASSENGER

```
PROCEDURE SelectPassengers (name: String30;
                                VAR Passengers: PassengerIdSet);
    VAR p:PassengerType;

BEGIN Empty(Passengers);
        FOREACH p IN Passenger
        WHERE     p.Name = name
        DO              Insert(p.Passenger#,Passengers)
        END
END     SelectPassengers
```

DEPARTURE

```
PROCEDURE SelectDepartures (Source, Destination: String3;
                                day:  DayType;
                                date: String8;
                                VAR Departures: DepartureIdSet);

    VAR d: DepartureType;
        SelectedFlights: FlightIdSet;

BEGIN Empty(Departures);
        SelectFlights(Source,Destination,
                        day, SelectedFlights);
        FOREACH d IN Departure
        WHERE     (d.Date = date)
        AND         Member(d.Flight#,SelectedFlights)
        DO          Insert(d.Departure#,Departures)
        END
END     SelectDepartures
```

FLIGHT

```
PROCEDURE SelectFlights (Source, Destination: String3;
                            day: DayType;
                            VAR SelectedFlights: FlightIdSet);

    VAR f: FlightType;

BEGIN Empty(SelectedFlights);
        FOREACH f IN Flight
        WHERE     (f.Source = Source)
        AND         (f.Destination = Destination)
        AND         (f.Day = day)
        DO          Insert(f.Flight#,SelectedFlights)
        END
END     SelectFlights
```

5 Environments, Submodels, and Access Rights

An application environment of any complexity can usually be subdivided into a collection of subenvironments, each of which consists of a collection of closely related activities performed by a group of users of the common database system. A subenvironment is represented by a submodel consisting of a collection of objects and a collection of actions upon those objects. In general, neither sets of objects of particular submodels nor their sets of actions are mutually disjoint. A submodel thus represents an *abstraction* of the model of the whole application environment (its view) that is suited to a particular group of users in that environment.

This abstraction is obtained by selecting only those objects and activities occurring in a particular subenvironment. Furthermore, only those properties of an object are abstracted in a submodel that are relevant to the subenvironment that the submodel represents. The submodel also specifies access rights (objects, their properties, and actions upon them) of groups of users of particular subenvironments.

An important overall design methodology suggests conceptual modeling of particular subenvironments first and then integration of the produced submodels into the overall model of the whole environment. This integration in fact produces the model that is structured into a collection of related submodels. Isolation of abstractions corresponding to particular subenvironments (submodels) is not only important from the semantic viewpoint, although such abstractions are certainly semantically more attractive to groups of users in particular application subenvironments; classification of complex application environments into subenvironments may be the only way to cope with the complexity of the overall design task.

Consider, for example, the flight-reservation application environment. What was done so far in terms of conceptual modeling of that particular application in fact applies to the booking environment specified below in terms of objects belonging to that particular environment and actions associated with those objects. But we can actually observe two more environments in the same manner:

(i) *Flight scheduling environment*

Objects:	FLIGHT	DEPARTURE
Properties:	Flight id Source, Destination Days of operation	Departure id Flight id Plane id Date Departure time, Arrival time
Actions:	Insert flight	Insert departure

Delete flight	Delete departure
Flight exists	Departure exists
Select flight	Select departure
Display flight	Display departure
Change source	Change date
Change destination	Change departure time
Change days of operation	Change arrival time

(ii) *Plane scheduling environment*

Objects:	PLANE	FLIGHT	DEPARTURE
Properties:	Plane id	Flight id	Departure id
	Type	Source, Destination	Flight id
		Days	Plane id
	Manufacturer		Date
	Capacity		Departure time,
	Distance		Arrival time

Actions:	Insert plane	Select flight	Select departure
	Delete plane	Display flight	Display departure
	Plane exists		Change plane id
	Select plane		Change maximum
			number of passengers

(iii) *Flight booking environment*

Objects:	PASSENGER	RESERVATION
Properties:	Passenger id	Reservation id
	Name	Passenger id
	Sex, Phone	Departure id
	Address	Status
	Number of	Expiration date
	reservations	

Actions:	Insert passenger	Insert reservation
	Delete passenger	Delete reservation
	Passenger exists	Reservation exists
	Select passenger	Select reservation
	Display passenger	Display reservation
	Change number	Change passenger id
	of reservations	Change departure id
		Change status
		Change expiration date

Objects:	FLIGHT	DEPARTURE
Properties:	Flight id	Departure id
	Source, Destination	Flight id
	Days of operation	Plane id

		Date
		Departure time, Arrival time
		Number of passengers
		Maximum passengers
Actions:	Select flight	Select departure
	Display flight	Display departure
	Flight exists	Departure exists
		Change occupancy
		Departure booked

Environments:

Flights

Planes

Reservations

Access rights. Specification of (sub-)environments has yet another extremely important aspect: Access rights of various groups of users
of a complex application environment in regard to their common database are, in general, quite different, as are their responsibilities and
the rules governing their conduct in that environment. This fact is
represented by abstractions or subenvironments (submodels) in the
following way:

(i) A submodel contains only those objects and their properties that are
relevant for the actions of the users of that submodel.
(ii) A submodel contains only those actions associated with the objects
of that submodel that the users of the submodel are responsible for
and authorized to perform.

Access rights associated with the Flight booking, Flight scheduling, and
Plane scheduling submodels are defined in accordance with these rules
and summarized in the diagrams below:

Access rights:

Flight booking

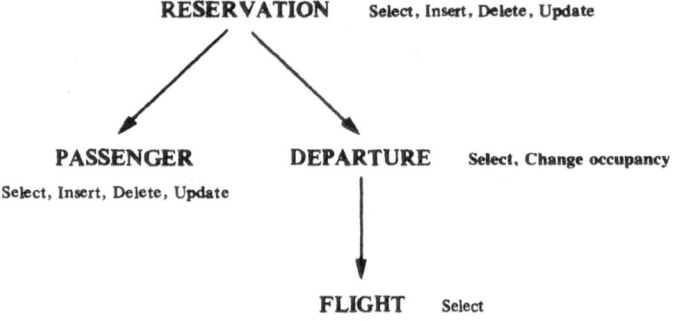

Flight scheduling

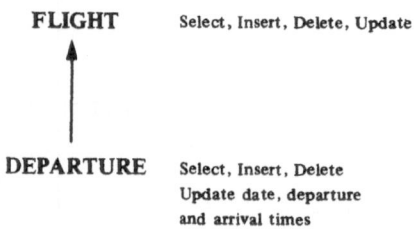

Plane scheduling

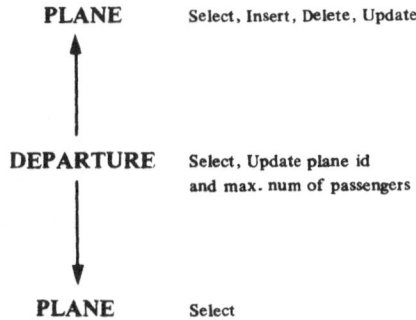

Users in the flight booking environment are thus allowed to perform all actions on the entity types RESERVATION and PASSENGER. They have no rights to perform any actions on the entity types DEPARTURE and FLIGHT other than selection (reading) of the attributes of these entity types that are relevant to the users of the flight booking environment, and increase and decrease occupancy of a departure. Enforcing these rights is achieved by giving users access to the definition module of their sub-environment as their interface to the common database.

Users of the flight scheduling environment are concerned only with the entity types FLIGHT and DEPARTURE, and the corresponding submodel thus contains only these two objects. Users of this submodel are permitted to perform all actions on the FLIGHT entity type. Their access rights with regard to the entity type DEPARTURE are somewhat more restricted. They include all actions except for reading and updating of those attributes that are of no concern to the users of that submodel (e.g., number of passengers). These access rights are reflected in the actions associated with the object types FLIGHT and DEPARTURE within the flight-scheduling submodel.

Plane scheduling involves three types of objects: PLANE, FLIGHT, and DEPARTURE. This activity requires all actions on the PLANE entity type. On the other hand, only reading of relevant attributes of entity types FLIGHT and DEPARTURE, and update of the plane identifier of the latter are permitted to the users of this submodel.

Representation of submodels (environments) is given below in terms of their definition modules:

DEFINITION MODULE Flights;

FROM Planes IMPORT PlaneId, DisplayPlane;

EXPORT QUALIFIED FlightType, FlightId,
                 FlightSelector, SelectFlight,

```
                        FlightExists, DisplayFlight,
                        InsertFlight, DeleteFlight, ChangeDays,

                        DepartureType, DepartureId,
                        DepartureSelector, SelectDeparture,
                        DepartureExists,
                        DisplayDeparture, DepartureBooked,
                        InsertDeparture, DeleteDeparture,
                        ChangeDate, ChangeTime,

                        PlaneId, DisplayPlane;

TYPE  FlightId          =  String7;
      DepartureId       =  String8;

      FlightType        =  RECORD Flight#:              FlightId;
                                  Source, Destination:  String3;
                                  Days:                 String7
                           END;

      DepartureType  =  RECORD Departure#:           DepartureId;
                               Flight#:              FlightId;
                               Plane#:               PlaneId;
                               Date:                 String8;
                               DepartureTime,
                               ArrivalTime:          String5;
                               NumPassengers:        Cardinal;
                               MaxNumPassengers: Cardinal
                           END;

      FlightSelector = PROCEDURE(flight: FlightType): Boolean;

      DepartureSelector = PROCEDURE(departure: DepartureType):
                                           Boolean;

PROCEDURE InsertFlight(flight: FlightType);

PROCEDURE DeleteFlight(flight#: FlightId);

PROCEDURE FlightExists(flight#: FlightId): Boolean;

PROCEDURE DisplayFlight(flight#: FlightId);

PROCEDURE SelectFlight(selector: FlightSelector;
                       VAR flight#: FlightId);

PROCEDURE ChangeDays(flight#: FlightId;
                     NewDays: String7);

PROCEDURE InsertDeparture(departure: DepartureType);

PROCEDURE DeleteDeparture(departure#: DepartureId);
```

PROCEDURE DepartureExists(departure#: DepartureId): Boolean;

PROCEDURE DisplayDeparture(departure#: DepartureId);

PROCEDURE SelectDeparture(selector: DepartureSelector;
                                        VAR departure#: DepartureId);

PROCEDURE DepartureBooked(departure#: DepartureId): Boolean;

PROCEDURE ChangeDate(departure#: DepartureId;
                                    NewDate: String8);

PROCEDURE ChangeTime(departure#: DepartureId;
                                    DepartureTime,
                                    ArrivalTime: String5);

END Flights.

DEFINITION MODULE Planes;

FROM Flights IMPORT FlightType, FlightId,
                    FlightSelector,
                    SelectFlight, DisplayFlight,

                    DepartureType, DepartureId,
                    DepartureSelector, SelectDeparture,
                    DisplayDeparture;

EXPORT QUALIFIED PlaneType, PlaneId,
                    PlaneSelector, SelectPlane, PlaneExists,
                    DisplayPlane,
                    InsertPlane, DeletePlane,

                    FlightType, FlightId,
                    FlightSelector, SelectFlight, DisplayFlight,

                    DepartureType, DepartureId,
                    DepartureSelector,
                    SelectDeparture, DisplayDeparture;

TYPE PlaneId   = String8;
     PlaneType = RECORD Plane#: PlaneId;
                        Plane: String4;
                        Manufacturer: String4;
                        Capacity: Cardinal;
                        Distance: Cardinal
                 END;
     PlaneSelector = PROCEDURE(plane: PlaneType): Boolean;

PROCEDURE InsertPlane(plane: PlaneType);

PROCEDURE DeletePlane(plane#: PlaneId);

PROCEDURE PlaneExists(plane#: PlaneId): Boolean;

PROCEDURE DisplayPlane(plane#: PlaneId);

PROCEDURE SelectPlane(selector: PlaneSelector;
                      VAR plane#: PlaneId);

PROCEDURE ChangePlane(departure#: DepartureId;
                      NewPlane: PlaneId);

PROCEDURE ChangeMaxOccupancy(departure#: DepartureId;
                             NewMax: Cardinal);

END Planes.

DEFINITION MODULE Bookings;

FROM Flights IMPORT FlightType, FlightId,
                    FlightSelector,
                    SelectFlight, DisplayFlight,

                    DepartureType, DepartureId,
                    DepartureSelector,
                    SelectDeparture, DisplayDeparture,
                    DepartureBooked;

EXPORT QUALIFIED FlightType, FlightId,
                 FlightSelector,
                 SelectFlight, DisplayFlight,

                 DepartureType, DepartureId,
                 DepartureSelector,
                 SelectDeparture, DisplayDeparture,
                 DepartureBooked,

                 ReservationType, ReservationId,
                 ReservationSelector, ReservationExists,
                 SelectReservation, DisplayReservation,

                 InsertReservation, DeleteReservation,
                 ChangePassenger, ChangeStatus,
                 ChangeExpiration, ChangeOccupancy,

                 PassengerType, PassengerId,
                 PassengerSelector, PassengerExists,
                 SelectPassenger, DisplayPassenger,

                 InsertPassenger, DeletePassenger,
                 ChangePhone, ChangeAddress,
                 ChangeNumReservations;

```
TYPE PassengerId        = String12;
      ReservationId     = String9;
      PassengerType     = RECORD Passenger#:        PassengerId;
                                 Name:              String30;
                                 Sex:               Char;
                                 Phone:             String10;
                                 Address:           String30;
                                 NumReservations:   Cardinal
                          END;

      ReservationType = RECORD Reservation#:        ReservationId;
                               Passenger#:          PassengerId;
                               Departure#:          DepartureId;
                               Status:              String2;
                               ExpDate:             String8
                        END;

      PassengerSelector = PROCEDURE(passenger: PassengerType):
                                    Boolean;

      ReservationSelector = PROCEDURE(reservation:
                                      ReservationType):
                                      Boolean;

PROCEDURE InsertPassenger(passenger: PassengerType);

PROCEDURE DeletePassenger(passenger#: PassengerId);

PROCEDURE PassengerExists(passenger#: PassengerId): Boolean;

PROCEDURE SelectPassenger(selector: PassengerSelector;
                          VAR passenger#: PassengerId);

PROCEDURE DisplayPassenger(passenger#: PassengerId);

PROCEDURE ChangePhone(passenger#: PassengerId;
                      NewPhone: String10);

PROCEDURE ChangeAddress(passenger#: PassengerId;
                        NewAddress: String30);

PROCEDURE ChangeNumReservations(passenger#: PassengerId;
                                difference: Integer);

PROCEDURE InsertReservation(reservation: ReservationType);

PROCEDURE DeleteReservation(reservation#: ReservationId);

PROCEDURE ReservationExists(reservation#: ReservationId):
                            Boolean;
```

PROCEDURE SelectReservation(selector: ReservationSelector;
                                                    VAR reservation#: ReservationId);

PROCEDURE DisplayReservation(reservation#: ReservationId);

PROCEDURE ChangePassenger(reservation#: ReservationId;
                                                    NewPassenger#: PassengerId);

PROCEDURE ChangeStatus(reservation#: ReservationId;
                                                    NewStatus: String2);

PROCEDURE ChangeExpiration(reservation#: ReservationId;
                                                    NewDate: String8);

PROCEDURE ChangeOccupancy(departure#: DepartureId;
                                                    difference: Integer);

END Bookings.

6 Design of Recursive Transactions

Our goal here is to illustrate the top-down design methodology and its
application in the development of a complex interactive, relational-oriented
transaction. The user of the transaction is an airline ticket agent, who
activates a transaction in order to perform booking of a complex itinerary
consisting of a number of connected flights (trips). The relational model
of the flight-reservation application environment has already been developed. Its definition module is presented below:

DEFINITION MODULE Booking;

EXPORT QUALIFIED FlightType, DepartureType,
                                ReservationType, PassengerType,

                                FlightId, DepartureId,
                                ReservationId, PassengerId,
                                DayType,

                                FlightSetType, DepartureSetType,
                                ReservationSetType, PassengerSetType,

                                Flight, Departure, Reservation, Passenger;

TYPE DayType   = (Mon,Tue,Wed,Thu,Fri,Sat,Sun);
        FlightId   = String7;
        DepartureId   = String8;
        ReservationId = String9;
        PassengerId   = String12;

```
FlightType          = RECORD Flight#:            FlightId;
                            Source, Destination: String3;
                            Days:      SET OF DayType
                    END;

DepartureType       = RECORD Departure#:         DepartureId;
                            Flight#:             FlightId;
                            Plane:               String5;
                            DepartureDate,
                            ArrivalDate:         String8;
                            DepartureTime,
                            ArrivalTime:         String5;
                            NumOfPassenger:      Cardinal;
                            MaxNumPassenger: Cardinal
                    END;

ReservationType = RECORD Reservation#:       ReservationId;
                            Passenger#:          PassengerId;
                            Departure#:          DepartureId;
                            Status:              String2;
                            ExpDate:             String8
                    END;

PassengerType       = RECORD Passenger#:         PassengerId;
                            Name:                String30;
                            Sex:                 Char;
                            Phone:               String8;
                            Address:             String30;
                            NumReservations:     [1..20]
                    END;

FlightSetType        = ENTITY SET OF FlightType;
DepartureSetType     = ENTITY SET OF DepartureType;
ReservationSetType = ENTITY SET OF ReservationType;
PassengerSetType     = ENTITY SET OF PassengerType;

VAR Flight:        FlightSetType;
    Departure:     DepartureSetType;
    Reservation:   ReservationSetType;
    Passenger:     PassengerSetType;

END Booking.
```

The chosen transaction is an example of the stepwise construction of a solution by repeated trial and error. The essential property of this method is that candidates for a solution are generated in a systematic manner and tested according to the criteria characterizing the solution. To do this, we represent trial solutions x in the form $[x_1, x_2, \ldots, x_n]$, such that x can be generated in steps that produce partial solutions:

$[x_1]$
$[x_1, x_2]$
.
.
.
$[x_1, x_2, \ldots, x_n]$

This decomposition of a trial solution x must satisfy the following conditions:

(i) Every step (a passage from $[x_1, \ldots, x_j]$ to $[x_1, \ldots, x_j, x_{j+1}]$) is considerably simpler than the computation of the entire solution x.
(ii) If $x = [x_1, x_2, \ldots, x_n]$ satisfies the specified criteria for the acceptable solution, then $[x_1]$, $[x_1, x_2]$, ..., $[x_1, x_2, \ldots, x_{n-1}]$ are necessarily partial solutions; that is, they also satisfy those criteria.

In other words, in order to obtain a full solution we generate partial solutions. Having constructed a partial solution $[x_1, x_2, \ldots, x_j]$ (a solution that is not full, but satisfies the specified criteria), we systematically generate its extensions $[x_1, x_2, \ldots, x_j, x_{j+1}]$ and test them against the given criteria. If we find an extension satisfying those criteria, then the $j+1$th step has been completed successfully, and we can proceed with further extensions. Sometimes, however, a partial solution $[x_1, x_2, \ldots, x_j]$ cannot be extended so that the specified criteria are satisfied; that is, while testing systematically all possible extensions of $[x_1, x_2, \ldots, x_j]$, we discover that not a single one of them is acceptable. If this happens for a partial solution of length j, we have to shorten it to $[x_1, x_2, \ldots, x_i]$, where $i < j$, and try a different acceptable extension of $[x_1, x_2, \ldots, x_i]$. This process is called *backtracking*.

   If we apply this general searching method to our particular problem, we can easily see that both criteria (i) and (ii) are satisfied. The complete itinerary is, by its very nature, represented as a sequence $(trip_1, trip_2, \ldots, trip_n)$.

   The criteria that characterize an acceptable itinerary, out of all possible itineraries, are specified by the passenger. The desired transaction displays various possible flights extending a partial itinerary, and the passenger is asked to choose an acceptable one. Extending a partial itinerary of length j is certainly considerably simpler than computing a complete and acceptable itinerary of length $j + 1$. On the other hand, if a complete itinerary is acceptable to the passenger, then certainly every portion of that itinerary is acceptable. If none of all possible flights (connections) extending a partial itinerary are acceptable, then that partial itinerary must be shortened. Extending a partial itinerary requires (a tentative) insertion of a reservation, and its shortening requires its deletion. This essential step in the overall algorithm is expressed as a recursive procedure ExtendReservation:

PROCEDURE ExtendReservation(source);

```
BEGIN Get next destination, day, and date;
        FOREACH departure with the given attributes
        DO IF appropriate THEN
              Insert reservation;
           IF NOT final destination
           THEN ExtendReservation (destination)
           END;
           IF Ticket not booked THEN
             Delete reservation END
           END
        END
END ExtendReservation
```

It is clear from the procedure ExtendReservation that candidates for a partial itinerary are generated systematically in the FOREACH statement and tested for acceptability. When an acceptable partial itinerary is composed, its extension is then attempted by a recursive call of Extend-Reservation. When an itinerary is completed (if at all), further recursive calls are not generated, and a sequence of returns occurs all the way back to the first call of ExtendReservation. Backtracking occurs when all candidates (flight departures) are tested and deemed unacceptable for the passenger. A return of the last call of ExtendReservation then occurs so that the last reservation (portion) of the itinerary is deleted before further systematic generation of other possible connections (flights) is resumed. If neither of the remaining candidates for an extension of the partial itinerary is acceptable to the passenger, further backtracking occurs, and a possibly complex revision of an itinerary constructed up to some point may be required. Note that each recursive call of ExtendReservation establishes an intermediate save point, which means that all the changes of the database performed by that transaction after that save point may be annulled if it turns out that those changes were not appropriate.

The first call of the recursive procedure ExtendItinerary occurs in the procedure BookItinerary, whose declaration is given below:

PROCEDURE BookItinerary(Source, FinalDestination: String3);

```
  VAR TicketBooked: Boolean;
        p: PassengerType;

      Itinerary: ItineraryType;

BEGIN TicketBooked : = false;
        ReadPassenger(p);

        ExtendReservation(Source);
        IF TicketBooked THEN PrintItinerary
        ELSE ReportFailure END
END BookItinerary
```

The only object in this procedure whose type has not been specified is Itinerary, and since it is of major interest to the external user (the passenger), its specification is given below, together with the specification of actions associated with it—ExtendItinerary, ShortenItinerary, and PrintItinerary:

```
TYPE ItineraryItem = RECORD Source,
                            Destination:   String3;
                            DepartureDate: String8;
                            DepartureTime: String5;
                            ArrivalDate:   String8;
                            ArrivalTime:   String5;
                            Flight#:       FlightId;
                            Plane:         String5
             END;

     ItineraryType = RECORD NumOfTrips: [1..20];
                            Trips: ARRAY [1..20]
                            OF ItineraryItem
             END;

PROCEDURE PrintItinerary;

  VAR i: Cardinal;

BEGIN WITH Itinerary DO
        FOR i := 1 TO NumOfTrips DO
           PrintItem(Trips[i])
        END
      END
END PrintItinerary;

PROCEDURE ShortenItinerary;

BEGIN WITH Itinerary DO
        NumOfTrips := NumOfTrips − 1
      END
END ShortenItinerary;

PROCEDURE PrintItem(Item: ItemType);

BEGIN WITH Item DO
        WriteLn;
        WriteString("Source: "); WriteString(Source);
        WriteLn;
        WriteString("Destination: "); WriteString(Destination);
        WriteLn;
        WriteString("DepartureDate: "); WriteString(DepartureDate);
        WriteLn;
        WriteString("DepartureTime: ");
        WriteString(DepartureTime);
```

```
            WriteLn;
            WriteString(" ArrivalDate: "); WriteString(ArrivalDate);
            WriteLn;
            WriteString(" ArrivalTime: "); WriteString(ArrivalTime);
            WriteLn;
            WriteString(" Flight: "); WriteString(Flight#);
            WriteLn;
            WriteString(" PlaneType: "); WriteString(Plane);
        END

END PrintItem;

PROCEDURE ExtendItinerary (f: FlightType;
                                    d: DepartureType);

    VAR Item: ItineraryItem;

BEGIN WITH Item DO
            Source : = f.Source;
            Destination : = f.Destination;
            DepartureDate : = d.DepartureDate;
            ArrivalDate : = d.ArrivalDate;
            DepartureTime : = d.DepartureTime;
            ArrivalTime : = d.ArrivalTime;
            Flight# : = f.Flight#;
            Plane : = f.Plane
        END;
        WITH Itinerary DO
          IF NumOfTrips < MaxNumTrips THEN
            NumOfTrips : = NumOfTrips + 1;
            Trips[NumOfTrips] : = Item
          END
        END

END ExtendItinerary
```

The specification of the relevant attributes of the passenger is given in the definition of its type PassengerType. The action ReadPassenger that is invoked in the procedure BookItinerary is specified below, together with the action PassengerExists, which is required in order to check whether the passenger data are already in the database so that reading in this case is necessary.

```
PROCEDURE ReadPassenger(VAR p: PassengerType);

BEGIN WriteLn; WriteString(" PassengerId: ")
        ReadString(p.Passenger#);
        IF NOT PassengerExists(p.Passenger#);
        THEN WriteLn;
            WriteString(" Passenger Name: ");
```

```
                    ReadString(p.Name);
                    WriteLn;
                    WriteString("Sex: M/F");
                    ReadCh(p.Sex);
                    WriteLn;
                    WriteString("Phone: ");
                    ReadString(p.Phone);
                    WriteLn;
                    WriteString("Address: ");
                    ReadString(p.Address);
                    p.NumReservations := 0
          END

END ReadPassenger;

PROCEDURE PassengerExists(passenger#: PassengerId):Boolean;

     VAR p: PassengerType;

BEGIN FOREACH p IN Passenger
          WHERE p.Passenger# = passenger#
          DO Return(true) END;
          Return(false)
END PassengerExists
```

We now turn to the further development of the abstract specification of the recursive procedure ExtendReservation. Systematic generation of candidates for an extension of a partial itinerary is achieved by the following nesting of FOREACH statements:

```
FOREACH f IN FlightType
WHERE     (f.Source = Source)
AND       (f.Destination = Destination)
AND       (day IN f.Days)
DO FOREACH d IN DepartureType
     WHERE     (d.Flight# = f.Flight#)
     AND       (d.Date = date)
     DO        Check whether acceptable
     END
END
```

The nesting of the FOREACH statements is necessary since we have to examine all departures on a given date (the inner loop) of all flights on a given day with the given source and destination (the outer loop).

Checking candidates for an extension of a partial itinerary in fact involves much more: getting a reservation if an acceptable connection is found, extending the itinerary composed that way if the final destination has not been reached yet, and dropping the reservation if all the attempts

to extend the partial itinerary until the final destination is reached fail.
So we obtain the following decomposition of the body of the nested FO-
REACH statement:

```
IF NOT Departure booked THEN
        IF acceptable THEN
           Get reservation;
           IF Final destination THEN
              Ticket booked
           ELSE ExtendReservation END
        END;
        IF Ticket booked THEN Exit
        ELSE Drop reservation END
END
```

```
PROCEDURE ExtendReservation(Source: String3);

   VAR Destination: String3;
       reservation#: ReservationId;
       day: DayType; date: String8;
       f: FlightType; d: DepartureType;

BEGIN GetDestination(Destination);
      GetDay(day); GetDate(date);

      FOREACH f IN Flight
      WHERE     (f.Source = Source)
      AND       (f.Destination = Destination)
      AND       (day IN f.Days)
      DO        FOREACH d IN Departure
                WHERE     (d.Flight# = f.Flight#)
                AND       (d.Date = date)
                DO IF NOT DepartureBooked(d.Departure#) THEN
                      DisplayDeparture(f.Flight#,
                                       d.DepartureTime,
                                       d.ArrivalTime);
                   IF Selected( ) THEN
                     GetReservation(f,d,reservation#)
                     IF destination = FinalDestination THEN
                       TicketBooked := true
                     ELSE ExtendReservation(destination) END
                   END;
                   IF TicketBooked THEN Exit
                   ELSE DropReservation(reservation#)
                   END
                END
             END
      END
```

END ExtendReservation

Specification of a number of actions that appear in the above procedure declaration as procedure calls, such as GetDestination, GetDay, GetDate, DisplayDeparture, DepartureBooked, and Selected, is straightforward and given below without any further explanations:

```
PROCEDURE GetDestination(VAR destination: String3);

BEGIN WriteString("Enter next destination");
      ReadString(destination)
END GetDestination;

PROCEDURE GetDay(VAR day: DayType);

  VAR d: String3;
BEGIN LOOP
        WriteString("Enter departure day");
        WriteString("Mon,Tue,Wed,Thu,Fri,Sat,Sun?>");
        ReadString(d);
        CASE d OF
          "Mon": day := Mon; Exit |
          "Tue": day := Tue; Exit |
          "Wed": day := Wed; Exit |
          "Thu": day := Thu; Exit |
          "Fri": day := Fri;  Exit |
          "Sat": day := Sat;  Exit |
          "Sun": day := Sun;  Exit
        ELSE WriteString("Wrong input, try again!")
        END
      END
END GetDay;

PROCEDURE GetDate(VAR date: String8);
BEGIN WriteString("Enter departure date");
      ReadString(date)
END GetDate;

PROCEDURE DisplayDeparture(flight#: FlightId;
                           DepartureTime, ArrivalTime;
                           String5);

BEGIN WriteString("Flight: ");
      WriteString(flight#);
      WriteLn;
      WriteString("Departure Time: ");
      WriteString(DepartureTime);
      WriteLn;
      WriteString("ArrivalTime: ");
      WriteString(ArrivalTime);
      WriteLn
```

END DisplayDeparture;

PROCEDURE Selected( ): Boolean;
  VAR ch: Char;
BEGIN WriteString(" Selected? Y/N ");
      ReadCh(ch);
      IF (ch = " Y ") OR (ch = " y ")
      THEN Return(true)
      ELSE Return(false) END
END Selected;

PROCEDURE DepartureBooked(departure#: DepartureId): Boolean;

  VAR d: DepartureType;

BEGIN FOREACH d IN Departure
      WHERE d.Departure# = departure#
      DO IF d.NumPassengers = d.MaxNumPassengers
         THEN Return(true)
         ELSE Return(false)
         END
      END

END DepartureBooked

Further refinement of the actions GetReservation and DropReservation
is more complex. Getting a reservation requires its insertion in the database
followed by an extension of the itinerary. Dropping a reservation requires
its deletion from the database, as well as the corresponding shortening of
the itinerary:

PROCEDURE GetReservation(f: FlightType; d: DepartureType;
                         VAR reservation#: ReservationId);

  VAR r: ReservationType;
      date: String5;

BEGIN GetReservationId(f.Flight#, d.Departure#,
                       p.Passenger#, reservation#);
      r.Reservation# := reservation#;
      r.Passenger# := p.Passenger#; (* global variable *)
      r.Departure# := d.Departure#;
      r.Status := "OK";
      GetExpirationDate(date);
      r.ExpDate := date;
      InsertReservation(r);
      ExtendItinerary(f,d);

END GetReservation;

PROCEDURE GetExpirationDate(VAR date: String5);

```
BEGIN WriteLn;
      WriteString(" Expiration date: ");
      ReadString(date)

END GetExpirationDate;

PROCEDURE DropReservation(reservation#: ReservationId);

BEGIN ShortenItinerary;
      DeleteReservation(reservation#)
END DropReservation;

PROCEDURE ReservationExists(reservation#: ReservationId): Boolean;
   VAR r: ReservationType;
BEGIN FOREACH r IN Reservation
      WHERE r.Reservation# = reservation#
      DO Return(true) END;
      Return(false)
END ReservationExists;

PROCEDURE GetReservationId(flight#:      FlightId;
                                departure#: DepartureId;
                                passenger#: PassengerId;
                       VAR reservation#:ReservationId);
```

(* This procedure generates a unique reservation identifier from flight#, departure# and passenger# *)

.
.
.

```
END GetReservationId
```

The final step of the development of the desired transaction is the specification of the actions InsertReservation and DeleteReservation in such a way that the integrity constraints of the database are preserved. This in particular means that, when a reservation is inserted, the number of occupied seats for that departure is increased, as well as the number of reservations held by the passenger. Deletion of a reservation is followed by decrease of those numbers:

```
PROCEDURE InsertReservation(r: ReservationType);
BEGIN Insert(r,Reservation);
      IncreaseNumReservations(r.Passenger#);
      IncreaseOccupancy(r.Departure#)
END InsertReservation;

PROCEDURE DeleteReservation(reservation#: ReservationId);
   VAR r: ReservationType;
```

```
BEGIN FOREACH r IN Reservation
       WHERE r.Reservation# = reservation#
       DO Delete(r,Reservation);
          DecreaseNumReservations(r.Passenger#);
          DecreaseOccupancy(r.Departure#)
       END

END DeleteReservation;

PROCEDURE IncreaseOccupancy(departure#: DepartureId);
  VAR d: DepartureType;

BEGIN FOREACH d IN Departure
       WHERE d.Departure# = departure#
       DO IF d.NumPassengers < d.MaxNumPassengers
          THEN d.NumPassengers := d.NumPassengers + 1
          ELSE Error END
       END
END IncreaseOccupancy;

PROCEDURE DecreaseOccupancy(departure#: DepartureId);
  VAR d: DepartureType;

BEGIN FOREACH d IN Departure
       WHERE d.Departure# = departure#
       DO IF d.NumPassengers > 0
          THEN d.NumPassengers :=
                  d.NumPassengers − 1
          END
       END
END DecreaseOccupancy;

PROCEDURE IncreaseNumReservations(passenger#: PassengerId);
  VAR p: PassengerType;
BEGIN FOREACH p IN Passenger
       WHERE p.Passenger# = passenger#
       DO IF p.NumReservations < 20
          THEN p.NumReservations :=
                  p.NumReservations + 1
          ELSE Error END
       END
END IncreaseNumReservations;

PROCEDURE DecreaseNumReservations(passenger#: PassengerId);
  VAR p: PassengerType;
BEGIN FOREACH p IN Passenger
       WHERE p.Passenger# = passenger#
       DO IF p.NumReservations > 0
```

```
        THEN p.NumReservations : =
              p.NumReservations − 1
    END
  END
END DecreaseNumReservations
```

Exercises

(1) Action and Transaction Modeling

(i) It has been suggested (by Brodie and Ridjanović (1984b)) that, for the purposes of action modeling of application environments, actions should be classified according to the following levels of abstraction:

—transactions,
—actions, and
—database alterations.

Database alterations are primitive actions upon the database that perform insert, delete, or update of particular object instances.

Actions refer to particular objects, but are defined in such a way that all integrity constraints associated with that object are maintained. An action associated with an object refers only to those objects immediately related to that object. Consequently, actions associated with those objects are used to decompose the desired action. A database-altering action is used to change the underlying object instance.

Transactions are application-environment, user-oriented actions, composed by using actions and other transactions. Transactions do not contain database alterations (they are carried out by actions that a transaction performs). Transactions do not necessarily refer to a particular object, but may refer to a collection of objects and sets of object instances.

(ii) In view of the above described classification of actions, skeletons for procedures representing actions and transactions have been proposed, intended to force application programmers to design actions and transactions in a disciplined manner. The proposed skeleton for an action has the following form:

PROCEDURE ActionName (Parameters);

  Declarations;

```
BEGIN IF NOT PreCondition
      THEN   ExceptionHandling
      ELSE   ActiveRole
      END;
      IF NOT PostCondition
      THEN   ExceptionHandling
```

```
        ELSE    DatabaseAlteration
        END
END    ActionName
```

Develop procedures for InsertEmployee, DeleteEmployee, and Up-dateSalary actions associated with the object type COURT-EMPLOYEE, which has the following immediate relationships with other objects

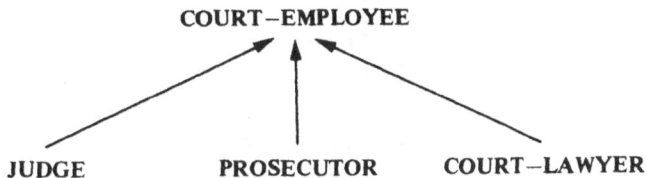

using the proposed skeleton. On the basis of the required development, analyze the appropriateness of the skeleton.

(iii) The skeleton proposed for transactions has the following form:

PROCEDURE TransactionName(Parameters);

Declarations;

```
BEGIN IF NOT PreCondition
        THEN    ExceptionHandling
        ELSE    ActiveRole
        END;
        IF NOT PostCondition
        THEN    ExceptionHandling
        ELSE    Success
        END
END    TransactionName
```

Observe that ActiveRole of an action upon an object is a composition of actions that refer to other, immediately related objects. ActiveRole of a transaction is a composition of actions and other transactions.

Using the proposed skeleton, develop typical transactions for the above submodel of the court application environment such as HireEmployees, FireEmployees, UpdateSalaries, etc. Analyze the appropriateness of the proposed skeleton on the basis of this development.

(2) Exception Handling

(i) Consider the following approach to exception handling: Each object type has an associated exception object type. Failure of Insert, Delete, or Update actions associated with the object type due to violation of integrity constraints causes insertion of the violating object instance into the set of exceptional object instances (see (Borgida, 1986a)). While actions associated with an object type are defined in such a way that all integrity constraints associated with that object type are maintained, actions associated with its exception object type allow unrestricted manipulation of exceptional object instances. For example, given the definition module Student, its associated definition module StudentException may be specified as follows:

DEFINITION MODULE StudentException;

FROM Student IMPORT StudentType, StudentSetType,
                    StudentId;

EXPORT QUALIFIED ExceptionalStudents,
                 InsertExceptionalStudent,
                 DeleteExceptionalStudent,
                 ModifyExceptionalStudent;

VAR ExceptionalStudents: StudentSetType;

PROCEDURE InsertExceptionalStudent(student: StudentType);
PROCEDURE DeleteExceptionalStudent(student#: StudentId);
PROCEDURE ModifyExceptionalStudent(student: StudentType);

END StudentException.

(ii) Observe that actions InsertExceptionalStudent, DeleteExceptional-Student, and ModifyExceptionalStudent do not raise any exception so that their implementation is immediate. Write the implementation module for the definition module StudentException given above.

(iii) Revise the implementation module of the object type Student, taking into account the existence of the module StudentException.

(iv) Give examples of corrective actions. Such an action would typically search the set ExceptionalStudents, perform some modification of an exceptional student instance, and attempt an insertion into the original StudentSet.

(3) Exceptional Properties

(i) The following definition module illustrates yet another approach to exception handling (see (Borgida, 1986a)):

DEFINITION MODULE Customer;

EXPORT QUALIFIED CustomerType, CustomerId, Attribute,
                 ExceptionAttr, Exception, ExceptionExists,
                 InsertExceptAttr, DeleteExceptAttr,
                 InsertCustomer, DeleteCustomer,
                 FindCustomer, ChangeAddress,
                 UpdateAmountDue, ChangeCreditLimit;

```
TYPE CustomerId    = String7;
     CustomerType  = RECORD Customer#: CustomerId;
                            Name: String30;
                            Address: String50;
                            AmountDue: Real;
                            CreditLimit: Real
                     END;
     Attribute     = (Customer#, Name, Address,
                      Meter#, AmountDue, CreditLimit);
     ExceptionAttr = RECORD Customer#: CustomerId;
                            ExceptionalAttribute:
                            Attribute
                     END;

VAR Exception: Boolean;

PROCEDURE InsertCustomer(customer: CustomerType);
PROCEDURE DeleteCustomer(customer#: CustomerId);
PROCEDURE FindCustomer(name: String30;
                       address: String50): CustomerId;
PROCEDURE ChangeAddress(customer#: CustomerId;
                        newaddress: String50);
PROCEDURE UpdateAmountDue(customer#: CustomerId;
                          addition: Real);
PROCEDURE ChangeCreditLimit(customer#: CustomerId;
                            NewCredit: Real);
PROCEDURE InsertExceptAttr(exception: ExceptAttr);
PROCEDURE DeleteExceptAttr(exception#: ExceptionId);
PROCEDURE ExceptionExists(customer#: CustomerId;
                          ExceptionalAttribute: Attribute):
                          Boolean;
END Customer.
```

(ii) Specify the declarations of procedures UpdateAmountDue and ChangeCreditLimit so that the integrity constraint

For each c in CustomerSet: (c.AmountDue $<=$ c.CreditLimit)

holds.

(iii) Consider the following two exception handling actions:

(a) If an exception occurs, the variable Exception is set appropriately, and the violating action is aborted.
(b) If an exception occurs, the terminal user who started the violating action is interrogated. If the user confirms that the exceptional value of an attribute is OK, the action is completed, and an indication of an exceptional value of an attribute of an object instance is inserted into the set of Exceptions (procedure InsertException).

(iv) Specify declarations of the procedures UpdateAmountDue and ChangeCreditLimit according to strategy (b) above.

(v) Specify the declaration of the procedures that print

(a) the names of all customers whose amount due is not exceptional,
(b) the names of all customers with an exceptional amount due, and
(c) the average exceptional amount due.

(vi) Specify procedure declarations of the update actions UpdateAmount-Due, ChangeCreditLimit, and ChangeAddress in such a way that, if the values of those attributes are exceptional, the corresponding exception is deleted first (DeleteException) and the update is then performed as described in strategy (b) from step (iii).

(vii) Specify the declaration of the procedure DisplayCustomer whose parameter is the customer identifier in such a way that each exceptional value of an attribute is indicated.

(4) Expert Systems

(i) Suppose our task is the design of an expert system required by a marriage agency. In accordance with the object-oriented approach, we specify the relevant objects of that particular application environment and actions associated with those objects as application procedures. Select appropriate attributes of objects Man and Woman that are relevant for this particular application environment. In other words, using the abstraction technique, specify only those attributes of objects Man and Woman that are relevant for selecting a marriage partner.

Specification of these two types leads to the database specified as follows:

Men: ENTITY SET OF Man;
Women: ENTITY SET OF Woman

(ii) To perform the service required by its end users, our database application system obviously requires its end users to express preference for their potential partners on the basis of the database designed in step (i) (see (Wirth, 1986)). This leads to a nonentity aggregation of the object types Men and Women specified as follows:

Preference   = RECORD Man#: PersonId;
                        Woman#: PersonId;
                        MansPreference: [1..n];
                        WomansPreference: [1..n]
               END
PreferenceSet = ENTITY SET OF Preference

Observe that the above specification is based on the assumption that each end user specifies preferable partners and assigns a rank in the range 1 to n to each of them. Specify ExpressMansPreference and ExpressWomans-Preference actions as application procedures that include appropriate communication with the end users in order to perform their task of constructing the nonentity aggregation set PreferenceSet.

(iii) Having designed the model consisting of two entity types Men and Women, and their nonentity aggregation Preference, consider the fundamental action of this application environment that attempts to find appropriate partners on the basis of the previously constructed PreferenceSet. This action, call it ConstructMarriageSet, inspects the set PreferenceSet and constructs another aggregation:

```
TYPE Marriage  =  RECORD Man#: PersonId;
                          Woman#: PersonId
                  END;
MarriageSet     =  ENTITY SET OF Marriage
```

Specify the action ConstructMarriageSet as a recursive application procedure that is based on the backtracking programming technique. Since the problem is symmetric, we can specify two symmetric recursive procedures FindPartner: One of them selects an appropriate woman in a man's order of preference, and the other selects an appropriate man in a woman's order of preference.

(iv) The join condition was defined as follows: A partner was acceptable to a person as long as he or she expressed some preference for that person (i.e., as long as his or her preference is recorded in the PreferenceSet), in addition to both being single (i.e., their marriage not being recorded in the MarriageSet). Of course, such a general join condition is a good example of the actual situations that occur in real applications for which the natural join is a very basic primitive. We make it even more complex by the following well-known requirement:

The stable marrying condition. The marriage set is unstable if there exists a man and a woman who would both prefer each other to their actual marriage partners specified in the marriage set. If no such pair exists, the marriage set is stable.

Modify the recursive procedure FindPartner specified in step (iv) so that the join condition is extended with the marriage stability condition. To do this, specify a Boolean function procedure Stable that checks this condition.

(v) Generalize the development in the previous steps in order to generalize all acceptable and stable marriage sets.

(5) Optimal Selection Problem

(i) Consider the problem of finding an optimal selection out of a given set of objects subject to some constraints. More specifically (see (Wirth,

1986)), suppose each object has attributes Weight and Value. The optimal (small) set of objects will be the one with the largest sum of values of its elements (object instances). The constraint is a given LimitWeight of the sum of weights of the selected object instances.

```
TYPE Object    = RECORD Object#: ObjectId;
                          {other attributes}
                          Weight, Value: Cardinal
                 END;
VAR ObjectSet = ENTITY SET OF Object
```

(ii) The general approach to this problem consists of systematic generation of candidate selections and the retention of the one that is optimal so far. The currently considered set and the optimal set constructed so far are represented as variables

```
VAR CurrentSet, OptimalSet: SET OF ObjectId;
    MaxValue: Cardinal
```

where MaxValue denotes the sum of values of objects in the optimal selection. To construct a candidate selection, we consider objects in turn, building partial candidate selections. We assume that a criterion Complete for completeness of a candidate selection is also given (e.g., an optimal selection is required to consist of n objects).

(iii) The procedure describing the process of investigating the suitability of an object instance is called recursively to investigate the next object until all objects have been considered. Analyze whether the following abstract procedure is appropriate for the above problem, and if not, propose the required modifications to obtain the appropriate one.

```
PROCEDURE NextObject;
  VAR o: Object;
BEGIN
  REPEAT SelectNext(o);
    IF Acceptable(o) THEN
      Insert(o,ObjectSet);
      IF NOT Complete(ObjectSet) THEN
        NextObject;
        IF NOT Successful THEN
          Delete(o,ObjectSet)
        END
      END
    END
  UNTIL Successful OR NoMoreObjects
END NextObject
```

Main algorithm

Empty(ObjectSet);
NextObject.

(iv) Consideration of each object instance has two possible outcomes: either inclusion of the investigated object instance in the current selection, or its exclusion. An object may be included in the current selection if the total weight after its inclusion is less than LimitWeight. If we consider exclusion of an object from a current selection, then the criterion for continuation of building up the current selection further is that the total value of objects in the current selection that is still achievable after the exclusion is not less than MaxValue. Indeed, such a continuation may produce an acceptable selection, but not the optimal one.

In view of the above considerations, specify the recursive procedure NextObject so that it has two parameters:

(a) the total weight of the selection constructed so far, and
(b) the still achievable value of that selection.

(v) Observe that the above proposed procedure NextObject requires the total value of all objects in ObjectSet. What is a suitable representation of this attribute of ObjectSet? Is it possible to define the procedure NextObject so that, instead of the still achievable value, its parameter is the achieved value, that is, the value of the current selection.

(vi) Write a complete module required by the above problem that performs the required import of database objects and associated procedures, as well as the required input/output (I/O) primitives.

(vii) The above described backtracking scheme with a limitation factor that reduces the growth of the potential search tree is known, in general, as the *branch and bound algorithm*. However, the described general strategy for reducing the number of investigated candidates may not be efficient enough for database applications. Consider further reduction of the complexity of the developed algorithm based on the assumption that selection of a set of objects of the same type with a given property (or properties) is in an efficient database action.

(6) Referential Integrity and Context-Dependent Actions

(i) Consider the object types Employee and Department, specified by the following two definition modules:

DEFINITION MODULE Employee;

EXPORT QUALIFIED EmployeeType, EmployeeId,
EmployeeSetType, Employees,
EmployeeExceptionType, EmployeeException;

```
TYPE EmployeeId      = String10;

     EmployeeType = RECORD employee#:   EmployeeId;
                            department#: DepartmentId;
                            (* other attributes *)
              END;

     EmployeeSetType = ENTITY SET OF EmployeeType;

VAR Employees: EmployeeSetType;

PROCEDURE InsertEmployee(employee: EmployeeType);

PROCEDURE DeleteEmployee(employee#: EmployeeId);

TYPE EmployeeExceptionType = (EmployeeOK, DuplicateEmployee,
                              NonExistentEmployee,
                              NonExistentDepartment);

VAR EmployeeException: EmployeeExceptionType;

END Employee.


DEFINITION MODULE Department;

FROM Employee IMPORT EmployeeId;

EXPORT QUALIFIED DepartmentType, DepartmentId,
                 DepartmentSetType, Departments;

TYPE Department Id    = String6;
     DepartmentType = RECORD department#: DepartmentId;
                             manager#:    EmployeeId;
                             (* other attributes *)
              END;

     DepartmentSetType = ENTITY SET OF DepartmentType;

VAR Departments: DepartmentSetType;

PROCEDURE InsertDepartment(department: DepartmentType);

PROCEDURE DeleteDepartment(department#: DepartmentId);

TYPE DepartmentException = (DepartmentOK,
                            DuplicateDepartmentId,
                            NonExistentDepartment,
                            NonExistentManager);

VAR DepartmentException: DepartmentExceptionType;

END Department.
```

(ii) Decomposition of actions InsertEmployee, DeleteEmployee, Insert-
Department, and DeleteDepartment reveals the following problem:

(a) InsertEmployee requires a reference to an existing department (department#). If it does not exist, the action is terminated with a request to perform InsertDepartment first.

(b) InsertDepartment requires a reference to an existing employee (manager#). If it does not exist, the action is terminated with a request to perform InsertDepartment first. So the cycle is completed.

(iii) The above problem indicates it is not always appropriate to enforce unconditionally the integrity constraints associated with an object type. The actual context determines whether some constraints should be suspended. Context-dependent actions (Brodie and Ridjanović, 1984b) may ignore the integrity constraints associated with an object type in order to avoid circularity demonstrated in the above example. In this particular case, this means that insertion of an employee invoked from the action InsertDepartment is allowed to ignore the referential integrity constraint relating an employee with an existing department. Symmetrically, the action InsertEmployee would ignore the integrity constraint relating a department with an existing manager.

(iv) Explore the possibilities and limitations of modules in terms of proper representation of the above cases, and revise the given example accordingly. Write up the implementation modules Department and Employee.

Bibliographical Notes

A classical reference on the top-down program development methodology is (Wirth, 1971). The presented object-oriented, top-down conceptual design methodology appeared in (Alagić, 1986). It grew out of previous work of Brodie and Ridjanović (1984a, 1984b). Exercise (1) is based on their approach to action and transaction modeling. The flight-reservation application was motivated by an example from Ullman (1980), but the overall object-action-oriented material developed in this book is original, including conceptual modeling, specification of environments in terms of modules, and the object-oriented versus relational-oriented procedures. The same applies to the material on the design of recursive transactions, although the applied general methodology is well known in programming; see, for example, (Wirth, 1971). The approaches to exception handling and exceptional properties presented in exercises (2) and (3) were motivated by Borgida (1986a). Exercises (4) and (5) are database generalizations of problems that appear in (Wirth, 1986).

CHAPTER 4
Standard Abstractions

1 Aggregation

The fundamental importance of the aggregation abstraction for the representation of objects comes from the fact that an object is obtained by aggregation of its attributes. An object type is, as far as its structure is concerned, represented as a record type whose components are object attributes and their types. This structural representation is then enriched by adding actions to objects represented as records, and thus, an object is represented by a module containing the definition of the record type of that object, together with the types of actions (procedures) that are applicable to that object. All of that has been done, however, for objects whose components are simple (attributes). Our goal now is to consider the general case of aggregation and its representation in terms of modules. In this general case, an object is defined in terms of the aggregation abstraction, where components of that object are not necessarily simple, but represent composite objects themselves.

So, in general, given entity types $E1, E2, ..., En$, we define their aggregate entity type E with the given entity types $E1, E2, ..., En$ as the attributes of E. $E1, E2, ..., En$ become component entity types of E. Conversely, given an entity type E, we perform its decomposition into entity types $E1, E2, ..., En$, which become attributes of E. In the programming language notation, the immediate representation of the entity type E would be as follows:

```
TYPE E = RECORD A1: E1;
                A2: E2;
```

.

.

.

An: En
END

Given an instance e of type E, its A*ith* component, which is of type Ei is denoted as e.Ai. This action is called *projection* and is fundamental to the aggregation abstraction. Conversely, given instances e1,e2,...,en of respective types E1,E2,...,En, they determine a unique instance e of type E with the property that e.A1 = e1, e.A2 = e2,...,e.An = en.

The graphical representation of aggregation given below is based on the fact that projections are in fact functions:

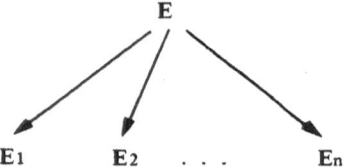

The problems associated with the above immediate representation of aggregation are well known and have been discussed to some extent in Chapter 1 when the relational model of data was introduced. Within the framework of that model, this immediate representation is not permitted since all attributes of entities are required to be of a simple type. That restriction avoids some anomalies of the above representation of aggregation such as follows: If an entity type A is a component of entity types A1,A2,...,An, then in the above immediate representation one and the same instance of A will be repeated as the value of the corresponding attributes of all the entity types A1,A2,...,An. This multiplication of the same instance of A is not only critical for reasons of storage economy, but also for reasons of data integrity. Indeed, update actions must then be defined in such a way that they guarantee consistent modifications of all those repeated instances, which is not always a trivial matter.

This problem is called the *update anomaly*. It is one of the reasons for a different representation of the aggregate entity type E whose components are E1,E2,...,En. Rather than taking E1,E2,...,En as attributes of E we take identifiers of the component entities E1#, E2#,...,En# as the attributes of the aggregate entity E to obtain a representation in accordance with the relational model of data. We will explore this representation from the viewpoint of action modeling since it imposes some important requirements on those actions with respect to the referential integrity constraints that this relational representation of aggregation has.

The framework we will consider is defined as follows: An entity type E, together with its actions, is represented as a module. E has component entities E1,E2,...,En that are likewise represented by the respective modules E1,E2,...,En. Our task is to develop a full representation of aggregation in terms of the definition and implementation modules. This full programming language notation will be developed for the following example of aggregation:

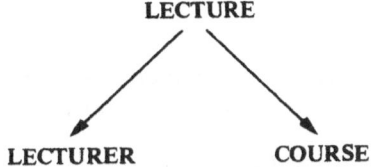

First consider the entity type LECTURE. Its attributes are in accordance with the above discussion:

LECTURE

Attributes: Lecture identifier
Lecturer identifier
Course identifier
Day
Time
Room

Actions: Insert lecture
Delete lecture
Select lecture
Reschedule lecture
Change lecture

The component objects have the following object-action-oriented specification

LECTURER

Attributes: Lecturer identifier
Name
Rank

Actions: Insert   lecturer
Delete   lecturer
Find   lecturer
Promote lecturer

COURSE

Attributes: Course identifier
Title
Level
Credit

Actions: Insert   course
             Delete   course
             Select   course
             Change title
             Change level
             Change credit

It is straightforward to express the above object-action type of specification
of our model in terms of definition modules as follows:

DEFINITION MODULE Lecture;

FROM Course   IMPORT CourseId;

FROM Lecturer IMPORT LecturerId;

EXPORT QUALIFIED LectureType, LectureId,
                 WorkDays, LectureHours,
                 WriteLecture,
                 LectureExists, SelectLecture,
                 InsertLecture, DeleteLecture,
                 ReScheduleLecture,
                 ChangeCourseLecturer, DeleteCourseLectures,
                 ReplaceLecturer,
                 RoomAvailable,
                 LecturerScheduled, CourseScheduled;

TYPE WorkDays   = (Mon,Tue,Wed,Thu,Fri);
     LectureHours = [9..16];
     LectureId   = String9;
     LectureType   = RECORD lecture#: LectureId;
                            lecturer#: LecturerId;
                            course#: CourseId;
                            day: WorkDays;
                            time: LectureHours;
                            room: String5
                     END;

     ExceptionType = (None, DuplicateLectureId,
                      NonExistentLecture,
                      NonExistentLecturer, NonExistentCourse,
                      NoRoom);

VAR Exception: ExceptionType;

PROCEDURE WriteLecture(lecture: LectureType);

PROCEDURE SelectLecture(VAR lecture#: LectureId);

PROCEDURE InsertLecture(lecture: LectureType);

PROCEDURE DeleteLecture(lecture#: LectureId);

PROCEDURE ReScheduleLecture(lecture#: LectureId;
                                day: WorkDays; time: LectureHours;
                                room: String5);

PROCEDURE LectureExists(lecture#: LectureId): Boolean;

PROCEDURE ChangeCourseLecturer(course#: CourseId;
                                newlecturer#: LecturerId);

PROCEDURE ReplaceLecturer(oldlecturer#,
                                newlecturer#: LecturerId);

PROCEDURE DeleteCourseLectures(course#: CourseId);

PROCEDURE RoomAvailable(day: WorkDays; time: LectureHours;
                                room: String5): Boolean;

PROCEDURE LecturerScheduled(lecturer#: LecturerId): Boolean;

PROCEDURE CourseScheduled(course#: CourseId): Boolean;

END Lecture.

DEFINITION MODULE Lecturer;

EXPORT QUALIFIED LecturerType, LecturerId,
                RankType, SpecialityType, LecturerExists,
                WriteLecturer, InsertLecturer, DeleteLecturer,
                SelectLecturer, FindLecturer, PromoteLecturer,
                ExceptionType, Exception;

TYPE RankType = (assistant, associate, full);
     SpecialityType = (Computers, Mathematics, Physics);
     LecturerId = String15;

     LecturerType = RECORD lecturer#: LecturerId;
                        name: String50;
                        rank: RankType;
                        speciality: SpecialityType
             END;

     ExceptionType = (None, DuplicateLecturerId,
                NonExistentLecturer, UnapplicableAct);

     VAR Exception: ExceptionType;

PROCEDURE LecturerExists(lecturer#: LecturerId): Boolean;

PROCEDURE WriteLecturer(lecturer: LecturerType);

PROCEDURE InsertLecturer(lecturer: LecturerType);

PROCEDURE DeleteLecturer(lecturer#: LecturerId);

PROCEDURE SelectLecturer(speciality: SpecialityType;
                         VAR lecturer#: LecturerId);

PROCEDURE FindLecturer(name: String50;
                       VAR lecturer#: LecturerId);

PROCEDURE PromoteLecturer(lecturer#: LecturerId);

END Lecturer.

DEFINITION MODULE Course;

EXPORT QUALIFIED CourseType, CourseId, LevelType,
                 ExceptionType, Exception,
                 InsertCourse, DeleteCourse,
                 ChangeLevel, ChangeCredit, CourseExists,
                 SelectCourse;

```
TYPE CourseId    = String4;
     LevelType   = String2;
     CourseType = RECORD course#: CourseId;
                         title:    String20;
                         level:    LevelType;
                         credit:   Cardinal
              END;

     ExceptionType = (None, DuplicateCourseId,
                      NonExistentCourse);
```

VAR Exception: ExceptionType;

PROCEDURE InsertCourse(course: CourseType);

PROCEDURE DeleteCourse(course#: CourseId);

PROCEDURE ChangeLevel(course#: CourseId;
                      level: LevelType);

PROCEDURE ChangeCredit(course#: CourseId; credit: Cardinal);

PROCEDURE CourseExists(course#: CourseId): Boolean;

PROCEDURE SelectCourse(title: String20;
                       VAR course#: CourseId);

END Course.

The above immediate and obvious specification of objects LECTURE, LECTURER, and COURSE, in terms of their definition modules, may have to be refined when the actions associated with those objects specified as procedure headings are actually decomposed. The decomposition of those actions may reveal, among other things, other types of exceptional situations that may occur while those actions are performed, so that the above definition modules may have to be revised with the definition of the appropriate type of exceptions that are detected in the course of execution of the procedures whose headings are specified in those modules.

Furthermore, the fact that LECTURE is an aggregate entity type whose component types are LECTURER and COURSE, together with the chosen structural representation of this abstraction in terms of object identifiers, will be reflected in the decomposition of actions associated with those objects. The decomposition of those actions will require further actions associated with the above objects that express the fact that they are related not only structurally, but also in terms of actions. This, in particular, indicates the following:

LECTURE. Insertion of a new lecture requires checking the uniqueness of its identifier (procedure LectureExists), the existence of the lecturer (procedure LecturerExists), and the course (procedure CourseExists) to which the new lecture refers. In addition to all this, a new lecture cannot be inserted if it is scheduled at the same time and in the same room as some other lecture (this requires the procedure RoomAvailable). Violation of the above conditions requires indication of the exception (error) that occurred. We will choose the following identifiers for the exceptions introduced thus far:

DuplicateLectureId,
NonExistentLecturer, NonExistentCourse,
NoRoom.

Our approach to action modeling will be to make all the actions for checking in advance violation of integrity constraints available to the users of an object. The same applies to selection of correct references to other objects before actions such as insertion or update are performed. This requires the functions LectureExists, CourseExists, and LecturerExists associated with the objects LECTURE, COURSE, and LECTURER, respectively, and the function RoomAvailable associated with the object LECTURE. The action SelectLecturer and SelectCourse were already introduced and permit selection of identifiers of existing objects required by the action InsertLecture.

Decomposition of the actions DeleteLecture and ReScheduleLecture does not present anything new, and the exceptions that may occur were already introduced. One of them occurs with an attempt to delete or update a lecture that does not exist (NonExistentLecture), and the other with an attempt to schedule a lecture in the same room and at the same time as some other, already scheduled lecture (RoomNotAvailable). On the other hand, decomposition of the action ChangeLecturer requires checking for a correct reference (procedure LecturerExists) to an existing lecturer.

LECTURER. Insertion of a lecturer requires checking whether the identifier of the new lecturer is acceptable, which may raise the exception DuplicateLecturerId. The procedure required for checking the existence of a lecturer with a given identifier (LecturerExists) has already been introduced, when its existence was required by the decomposition of the action InsertLecture.

Deletion of a lecturer is more subtle. This subtlety is caused by the fact that the lecturer may appear as a component of a lecture. Such a lecturer may not be simply deleted. So we must first check whether the lecturer to be deleted is scheduled to give any lectures. This requires the action (function) LecturerScheduled associated with the entity type LECTURE. If a lecturer is scheduled to give lectures (i.e., its identifier occurs in some lecture instances), we have to select a replacement. Our assumption is that the application environment permits scheduling of lectures with an unknown lecturer so that the replacement may be void. This requires a new action ReplaceLecturer associated with the object LECTURE that performs the desired replacement of the lecturer to be deleted with the selected replacement. It is only then that we may delete the lecturer.

COURSE. The analysis of the decomposition of Insert and Delete actions given for the LECTURER entity type applies to the COURSE entity type as well. Decomposition of other actions is straightforward. The complete implementation module is given below:

IMPLEMENTATION MODULE Lecture;

FROM Lecturer   IMPORT LecturerExists;
FROM Course   IMPORT CourseExists;
FROM StandardIO IMPORT ReadCh,
                              WriteCard, WriteString, WriteLn;

TYPE LectureSetType = ENTITY SET OF LectureType;

  VAR lecture: LectureSetType;

PROCEDURE WriteLecture(1: LectureType);

BEGIN WriteLn;
        WriteString(" Lecture#: "); WriteString(1.lecture#);
        WriteLn;
        WriteString(" Lecturer#: "); WriteString(1.lecturer#);
        WriteLn;
        WriteString(" Course#: "); WriteString(1.course#);
        WriteLn;
        WriteString(" Day: "); WriteCard(Ord(1.day) + 1,1);
        WriteLn;
        WriteString(" Time: "); WriteCard(1.time,2);
        WriteLn;
        WriteString(" Room: "); WriteString(1.room)
END WriteLecture;

```
PROCEDURE InsertLecture(1:LectureType);

  PROCEDURE PreConditions( ):Boolean;

  BEGIN IF        LectureExists(1.lecture#) THEN
                  Exception := DuplicateLectureId;
                  Return(false)
          ELSIF NOT LecturerExists(1.lecturer#) THEN
                  Exception := NonExistentLecturer;
                  Return(false)
          ELSIF NOT CourseExists(1.course#) THEN
                  Exception := NonExistentCourse;
                  Return(false)
          ELSE  Return(true)
          END
  END PreConditions;

BEGIN IF PreConditions ( ) THEN
          Insert(1,lecture);
          Exception := None
        END
END InsertLecture;

PROCEDURE DeleteCourseLectures(course#: CourseId);

  VAR 1: LectureType;

BEGIN FOREACH 1 IN Lecture
        WHERE   1.course# = course#
        DO      Delete(1,lecture)
        END
END DeleteCourseLectures;

PROCEDURE DeleteLecture(lecture#: LectureId);

  VAR 1: LectureType;

BEGIN Exception := NonExistentLecture;
        FOREACH 1 IN lecture
        WHERE   1.lecture# = lecture#
        DO      Exception := None;
                Delete(1,lecture)
        END
END DeleteLecture;

PROCEDURE LectureExists(lecture#: LectureId): Boolean;

  VAR 1: LectureType;

BEGIN FOREACH 1 IN lecture
        WHERE   1.Lecture# = lecture#
        DO      Return(true)
```

```
            END;
            Return(false)
      END LectureExists;

      PROCEDURE ReplaceLecturer(oldlecturer#,newlecturer#:
                                                      LecturerId);

         VAR 1: LectureType;

      BEGIN FOREACH 1 IN lecture
            WHERE     1.lecturer# = oldlecturer#
            DO        1.lecturer# := newlecturer#
            END
      END ReplaceLecturer;

      PROCEDURE RoomAvailable(day:WorkDays; time: LectureHours;
                              room: String5): Boolean;

         VAR 1: LectureType;

      BEGIN
         FOREACH 1 IN lecture
         WHERE    (1.day = day)
         AND      (1.time = time)
         AND      (1.room = room)
         DO Return(false) END;
         Return(true)
      END RoomAvailable;


      PROCEDURE ReScheduleLecture(lecture#: LectureId;
                                  day: WorkDays;
                                  time: LectureHours;
                                  room: String5);

         VAR 1: LectureType;

      BEGIN IF RoomAvailable(day,time,room) THEN
            FOREACH 1 IN lecture
            WHERE     1.lecture# = lecture#
            DO        1.day := day;
                      1.time := time;
                      1.room := room;
                      Exception := None
            END
         ELSE Exception := NoRoom END
      END ReScheduleLecture;

      PROCEDURE LecturerScheduled(lecturer#: LecturerId): Boolean;

         VAR 1: LectureType;
```

```
BEGIN FOREACH l IN lecture
      WHERE    l.lecturer# = lecturer#
      DO       Return(true)
      END;
      Return(false)
END LecturerScheduled;
```

```
PROCEDURE CourseScheduled(course#: CourseId): Boolean;

   VAR l: LectureType;

BEGIN FOREACH l IN lecture
      WHERE    l.course# = course#
      DO Return(true) END;
      Return(false)
END CourseScheduled;
```

```
PROCEDURE ChangeCourseLecturer(course#: CourseId;
                                    newlecturer#: LecturerId);

   VAR l: LectureType;

BEGIN FOREACH l IN lecture
      WHERE    l.course# = course#
      DO       l.lecturer# : = newlecturer#
      END
END ChangeCourseLecturer;
```

```
PROCEDURE LecturerScheduled(lecturer#: LecturerId): Boolean;

   VAR l: LectureType;

   PROCEDURE Selected( ): Boolean;
     VAR ch: Char;
   BEGIN WriteString(" Is this the desired tuple? Y/N ");
         ReadCh(ch);
         IF (ch = " Y ") OR (ch = " y ") THEN Return(true)
         ELSE Return(false) END
END Selected;

BEGIN lecture# : = EmptyString;
      FOREACH l IN lecture
      DO WriteLecture(l);
         IF Selected( ) THEN lecture#: = l.lecture#;
           Exit
         END
      END
END SelectLecture;
```

```
BEGIN Exception : = None
END Lecture.
```

IMPLEMENTATION MODULE Lecturer;

FROM Lecture IMPORT LecturerScheduled, ReplaceLecturer;
FROM StandardIO IMPORT ReadCh, WriteString, WriteLn;

TYPE LecturerSetType = ENTITY SET OF LecturerType;

VAR lecturer: LecturerSetType;

PROCEDURE WriteLecturer(l: LecturerType);

```
  PROCEDURE WriteRank(r: RankType);
  BEGIN CASE r OF
          assistant: WriteString("Assistant Professor")  |
          associate: WriteString("Associate Professor")  |
          full:      WriteString("Professor")
        END
  END WriteRank;

  PROCEDURE WriteSpeciality(s: SpecialityType);
  BEGIN CASE s OF
          Computers:   WriteString("Computers")  |
          Mathematics: WriteString("Mathematics")  |
          Physics:     WriteString("Physics")
        END
  END;
  BEGIN WriteLn;
        WriteString("Lecturer#: "); WriteString(l.lecturer#);
        WriteLn;
        WriteString("Name: "); WriteString(l.name);
        WriteLn;
        WriteString("Rank: "); WriteRank(l.rank);
        WriteLn;
        WriteString("Speciality: ");
        WriteSpeciality(l.speciality);
        WriteLn;

END WriteLecturer;

PROCEDURE InsertLecturer(l: LecturerType);

BEGIN IF LecturerExists(l.lecturer#)
      THEN Exception := DuplicateLecturerId
      ELSE Insert(l,lecturer);
           Exception := None
      END
END InsertLecturer;

PROCEDURE DeleteLecturer(lecturer#: LecturerId);

  VAR replacement#: LecturerId; l: LecturerType;
```

```
BEGIN Exception : = NonExistentLecturer;
        FOREACH l IN lecturer
        WHERE l.lecturer# = lecturer#
        DO IF LecturerScheduled(lecturer#)
            THEN SelectLecturer(l.speciality, replacement#);
              IF replacement < > EmptyString THEN
                ReplaceLecturer(lecturer#, replacement#);
                Delete(l,lecturer);
                Exception : = None
              END
            END
        END
END DeleteLecturer;

PROCEDURE LecturerExists(lecturer#: LecturerId): Boolean;

  VAR l: LecturerType;
BEGIN FOREACH l IN lecturer
        WHERE     l.lecturer# = lecturer#
        DO Return(true) END;
        Return(false)
END LecturerExists;

PROCEDURE SelectLecturer(speciality: SpecialityType;
                          VAR lecturer#: LecturerId);

  VAR l: LecturerType;
  PROCEDURE Selected( ): Boolean;
    VAR ch: Char;
  BEGIN WriteString("Is this the desired tuple? Y/N");
        ReadCh(ch);
        IF (ch = "Y") OR (ch = "y") THEN Return(true)
        ELSE Return(false) END
  END Selected;

BEGIN lecturer# : = EmptyString;
        FOREACH l IN lecturer
        WHERE l.speciality = speciality
        DO WriteLecturer(l);
            IF Selected( ) THEN
              lecturer# : = l.lecturer#;
              Exit
            END
        END
END SelectLecturer;

PROCEDURE PromoteLecturer(lecturer#: LecturerId);

  VAR l: LecturerType;
```

```
BEGIN Exception : = None;
       FOREACH l IN lecturer
       WHERE      l.lecturer# = lecturer#
       DO             CASE l.rank OF
                        assistant: l.rank : = associate  |
                        associate:l.rank : = full  |
                        full:       Exception : = UnapplicableAct
                      END
       END
END PromoteLecturer;
```

```
PROCEDURE FindLecturer(name: String50;
                             VAR lecturer#: LecturerId);

  VAR l: LectureType;

  PROCEDURE Selected( ): Boolean;

    VAR ch: Char;
  BEGIN WriteString("Is this the desired tuple? Y/N");
        ReadCh(ch);
        IF (ch = "Y") OR (ch = "y") THEN Return(true)
        ELSE Return(false) END
  END Selected;

BEGIN lecturer# : = EmptyString;
       FOREACH l IN lecturer
       WHERE      l.name = name
       DO             WriteLecturer(l);
                      IF Selected( ) THEN
                        lecturer# : = l.lecturer#;
                        Exit
                      END
       END
END FindLecturer;
```

```
BEGIN Exception : = None
END Lecturer.
```

```
IMPLEMENTATION MODULE Course;
```

```
FROM Lecture IMPORT CourseScheduled, DeleteCourseLectures;
FROM StandardIO IMPORT ReadCh,
                             WriteCard, WriteString, WriteLn;
```

```
TYPE CourseSetType = ENTITY SET OF CourseType;
```

```
VAR course: CourseSetType;
```

```
PROCEDURE WriteCourse(c: CourseType);
```

```
BEGIN WriteLn;
      WriteString(" Course#: "); WriteString(c.course#);
      WriteLn;
      WriteString(" Title: "); WriteString(c.title);
      WriteLn;
      WriteString(" Level: "); WriteString(c.level);
      WriteLn;
      WriteString(" Credit: "); WriteCard(c.credit,1);
END WriteCourse;

PROCEDURE CourseExists(course#: CourseId): Boolean;

  VAR c: CourseType;

BEGIN FOREACH c IN course
      WHERE    c.course# = course#
      DO Return(true) END;
      Return(false)
END CourseExists;

PROCEDURE InsertCourse(course: CourseType);

BEGIN IF CourseExists(c.course#) THEN
          Exception := DuplicateCourseId;
      ELSE Exception := None;
              Insert(c,course)
      END
END InsertCourse;

PROCEDURE DeleteCourse(course#: CourseId);

  VAR c: CourseType;

BEGIN Exception := NonExistentCourse;
      IF CourseScheduled(course#) THEN
          DeleteCourseLectures(course#)
      END;
      FOREACH c IN course
      WHERE    c.course# = course#
      DO Exception := None;
          Delete(c,course)
      END
END DeleteCourse;

PROCEDURE ChangeLevel(course#: CourseId;
                             level: LevelType);
  VAR c: CourseType;

BEGIN Exception := NonExistentCourse;
      FOREACH c IN course
```

```
                WHERE       c.course# = course#
                DO          c.level := level;
                            Exception := None
            END
        END ChangeLevel;

        PROCEDURE ChangeCredit(course#: CourseId; credit: Cardinal);

            VAR c: CourseType;
        BEGIN Exception := NonExistentCourse;
                FOREACH c IN course
                WHERE       c.course# = course#
                DO Exception := None;
                    c.credit := credit
                END
        END ChangeCredit;

        PROCEDURE SelectCourse(title: String20;
                                        VAR course#: CourseId);
            VAR c:CourseType;

            PROCEDURE Selected( ): Boolean;
            VAR ch: Char;
            BEGIN WriteString(" Is this the desired tuple? Y/N ");
                    ReadCh(ch);
                    IF (ch = "Y") OR (ch = "y") THEN Return(true)
                    ELSE Return(false) END
            END Selected;

        BEGIN course# := EmptyString;
                FOREACH c IN course
                WHERE       c.title = title
                DO WriteCourse(c);
                    IF Selected( ) THEN
                        course# := c.course#;
                        Exit
                    END
                END
        END SelectCourse;

        BEGIN Exception := None
        END Course.
```

2 Generalization

Given entity types E1,E2,...,En, we define their generic entity type E with the attributes common to all Ei (i = 1,2,...,n). E1,E2,...,En become subtypes of the entity type E. So all the properties of E are also the properties of each of its subtypes. This is called *full property inheritance*. Conversely, given an entity type E, we may define its subtype Ei introducing those properties of Ei, in addition to the properties of E, that are specific to Ei (*specialization*). The graphical representation given below indicates that E is equipped with a collection of injective functions Ei → E ($i = 1,2,...,n$) that are of fundamental importance to the generalization abstraction:

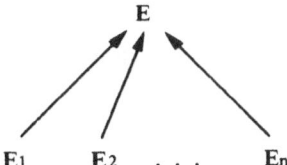

These functions are defined as follows: Suppose type E has attributes A1,A2,...,An, and its subtype Ei has additional attributes B1,B2,...,Bm. Now e in E has components e.A1,e.A2,...,e.An, and ei in Ei has components ei.A1,ei.A2,...,ei.An, ei.B1,ei.B2,...,ei.Bm. The function Ei → E maps ei → e, where e.A1 = ei.A1, e.A2 = ei.A2, and e.An = ei.An, which defines a unique element e of E given an element ei of Ei. If E and Ei are actual sets of objects in an application environment, then we would like to guarantee the existence of the above injective functions at any moment of time; that is, given ei in Ei, e in E, which represents its image, must exist in E. In other words, given an instance of the entity subtype Ei, its generic instance of the generic type E must exist in E. The converse, in general, does not have to hold. Given an instance of E, there is nothing in our approach to generalization requiring existence of instances e1,e2,...,en of respective subtypes E1,E2,...,En, such that e is the image of ei for $i = 1,2,...,n$. This stronger condition however, may in fact be required in particular application environments, as will be illustrated later in an example.

The above programming language notation refers only to the attributes of the generic entity type E and its subtypes E1,E2,...,En and says nothing about the actions associated with these entity types. To complete the model, we represent E and its subtypes E1,E2,...,En as modules so that the actions associated with these types will be procedures declared within their respective modules. The full programming language notation will be developed for the following example of generalization:

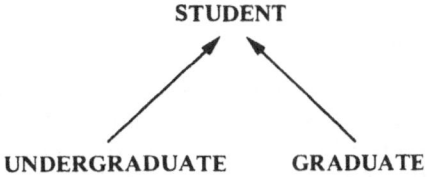

The generic entity type STUDENT is assumed to have the following attributes and associated actions:

STUDENT

Attributes: Student identifier
            Name
            Age
            Address
            Phone
            Level (graduate or undergraduate)
Actions: Enroll student
            Drop student
            Find student
            Change address
            Change phone
            Change level

The attributes and the actions associated with the entity subtypes GRADUATE and UNDERGRADUATE are as follows:

GRADUATE

Attributes: All attributes of STUDENT
            Program (MSc or PhD)
            Advisor
            Department

Actions: Enroll graduate
            Drop graduate
            Change program
            Change advisor
            Change department

UNDERGRADUATE

Attributes: All attributes of STUDENT
            Status (full time or part time)
            School
            Year

Actions: Enroll undergraduate
            Drop undergraduate
            Change status
            Change year
            Change school

The above specification of attributes and actions associated with the objects STUDENT, UNDERGRADUATE, and GRADUATE is mapped below to a relational representation given in the programming language notation in terms of the definition modules of the above three objects:

```
DEFINITION MODULE Student;

EXPORT QUALIFIED StudentType, StudentId,
                 LevelType, AgeType,
                 StudentSetType, student,
                 ExceptionType, StudentExcept,
                 FindStudent, StudentExists,
                 EnrollStudent, DropStudent,
                 ChangeAddress, ChangePhone, ChangeLevel;

TYPE LevelType   = (undergraduate, graduate);
     AgeType     = [12..80];
     StudentId   = String5;
     StudentType = RECORD student#: StudentId;
                          name:     String30;
                          age:      AgeType;
                          address:  String50;
                          phone:    String7;
                          level:    LevelType
                   END;

     ExceptionType = (None, DuplicateStudentId,
                      NonExistentStudent, UnapplicableAct,
                      NonExistentGrad, NonExistentUndergrad);


  VAR StudentExcept: ExceptionType;

TYPE StudentSetType = ENTITY SET OF StudentType;

VAR student: StudentSetType;

PROCEDURE StudentExists(student#: StudentId): Boolean;

PROCEDURE EnrollStudent(student: StudentType);

PROCEDURE DropStudent(student#: StudentId);

PROCEDURE ChangeAddress(student#: StudentId;
                        NewAddress: String50);

PROCEDURE ChangePhone(student#: StudentId;
                      phone: String7);

PROCEDURE FindStudent(name: String30;
                      VAR student#: StudentId);

PROCEDURE ChangeLevel(student#: StudentId);
END Student.

DEFINITION MODULE Graduate;

FROM Student IMPORT StudentId, ExceptionType;
```

```
EXPORT QUALIFIED GraduateType, StudentId, ProgramType,
                 GraduateSetType, graduate,
                 GraduateExists, EnrollGraduate,
                 DropGraduate,
                 ChangeLevel, ChangeAdvisor,
                 ChangeDepartment,
                 GraduateExcept, ExceptionType;

TYPE ProgramType  = (MSc,PhD);
     GraduateType = RECORD student#:    StudentId;
                           program:     ProgramType;
                           advisor:     String30;
                           department:  String20
                    END;

VAR GradExcept: ExceptionType;

TYPE GraduateSetType = ENTITY SET OF GraduateType;

VAR graduate: GraduateSetType;

PROCEDURE GraduateExists(student#: StudentId): Boolean;

PROCEDURE EnrollGraduate(student: GraduateType);

PROCEDURE DropGraduate(student#: StudentId);

PROCEDURE ChangeProgram(student#: StudentId);

PROCEDURE ChangeAdvisor(student#: StudentId;
                        NewAdvisor: String30);

PROCEDURE ChangeDepartment(student#: StudentId;
                           NewDepartment: String20);

END Graduate.

DEFINITION MODULE Undergraduate;

FROM Student IMPORT StudentId, ExceptionType;

EXPORT QUALIFIED SchoolType, YearType, StatusType,
                 UndergraduateType, StudentId,
                 UndergraduateExists,
                 UndergraduateSetType, undergraduate,
                 EnrollUndergraduate, DropUndergraduate,
                 ChangeStatus, ChangeYear, ChangeSchool,
                 UndergradExcept, ExceptionType;

TYPE SchoolType = (Arts, Sciences, Engineering, Medicine);
     YearType   = (freshman, junior, sophomore, senior);
     StatusType = (fulltime, parttime);
```

```
UndergraduateType  =  RECORD student#: StudentId;
                                status:    StatusType;
                                school:    SchoolType;
                                year:      YearType
                 END;
```

VAR UndergradExcept: ExceptionType;

TYPE UndergraduateSetType = ENTITY SET OF
                                      UndergraduateType;

VAR undergraduate: UndergraduateSetType;

PROCEDURE UndergraduateExists(student#: StudentId): Boolean;

PROCEDURE EnrollUndergraduate(student: UndergraduateType);

PROCEDURE DropUndergraduate(student#: StudentId);

PROCEDURE ChangeStatus(student#: StudentId);

PROCEDURE ChangeYear(student#: StudentId);

PROCEDURE ChangeSchool(student#: StudentId;
                       NewSchool: SchoolType);

END Undergraduate.

A major design effort in the specification of the implementation modules
of the objects STUDENT, UNDERGRADUATE, and GRADUATE is
required for the decomposition of actions associated with the above three
objects. This decomposition is affected by the integrity constraints introduced for generalization in general and specific constraints that follow
from the chosen application environment.

STUDENT:

EnrollStudent. Insertion of a student requires checking its identifier,
which may raise the exception DuplicateStudentId. If the exception does
not occur, a new instance of STUDENT is inserted. In accordance with
our approach to generalization, this insertion is not necessarily followed
by insertion of the associated instances of either the entity type GRAD-
UATE or the entity type UNDERGRADUATE (depending on the value
of the attribute level of the newly inserted instance of STUDENT). This
approach permits the existence of the generic student data without the
existence of the specific (graduate or undergraduate) data. In order to
insert the additional data, it is necessary to invoke actions associated with
entity subtypes UNDERGRADUATE (EnrollUndergraduate) and
GRADUATE (EnrollGraduate). Perhaps this decision is not appropriate
for this particular application environment, but has been made deliberately

to illustrate the meaning of the integrity constraint introduced for the generalization abstraction in general.

DropStudent. Decomposition of this action completes our discussion of the above integrity constraint. Indeed, deletion of a student is necessarily followed by deletion of its associated subtype instance (if it exists) either of the type UNDERGRADUATE (DropUndergraduate) or GRADUATE (DropGraduate). In other words, existence of specific student data are not permitted if the generic data about that student do not exist as well. For the same reason, the update action ChangeLevel invokes the actions DropGraduate and DropUndergraduate.

GRADUATE:

EnrollGraduate. The above discussion continues in the same fashion as we consider decomposition of actions associated with the entity subtypes GRADUATE and UNDERGRADUATE. Insertion of an instance of the entity type GRADUATE requires checking the existence of the associated generic instance of the type STUDENT. If the generic student data do not exist, they have to be inserted (action InsertStudent) prior to inserting the specific graduate data.

DropGraduate. Deletion of specific, graduate data does not necessarily mean the general student data should be deleted as well. For example, when a student changes from undergraduate to graduate (action ChangeLevel of the module Student), the undergraduate data should be dropped (DropUndergraduate), but there is no need to drop the student's general data.

UNDERGRADUATE:

The above analysis of the implementation module Graduate applies to the implementation module Undergraduate as well. Insertion of undergraduate data requires the existence of the generic student data. Deletion of undergraduate data does not necessarily require deletion of the generic data.

IMPLEMENTATION MODULE Student;

FROM Undergraduate IMPORT DropUndergraduate;
FROM Graduate   IMPORT DropGraduate;

PROCEDURE StudentExists(student#: StudentId);
(* block *)

PROCEDURE EnrollStudent(s: StudentType);

BEGIN IF StudentExists(s.student#) THEN
            StudentExcept : = DuplicateStudentId
        ELSE Insert(s,student);
            StudentExcept : = None
END
END EnrollStudent;

```
PROCEDURE DropStudent(student#: StudentId);

   VAR s: StudentType;

BEGIN StudentExcept : = NonExistentStudent;
      FOREACH s IN student
      WHERE s.student# = student#
      DO Delete(s,student);
          StudentExcept : = None;
          CASE level OF
            undergraduate: DropUndergraduate(student#)  |
            graduate:        DropGraduate(student#)
          END
      END
END DropStudent;

PROCEDURE ChangeAddress(student#: StudentId;
                        NewAddress: String50);

   VAR s: StudentType;

BEGIN StudentExcept : = NonExistentStudent;
      FOREACH s IN student
      WHERE s.student# = student#
      DO StudentExcept : = None;
          s.address : = NewAddress
      END
END ChangeAddress;

PROCEDURE ChangePhone(student#: StudentId;
                      phone: String7);

   VAR s: StudentType;

BEGIN StudentExcept : = NonExistentStudent;
      FOREACH s IN student
      WHERE s.student# = student#
      DO StudentExcept : = None;
          s.phone : = phone
      END
END ChangePhone;

PROCEDURE FindStudent(name: String30;
                      VAR student#: StudentId);

   VAR s: StudentType;

   PROCEDURE Selected( ): Boolean;

    VAR ch: Char;
BEGIN WriteString(''Is this the desired tuple? Y/N'');
      ReadCh(ch);
```

```
                    IF (ch = "Y") OR (ch = "y") THEN
                    Return(true) ELSE Return(false)
                    END
      END Selected;

BEGIN student# : = EmptyString;
         FOREACH s IN student
         WHERE     s.name = name
         DO WriteStudent(s);
             IF Selected( ) THEN student# : = s.student#;
               Exit
             END
         END
END FindStudent;

PROCEDURE ChangeLevel(student#: StudentId);

   VAR s: StudentType;

BEGIN StudentExcept : = NonExistentStudent;
         FOREACH s IN student
         WHERE s.student# = student#
         DO StudentExcept : = None;
             CASE level OF
               undergraduate: s.level : = graduate;
                              DropUndergraduate(student#)  |

               graduate:      s. level : = undergraduate;
                              DropGraduate(student#)

           END
         END
END ChangeLevel;

BEGIN StudentExcept : = None
END Student.

IMPLEMENTATION MODULE Graduate;

FROM Student IMPORT StudentExists;

PROCEDURE GraduateExists(student#: StudentId): Boolean;
(* block *)

PROCEDURE EnrollGraduate(g: GraduateType);

BEGIN IF NOT StudentExists(g.student#) THEN
         GradExcept : = NonExistentStudent
      ELSE Insert(g,graduate);
             GradExcept : = None
      END
```

```
END EnrollGraduate;

PROCEDURE DropGraduate(student#: StudentId);

   VAR g: GraduateType;

BEGIN GradExcept : = NonExistentGrad;
       FOREACH g IN graduate
       WHERE    g. student#  =  student#
       DO       GradExcept : = None;
                Delete(g,graduate)
       END
END DropGraduate;

PROCEDURE ChangeProgram(student#: StudentId);

   VAR g: GraduateType;

BEGIN GradExcept : = NonExistentGrad;
       FOREACH g IN graduate
       WHERE    g.student#  =  student#
       DO       GradExcept : = None;
                CASE g.program OF
                  MSc: g.program : = PhD  |
                  PhD: g.program : = MSc
                END
       END
END ChangeProgram;

PROCEDURE ChangeAdvisor(student#: StudentId;
                              NewAdvisor:String30);

   VAR g: GraduateType;

BEGIN GradExcept : = NonExistentGrad;
       FOREACH g IN graduate
       WHERE    g.student#  =  student#
       DO       GradExcept : = None;
                g.advisor : = NewAdvisor
       END
END ChangeAdvisor;

PROCEDURE ChangeDepartment(student#: StudentId;
                              NewDepartment: String30);

   VAR g: GraduateType;

BEGIN GradExcept : = NonExistentGrad;
       FOREACH g IN graduate
       WHERE    g.student#  =  student#
```

```
        DO          GradExcept : = None;
                    g.department : = NewDepartment
        END
END ChangeDepartment;

BEGIN GradExcept : = None
END Graduate.
```

IMPLEMENTATION MODULE Undergraduate;

FROM Student IMPORT StudentExists;

PROCEDURE UndergraduateExists(student#: StudentId): Boolean;
(* block *)

PROCEDURE EnrollUndergraduate(u: UndergraduateType);

```
BEGIN IF NOT StudentExists(u.student#)
        THEN   UndergradExcept : = NonExistentStudent
        ELSE   Insert(u,undergraduate);
               UndergradExcept : = None
        END
END EnrollUndergraduate;
```

PROCEDURE DropUndergraduate(student#: StudentId);

   VAR u: UndergraduateType;

```
BEGIN UndergradExcept : = NonExistentUndergrad;
        FOREACH u IN undergraduate
        WHERE   u.student#  = student#
        DO          UndergradExcept : = None;
                    Delete(u,undergraduate)
        END
END DropUndergraduate;
```

PROCEDURE ChangeStatus(student#: StudentId);

   VAR u: UndergraduateType;

```
BEGIN UndergradExcept : = NonExistentUndergrad;
        FOREACH u IN undergraduate
        WHERE   u.student#  = student#
        DO          UndergradExcept : = None;
                    CASE u.status OF
                      fulltime: u.status : = parttime  |
                      parttime: u.status : = fulltime
                    END
        END
END ChangeStatus;
```

PROCEDURE ChangeYear (student#: StudentId);

```
    VAR u: UndergraduateType;

BEGIN UndergradExcept : = NonExistentUndergrad;
      FOREACH u IN undergraduate
      WHERE     u.student# = student#
      DO        UndergradExcept : = None;
                CASE u.year OF
                    freshman:   u.year : = junior  |
                    junior:     u.year : = sophomore  |
                    sophomore: u.year : = senior  |
                    senior:     UndergradExcept : =
                                    UnapplicableAct
                END
      END
END ChangeYear;

PROCEDURE ChangeSchool( student#:    StudentId;
                        NewSchool: SchoolType);

    VAR u: UndergraduateType;

BEGIN UndergradExcept : = NonExistentUndergrad;
      FOREACH u IN undergraduate
      WHERE     u.student# = student#
      DO        UndergradExcept : = None;
                u.school : = NewSchool
      END
END ChangeSchool;

BEGIN UndergradExcept : = None
END Undergraduate.
```

We conclude this section with an example of a client of the modules Student and Graduate that prints the names of all graduate students of a given department together with the names of their advisors.

```
MODULE GraduatesAndAdvisors;

FROM Student       IMPORT StudentType,StudentId, LevelType,
                          student,StudentSetType;
FROM Graduate      IMPORT GraduateType,
                          GraduateSetType, graduate;
FROM StandardIO IMPORT ReadString, WriteString, WriteLn;

    VAR s: StudentType; g: GraduateType;
        department: String20;

BEGIN WriteString(" Select graduate department ");
      ReadString(department);
      FOREACH s IN student, g IN graduate
      WHERE     (s.level = graduate)
```

```
AND          (s.student# = g.student#)
AND          (g.department# = department)
DO           WriteString(s.name); WriteString(" ");
             WriteString(g.advisor); WriteLn
END
END GraduatesAndAdvisors.
```

3 Recursion and Covering

Given entity types E and M, E is a covering of M if every instance of E is a set of instances (possibly empty) of the entity type M, where this set is not determined at the model definition time. E is called *cover entity type*, and M *member entity type*. Note that this association of a set of member instances with an instance of the cover is not partitioning of the member entity type M into disjoint subsets, one subset of members per instance of the cover entity type E. The covering abstraction in fact establishes a correspondence between the entity type E and $\mathcal{P}(M)$. For example, consider the association of the entity types PRODUCT and PART, which defines PRODUCT as the cover type of its member type PART:

PRODUCT

Cover (PART)

The meaning of the above association is quite clear: Each product is defined as a set of parts. A more realistic approach requires the use of both aggregation and covering abstractions so that the entity type PRODUCT is defined as an aggregation of its attributes, one of which is not simple but represents a set of parts. Applying aggregation and covering, we may define an entity type E as a cover aggregation of entity types M1, M2,...,Mn, which means that an instance of E has subsets of instances of M1, M2,...,Mn as the values of its attributes. As an illustration, we generalize our example of covering and aggregation so that PRODUCT becomes the cover type of its associated member types PART and OPERATION, where the instances of the latter entity type are working operations that are necessary for manufacturing products.

PRODUCT

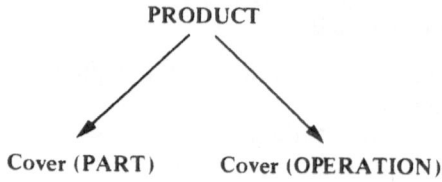

Cover (PART)   Cover (OPERATION)

Now we have that each instance of the entity type PRODUCT is an aggregate of its simple attributes, a set of parts, and a set of working operations that are necessary for manufacturing a product. We could generalize this example further by introducing an entity type TOOL, whose instances are tools used to manufacture a product, but this would not introduce anything new from the conceptual viewpoint, although the example would probably be closer to the actual application environment.

As was already shown in Section 5 of Chapter 2, this particular example is interesting since it involves another abstraction of fundamental importance—*recursion*. Indeed, as already noted, the entity types PRODUCT and PART may in fact be identified since each PART may, in general, be a product, so that the entity type PRODUCT is in fact defined recursively. Putting this all together, we have defined the entity type PRODUCT in terms of classification, aggregation, covering, and recursion abstractions.

PRODUCT

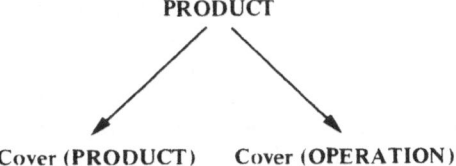

Cover (PRODUCT)   Cover (OPERATION)

Product Entity
    with Attributes

        Product Identifier
        Product name
        Quantity
        Price

        Set of parts each of which is
           Product Entity

        Set of operations each of which is
           Operation Entity

Operation Entity
    with Attributes

        Operation identifier
        Description
        Price

The fundamental conceptual simplicity of the relational model derives from the fact that it is based on a single type of abstraction—aggregation. Conceptual modeling methodology using the relational model requires representation of other types of abstraction in terms of aggregation. Furthermore, the basic relational model permits only a particular representation of aggregation (simple types of attributes). The purpose of this section is to reconsider the application example introduced in this chapter from the viewpoint of relational representation. Such consideration will in fact lead to a further generalization of the conceptual model developed thus far, which may come as a surprise in view of the fact that the generalized model will contain only one explicit form of abstraction—aggregation.

Structure modeling. We start our analysis with the observation that the model developed thus far is not relational. Indeed, it contains a rather immediate representation of covering in which the entity type PRODUCT has attributes Parts and Operations whose values are sets of product and operation identifiers. The use of small-set types of attributes (i.e., sets of simple values) is an obvious extension of the relational model, but it is not permitted because of the strict requirement of that model for simple types of attributes. Formally, entity types in the relational model are in the algebraic sense defined only in terms of the Cartesian product operation, while the use of the power set is not permitted. On the other hand, the use of simple sets allows not only a rather obvious representation of covering, but also of the hierarchical, recursive structure of the fundamental entity type in our application. Indeed, we could argue that it is a quite natural representation in which the attribute of a product entity is a set of references to its immediate subproducts, to which the same rule applies since they are products themselves. But all of this can now be viewed as an intermediate step in the development of the relational representation, where the latter is in that sense on the lower conceptual level of abstraction than the model developed thus far. The two independent (kernel) entity types PRODUCT and OPERATION of this application environment remain, but we now elaborate their relationships further and represent them in terms of aggregation.

The relationship among the entity types PRODUCT and OPERATION is M : N, which means that a product requires N working operations, and one and the same working operation participates in M products. This relationship is called LABOR and has attributes of its own, such as the quantity of a given working operation (in working hours) required in manufacturing a given product.

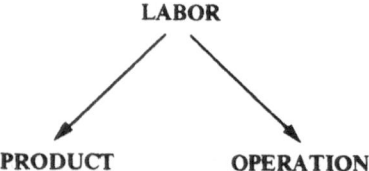

Thus, LABOR is defined as an aggregation of PRODUCT and OPERATION.

In the assembly of products relational schema, this relationship is represented in such a way that PRODUCT# (the product identifier) and OPERATION# (the operation identifier) become attributes of the entity type LABOR.

Now consider the nested (recursive) structure of the entity type PRODUCT. As explained, each product is assumed to have (at least potentially) a complex structure consisting of its subproducts, which are also products, assumed to have subproducts, and so on. This is in fact an M : N relationship of the entity type PRODUCT with itself. This means that a given product participates in M other products as their subproduct (part), and each product has N subproducts (parts). The relationship is called ASSEMBLY and is represented in the following diagram in terms of aggregation:

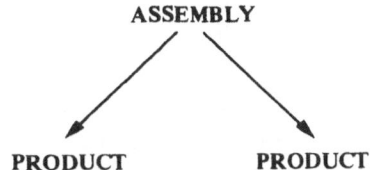

The relationship ASSEMBLY has attributes of its own, such as the quantity of a given subproduct (part) that is required in a given product. Its attributes in the relational schema will also be the product identifier PRODUCT# and subproduct (part) identifier PART#.

4 Sample Database: Assembly of Products

The definition module AssemblyOfProducts given below is based on the above described relational (Cartesian) representation.

DEFINITION MODULE AssemblyOfProducts;

EXPORT QUALIFIED ProductType, OperationType, AssemblyType, LaborType,

ProductSetType, OperationSetType, AssemblySetType, LaborSetType,

Product, Operation, Assembly, Labor, ReadProduct, WriteProduct, ReadOperation, WriteOperation,

InsertProduct, DeleteProduct, UpdateProductPrice, DisplayProductStructure, ProductExists,

InsertOperation, DeleteOperation, UpdateOperationPrice, DisplayOperationProducts, OperationExists;

TYPE ProductId   = String6;
     OperationId = String4;

```
        ProductType      = RECORD
                              product#:   ProductId;
                              name:       String30;
                              class#:     String10;
                              quantity:   Real;
                              price:      Real
                           END;

        AssemblyType    = RECORD
                              product#:   ProductId;
                              part#:      ProductId;
                              quantity:   Real
                           END;

        OperationType   = RECORD
                              operation#: OperationId;
                              description: String30;
                              price:      Real
                           END;

        LaborType       = RECORD
                              operation#: OperationId;
                              product#:   ProductId;
                              quantity:   Real
                           END;

        ProductSetType    = ENTITY SET OF ProductType;
        AssemblySetType   = ENTITY SET OF AssemblyType;
        OperationSetType  = ENTITY SET OF OperationType;
        LaborSetType      = ENTITY SET OF LaborType;

VAR Product:    ProductSetType;
    Operation: OperationSetType;
    Assembly:  AssemblySetType;
    Labor:     LaborSetType;

TYPE ExceptionType = (None, NonExistentProduct,
                      NonExistentOperation,
                      DuplicateProductId, DuplicateOperationId,
                      RefIntegrity);

VAR Exception: ExceptionType;

PROCEDURE ReadProduct(VAR p: ProductType);

PROCEDURE WriteProduct(p: ProductType);

PROCEDURE ProductExists(product#: ProductId): Boolean;

PROCEDURE InsertProduct(p: ProductType);

PROCEDURE DeleteProduct(product#: ProductId);

PROCEDURE UpdateProductPrice(product#: ProductId;
                             newprice: Real);
```

PROCEDURE DisplayProductStructure(product#: ProductId);

PROCEDURE ReadOperation(VAR o: OperationType);

PROCEDURE OperationExists(operation#: OperationId): Boolean;

PROCEDURE WriteOperation(o: OperationType);

PROCEDURE InsertOperation(o: OperationType);

PROCEDURE DeleteOperation(operation#: OperationId);

PROCEDURE UpdateOperationPrice(operation#: OperationId;
                                        newprice: Real);

PROCEDURE DisplayOperationProducts(operation#: OperationId);

END AssemblyOfProducts.

A very important matter related to the entity sets LABOR and AS-SEMBLY is whether they should be treated as entity types or nonentity aggregations. To illustrate the latter, we choose to represent LABOR and ASSEMBLY as nonentity aggregations. This decision, however, is reflected in the developed relational schema, in which LABOR and AS-SEMBLY do not have distinct identifiers of their own. Thus, pairs of attributes of entity types that participate in those aggregations will serve as the identifiers of the associations (product# and part# in ASSEMBLY, and operation# and product# in LABOR). This decision has some implications on action modeling: First, an instance of a nonentity aggregation is permitted to exist as long as the instances participating in the aggregation also exist in the database. So actions associated with the developed relational structure must reflect this requirement. In addition, if ASSEMBLY and LABOR are nonentity aggregations, we may choose not to offer any actions upon them to the users of the module AssemblyOfProducts.

Action Modeling. The definition module of the assembly of the products application environment contains declarations of procedures corresponding to some typical actions in that environment (Insert, Delete, Update, and Display). The major task in action modeling is the development of the procedural decomposition of the above actions given the relational result of the structure modeling phase. Although it is certainly possible to perform that decomposition starting from the developed relational model, we will attempt to do it top-down starting from the conceptual level of abstraction, in which the entity type PRODUCT is defined as the cover aggregate of the entity types OPERATION and PRODUCT itself:

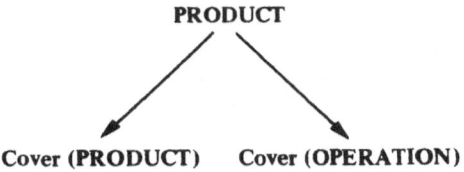

PRODUCT

Cover (PRODUCT)   Cover (OPERATION)

Consequently the abstract algorithms for the actions associated with the
entity types PRODUCT and OPERATION follow the pattern proposed
in Section 3.

PRODUCT

InsertProduct: Get product attributes;
　　　　　　　Check if acceptable;
　　　　　　　Insert product;
　　　　　　　For each of its required subproducts,
　　　　　　　　InsertProduct;
　　　　　　　For each of its required working operations,
　　　　　　　　InsertOperation

DeleteProduct: Get product identifier;
　　　　　　　Check if it exists;
　　　　　　　If that product participates in any other product, then
　　　　　　　　display those products, else delete it

UpdatePrice:　Get product identifier;
　　　　　　　Check if it exists;
　　　　　　　Get new price;
　　　　　　　Check if acceptable;
　　　　　　　Update price;
　　　　　　　For each product in which the given product
　　　　　　　　participates, apply
　　　　　　　UpdatePrice

DisplayProductStructure: Get product identifier;
　　　　　　　　　Check if it exists;
　　　　　　　　　Display product attributes;
　　　　　　　　　For each of its subproducts,
　　　　　　　　　DisplayProductStructure

OPERATION

InsertOperation: Get operation attributes;
　　　　　　　　Check if acceptable;
　　　　　　　　Insert operation

DeleteOperation: Get operation identifier;
　　　　　　　　Check if it exists;
　　　　　　　　If operation does not participate in any product, then
　　　　　　　　　delete operation, else display the products in which
　　　　　　　　　the given operation participates

UpdatePrice:　　Get operation identifier;
　　　　　　　　Check if it exists;
　　　　　　　　Get new price;
　　　　　　　　Check if acceptable;

Update operation price;
For each product in which the given operation
   participates, apply UpdatePrice.

DisplayOperationProducts: Get operation identifier;
                                     Check if it exists;
                                     For each product in which the given
                                        operation participates,
                                     Display product attributes and the
                                        quantity of participation.

Our task now is to represent (implement) the above conceptual-level algorithms as procedures declared in the implementation module Assembly-OfProducts that operate on the developed relational model specified in the corresponding definition module. The best way to see what this mapping to the relational representation involves is first to consider the decomposition of the action DisplayProductStructure. When the currently considered product is displayed at the appropriate place, the same action should be applied recursively to all its immediate subproducts (parts) whose identifiers are found in the ASSEMBLY relation. This requires the natural join of the relations PRODUCT and ASSEMBLY, which is implicit in the declaration of the procedure AnalyzeProduct since the identifier of a subproduct (part#) is passed as the actual parameter in the recursive call of AnalyzeProduct.

```
PROCEDURE AnalyzeProduct (product#: ProductId;
                          level:    Cardinal);
    VAR a: AssemblyType;

BEGIN DisplayProduct(product#);
      FOREACH a IN Assembly
      WHERE    a.product# = product#
      DO       AnalyzeProduct(a.part#, level + 1)
      END
END AnalyzeProduct
```

The procedure DisplayProduct is in fact declared local to Analyze-Product, as exhibited later on. The above declaration of the procedure AnalyzeProduct makes it clear that it is in fact an action on the nonentity aggregation ASSEMBLY according to the relational representation of the recursive structure of the entity type PRODUCT in terms of aggregation:

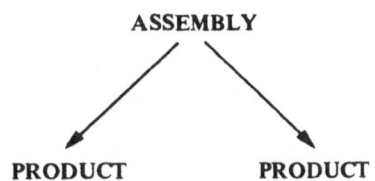

ASSEMBLY

PRODUCT   **PRODUCT**

IMPLEMENTATION MODULE AssemblyOfProducts;

FROM StandardIO IMPORT ReadCh, ReadString, ReadReal, WriteCh,
                                  WriteString, WriteReal, WriteLn;

PROCEDURE ReadProduct(VAR p: ProductType);
(* block *)

PROCEDURE WriteProduct (p: ProductType);
(* block *)

PROCEDURE ProductExists(product#: ProductId): Boolean;
(* block *)

PROCEDURE InsertProduct (p: ProductType);

PROCEDURE LastOperation( ): Boolean;
  VAR ch: Char;
BEGIN WriteLn; WriteString("Last operation <Y/N>?>");
      WriteLn; ReadCh(ch);
      IF (ch = "Y") OR (ch = "y")
      THEN Return(true)
      ELSE Return(false)
      END
END LastOperation;

PROCEDURE LastSubProduct ( ): Boolean;
  VAR ch: Char;
BEGIN WriteLn;
      WriteString("Last subproduct <Y/N>?>");
      ReadCh(ch);
      IF (ch = "Y") OR (ch = "y")
      THEN Return(true)
      ELSE Return(false) END
END LastSubProduct;

PROCEDURE InsertLabor(product#: ProductId;
                              operation#: OperationId);

    VAR p: LaborType; quantity: Real;

  PROCEDURE RequestQuantity(operation#: OperationId;
                                product#: ProductId);
BEGIN WriteLn; WriteString("Enter quantity of operation:");
      WriteString(operation#); WriteString("required for product:");
      WriteString(product#); WriteLn
END RequestQuantity;

BEGIN RequestQuantity(operation#,product#);
      ReadReal(quantity);
      p.product# := product#;

```
                p.operation# : = operation#;
                p.quantity : = quantity;
                Insert(p,Labor)
END InsertLabor;

PROCEDURE InsertAssembly(product#,part#: ProductId);

    VAR a: AssemblyType;

PROCEDURE RequestQuantity(part#,product#: ProductId);

BEGIN WriteLn; WriteString(" Enter quantity of part: ");
        WriteString(part#); WriteString(" in product: ");
        WriteString(product#); WriteLn
END RequestQuantity;

BEGIN RequestQuantity(part#,product#);
        ReadReal(a.quantity);
        a.product# : = product#;
        a.part# : = part#;
        Insert(a,Assembly)

END InsertAssembly;

PROCEDURE ReadOperation (VAR o: OperationType);
(* block *)

PROCEDURE WriteOperation(o: OperationType);
(* block*)

PROCEDURE InsertOperations(product#: ProductId);
PROCEDURE RequestOperation(product#: ProductId);
BEGIN WriteLn;
        WriteString(" Enter working operation for product: ");
        WriteString(product#)
END RequestOperation;

VAR x,o: OperationType;
    notfound: Boolean;

BEGIN WHILE NOT LastOperation( ) DO
        RequestOperation(product#);
        ReadOperation(o);
        notfound : = true;
        FOREACH x IN Operation
        WHERE    x.operation# = o.operation#
        DO notfound : = false;
            InsertLabor(product#, o.operation#)
        END
        IF notfound THEN
            Insert(o, Operation);
```

```
                InsertLabor(product#, o.operation#)
            END
        END
END InsertOperations;

PROCEDURE InsertSubProducts(product#: ProductId);

    PROCEDURE LastPart( ): Boolean;
        VAR ch: Char;
    BEGIN WriteLn;
            WriteString(" Last part ⟨Y/N⟩?> ");
            IF (ch = "Y") OR (ch = "y")
            THEN Return(true)
            ELSE Return(false) END
    END LastPart;

    PROCEDURE RequestPart(product#: ProductId);

    BEGIN WriteLn;
            WriteString(" Enter immediate subproduct of product: ");
            WriteString(p.product#)
    END RequestPart;

    VAR x,p: ProductType; a: AssemblyType;

BEGIN WHILE NOT LastPart( ) DO
            RequestPart(product#);
            ReadProduct(p);
            notfound := true;
            FOREACH x IN product
            WHERE    x.product# = p.product#
            DO notfound := false;
                InsertAssembly(product#, p.product#)
            END;
            IF notfound THEN
              InsertProduct(p);
              InsertAssembly(product#, p.product#)
            END;

            FOREACH a IN Assembly
            WHERE    a.product# = product#
            DO            InsertSubProducts(a.part#)
            END
        END (* WHILE *)
END InsertSubProducts;

BEGIN (* InsertProduct *)
        Exception := None;
```

```
IF NOT ProductExists(p.product#) THEN
   Insert(p,Product);
   InsertOperations(p.product#);
   InsertSubProducts(p.product#)
ELSE Exception := DuplicateProductId
END
END InsertProduct;

PROCEDURE DeleteProduct(product#: ProductId);

PROCEDURE WriteMessage(part#, product#: ProductId);

   BEGIN WriteLn; WriteString("Product");
         WriteString(part#);
         WriteString("participates in product:");
         WriteString(product#)
   END WriteMessage;

PROCEDURE DeleteProductLabor(product#: ProductId);
   VAR l: LaborType;
BEGIN FOREACH l IN Labor
         WHERE    l.product# = product#
         DO       Delete(l,Labor)
         END
END DeleteProductLabor;

PROCEDURE PerformDelete(product#: ProductId);
   VAR p: ProductType; a: AssemblyType;

BEGIN Exception := None;
         FOREACH p IN Product
         WHERE    p.product# = product#
         DO       Delete(p,Product)
         END;
         FOREACH a IN Assembly
         WHERE    a.product# = product#
         DO       Delete(a,Assembly)
         END
END PerformDelete;

PROCEDURE Descend (product#, owner#: ProductId);
   VAR a: AssemblyType; notfound: Boolean;
BEGIN notfound := true;
         FOREACH a IN Assembly
         WHERE    a.part# = product#
         DO IF a.product# < > owner# THEN
                  notfound := false;
```

```
                    Exception : = RefIntegrity;
                    WriteMessage(product#, a.part#)
                END;
            END
            IF notfound THEN
                FOREACH a IN Assembly
                WHERE      a.product# = product #
                DO              Descend(a.part#,product#)
                END;
                PerformDelete(product#);
                DeleteProductLabor(product#)
            END
    END Descend;

    BEGIN Exception : = NonExistentProduct;
          Descend(product#,EmptyString)
    END DeleteProduct;

    PROCEDURE UpdateProductPrice(product#: ProductId;
                                            newprice: Real);

        VAR p: ProductType; a: AssemblyType;
            price, oldprice: Real;

    BEGIN FOREACH p IN Product
            WHERE      p.product# = product#
            DO              oldprice : = p.price;
                            p.price : = newprice
            END;
            FOREACH a IN Assembly
            WHERE      a.part# = product#
            DO FOREACH p IN Product
                WHERE      p.product# = a.product#
                DO price : = p.price + (newprice − oldprice) * a.quantity;
                    UpdateProductPrice(p.product#, price)
                END
            END
    END UpdateProductPrice;

    PROCEDURE DisplayProductStructure(product#: ProductId);

    PROCEDURE WriteHead(product#: ProductId);
    BEGIN WriteLn;
          WriteString(" ASSEMBLY OF PRODUCT: ");
          WriteString(product#); WriteLn;
          WriteString(" Product#      Name ");
          WriteLn
```

```
END WriteHead;

PROCEDURE AnalyzeProduct(product#: ProductId;
                                    level: Cardinal);
  VAR p: ProductType;
      a: AssemblyType;

PROCEDURE WriteProduct(p: ProductType);
  VAR i: Cardinal;
BEGIN FOR i := 1 TO level DO WriteCh(" ") END;
      WriteCh(">");
      WriteString(p.product#);
      WriteString(p.name); WriteLn
END WriteProduct;

BEGIN FOREACH p IN Product
      WHERE    p.product# = product#
      DO WriteProduct(p)
      END;

      FOREACH a IN Assembly
      WHERE    a.product# = product#
      DO AnalyzeProduct(a.part#, level + 1)
      END
END AnalyzeProduct;

BEGIN WriteHead(product#);
      AnalyzeProduct(product#, 0)

END DisplayProductStructure;

PROCEDURE OperationExists(operation#: OperationId): Boolean;
(* block *)

PROCEDURE InsertOperation(o: OperationType);

BEGIN IF OperationExists(o.operation#)
      THEN Exception := DuplicateOperationId
      ELSE Insert(o,Operation);
           Exception := None
      END
END InsertOperation;

PROCEDURE DeleteOperation(operation#: OperationId);

  VAR l: LaborType; o: OperationType;
      found: Boolean;

PROCEDURE WriteMessage(operation#: OperationId;
                                product#: ProductId);
```

```
   BEGIN WriteLn;
         WriteString("Operation");
         WriteString(operation#);
         WriteString("participates in product");
         WriteString(product#)
   END WriteMessage;

BEGIN found := false;
      Exception := NonExistentOperation;
      FOREACH l IN Labor
      WHERE    l.operation# = operation#
      DO found := true;
          Exception := RefIntegrity;
          WriteMessage(operation#, l.product#)
      END;
      IF NOT found THEN
        FOREACH o IN Operation
        WHERE    o.operation# = operation#
        DO       Exception := None;
                 Delete(o,Operation)
        END
      END
END DeleteOperation;

PROCEDURE UpdateOperationPrice(operation#: OperationId;
                                   newprice: Real);

   VAR o: OperationType; l: LaborType;
       p: ProductType; oldprice: Real;

BEGIN Exception := NonExistentOperation;
      FOREACH o IN Operation
      WHERE    o.operation# = operation#
      DO       Exception := None;
               oldprice := o.price;
               o.price := newprice;
      END;

      FOREACH l IN Labor
      WHERE    l.operation# = operation#
      DO       FOREACH p IN Product
               WHERE    p.product# = l.product#
               DO p.price := p.price − l.quantity * oldprice;
                   p.price := p.price + l.quantity *o.price
               END
      END
END UpdateOperationPrice;
```

```
PROCEDURE DisplayOperationProducts(operation#: OperationId);

    VAR p: ProductType; l: LaborType;

  PROCEDURE WriteQuantity(quantity: Real);
  BEGIN WriteLn;
        WriteString(" participation quantity: ");
        WriteReal(quantity,4)
  END WriteQuantity;

BEGIN IF OperationExists(operation#)
        THEN Exception : = None;
        FOREACH l IN Labor
        WHERE     l.operation# = operation#
        DO        FOREACH p IN Product
                  WHERE     p.product# = l.product#
                  DO        WriteProduct(p);
                            WriteReal(l.quantity,6)
                  END
        END
        ELSE Exception : = NonExistentOperation END
END DisplayOperationProducts;

BEGIN Exception : = None
END AssemblyOfProducts.
```

Observe that the hierarchical product structure is displayed (printed out) in such a way that the description of the specified product is displayed (or printed out) appropriately. After that the description of its immediate constituent parts (subproducts) is displayed (printed out) on the same hierarchical level (i.e., with the same indentation), and the same procedure is applied to those parts (subproducts) themselves.

5 A Complex Application Module

The final example in this chapter is an application module that displays (prints out) the descriptions and quantities of all products (parts) and working operations required in manufacturing a specified product. To do this the procedure accesses all the relations in the assembly of the product's database, performing appropriate natural joins of those relations as explained below.

Abstract algorithm

```
MODULE PartsAndLabor;
PROCEDURE PartAndLaborAnalysis:
                Print product description;
```

```
        Accumulate the required working operations;
        For each of its subproducts
        (Accumulate the required subproducts;
        Call the procedure PartAndLaborAnalysis)
```

END PartAndLaborAnalysis;

```
BEGIN Get product identifier;
        Call the procedure PartAndLaborAnalysis;
        Print the accumulated working operations;
        Print the accumulated parts
```

END PartsAndLabor.

The results of the part and labor analysis of a given product are accumulated in two temporary (local) relations ReqMaterials and ReqOperations defined as follows:

```
TYPE ReqMatType      = RECORD material#:   ProductId;
                              description: String30;
                              quantity:    Real
                       END;
     ReqOpType       = RECORD operation#: OperationId;
                              description: String30;
                              quantity:    Real
                       END;
     ReqMatSetType = ENTITY SET OF ReqMatType;
     ReqOpSetType  = ENTITY SET OF ReqOpType;

VAR ReqMaterials:   ReqMatSetType;
    ReqOperations: ReqOpSetType;
```

The data accumulated in the variables ReqMaterials and ReqOperations are printed out at the end of the desired application procedure. Note that the required output contains not only the attributes of the entity types PRODUCT and OPERATION, but also the attributes of the nonentity aggregations ASSEMBLY and LABOR (quantity of participation of a subproduct and of a working operation in a given product).

Thus, the development of this application procedure obviously requires appropriate procedures acting on two nonentity aggregations ASSEMBLY and LABOR. The action on the nonentity aggregation ASSEMBLY

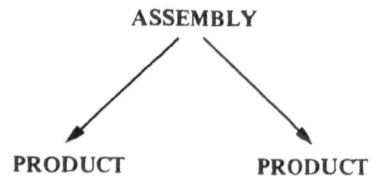

performs the analysis of the given product in terms of its subproducts. Since the result of structure modeling is relational, this action (procedure AnalyzeProductStructure) will require the natural join of the relation PRODUCT with itself via the relation ASSEMBLY. Given our former experience with recursively defined actions on the recursively defined entity type PRODUCT, we have to remember that the above nonentity aggregation is in fact a representation of the recursive structure of the entity type PRODUCT in the relational framework. Following that logic, the algorithm AnalyzeProductStructure will not be symmetric, as it appears from the above aggregation of the entity type PRODUCT with itself. It will be written as an action on ASSEMBLY, which contains a join of that relation with the relation PRODUCT in order to get immediate subproducts of the currently considered product that is displayed first. The same procedure is then invoked recursively (applied to those immediate subproducts) so that one of the required joins is performed via parameter passing.

```
PROCEDURE AnalyzeProductStructure(product#: ProductId);

   VAR p: ProductType;
       a: AssemblyType;

BEGIN DisplayProduct(product#);
      FOREACH a IN Assembly
      WHERE    a.product# = product#
      DO       FOREACH p IN Product
               WHERE a.part# = p.product#
               DO AddMaterial(p.product#, p.name, a.quantity);
                  AnalyzeOperations (product#);
                  AnalyzeProductStructure(a.part#, level + 1)
               END
      END
END AnalyzeProductStructure;

PROCEDURE DisplayProduct(product#: ProductId);
   VAR p: ProductType;
BEGIN FOREACH p IN Product
      WHERE    p.product# = product#
      DO       WriteProduct(p)
      END
END DisplayProduct
```

For each product encountered during the above described recursive search, data about the required materials (procedure AddMaterial) and operations (AnalyzeOperations) are accumulated in the local entity set variables ReqMaterials and ReqOperations. Adding all the required work-

ing operations of a product, however, is not so simple. This is an action
(procedure AnalyzeOperations) on the nonentity aggregation LABOR:

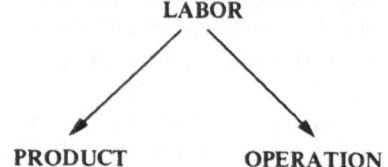

Indeed, for a given product, its associated working operations are obtained
by a natural join of the relations LABOR and OPERATION, and all those
operations are added to the set ReqOperations calling the procedure
AddOperation.

PROCEDURE AnalyzeOperations(product#: ProductId);

VAR l: LaborType;
      o: OperationType;

BEGIN FOREACH l IN Labor
        WHERE   l.product# = product#
        DO   FOREACH o IN Operation
                     WHERE   o.operation# = l.operation#
                     DO   AddOperation(o.operation#, o.description,
                                                        l.quantity)
        END
END AnalyzeOperations;

A complete module PartsAndLabor is now given below:

MODULE PartsAndLabor;

FROM AssemblyOfProducts IMPORT
        ProductType,OperationType,AssemblyType,LaborType,
        ProductSetType,OperationSetType,AssemblySetType,LaborSetType,
        Product,Operation,Assembly,Labor;

FROM StandardIO IMPORT ReadCh,ReadCard,
                                    WriteCh,WriteCard,WriteReal,WriteString,WriteLı

TYPE ReqMatType = RECORD materials#: ProductId;
                                      description: String30;
                                      quantity: Real
                          END;
      ReqOpType   = RECORD operation#: OperationId;
                                      description: String30;
                                      quantity: Real
                          END;

      ReqMatSetType = ENTITY SET OF ReqMatType;

```
    ReqOpSetType   = ENTITY SET OF ReqOpType;

VAR ReqMaterials:   ReqMatSetType;
    ReqOperations: ReqOpSetType;
    product#:       ProductId;

PROCEDURE WriteHead(VAR product#: ProductId);
  VAR i: Cardinal;

BEGIN WriteLn;
        WriteString(" Part and labor analysis for product: ");
        ReadString(product#); WriteLn;
        For i := 1 TO 21 DO WriteCh("_") END;
        WriteLn;
        WriteString(" Assembly for product: ");
        WriteString(product#); WriteLn
END WriteHead;

PROCEDURE WriteOperations;

  PROCEDURE WriteOperation(o: ReqOpType);

  BEGIN WriteLn;
        WriteString(o.operation#); WriteString("  ");
        WriteString(o.description); WriteString("  ");
        WriteReal(o.quantity,4);
        WriteLn
  END WriteOperation;

  PROCEDURE WriteHead;
    VAR i: Cardinal;
  BEGIN WriteLn; WriteString(" Operations for product: ");
        WriteString(product#); WriteLn;
        WriteString(" Operation# "); WriteString("  ");
        WriteString(" Description ");
        FOR i := 1 TO 21 DO WriteCh("_") END;
        WriteString(" Quantity ");
        WriteLn
  END WriteHead;

    VAR o: ReqOpType;

  BEGIN WriteHead;
        FOREACH o IN ReqOperations DO
          WriteOperation(o)
        END
  END WriteOperations;

PROCEDURE WriteMaterials;
```

```
PROCEDURE WriteHead;
   VAR i: Cardinal;
BEGIN    WriteLn;
         WriteString(" Materials for product:  ");
         WriteString(product#);
         WriteLn;
         WriteString(" Material "); WriteString("  ");
         WriteString(" Description ");
         FOR i := 1 TO 21 DO WriteCh("__") END;
         WriteString(" Quantity ");
         WriteLn
END WriteHead;

PROCEDURE WriteMaterial(m: ReqMatType);
BEGIN        WriteLn;
             WriteString(m.material#); WriteString("  ");
             WriteString(m.description); WriteString("  ");
             WriteReal(m.quantity,6);
             WriteLn
END WriteMaterial;

VAR m: ReqMatType;

BEGIN WriteHead;
      FOREACH m IN ReqMaterials DO
         WriteMaterial(m)
      END
END WriteMaterials;

PROCEDURE AddOperation (operation#: OperationId;
                                description: String30;
                                quantity:    Real);

VAR    o:       ReqOpType;
       notfound: Boolean;
BEGIN notfound := true;
      FOREACH o IN ReqOperations
      WHERE    o.operation# = operation#
      DO       notfound := false;
               o.quantity := o.quantity + quantity
      END;
      IF notfound THEN
         o.operation# := operation#;
         o.description := description;
         o.quantity := quantity;
         Insert(o,ReqOperations)
END
END AddOperation;
```

```
PROCEDURE AddMaterial (material#:  ProductId;
                                 description: String30;
                                 quantity:    Real);

  VAR m: ReqMatType;
        notfound: Boolean;
BEGIN notfound : = true;
        FOREACH m IN ReqMaterials
        WHERE    m.material# = material#
        DO         notfound : = false;
                      m.quantity : = m.quantity + quantity
        END;
        IF notfound THEN
          m.material# : = material#;
          m.description : = description;
          m.quantity : = quantity;
          Insert(m,ReqMaterials)
        END
END AddMaterial;

PROCEDURE AnalyzeOperations(product#: ProductId);

  VAR l:  LaborType;
        o: OperationType;

BEGIN FOREACH l IN Labor
        WHERE    l.product# = product#
        DO FOREACH o IN Operation
            WHERE o.operation# = l.operation#
            DO AddOperation(o.operation#, o.description, l.quantity)
            END
        END
END AnalyzeOperations;

PROCEDURE AnalyzeProductStructure(product#: ProductId;
                                               level: Cardinal);

  VAR p: ProductType;
        a: AssemblyType;

PROCEDURE WriteProduct(p: ProductType);
  VAR i: Cardinal;
BEGIN FOR i : = 1 TO level DO
        WriteCh(" "); WriteCh(" > ")
        END;
        WriteString(p.product#); WriteCh(" ");
        WriteString(p.name); WriteLn
END WriteProduct;
```

```
BEGIN FOREACH p IN Product
      WHERE    p.product# = product#
      DO       WriteProduct(p)
      END;

      FOREACH a IN Assembly
      WHERE    a.product# = product#
      DO       FOREACH p IN Product
               WHERE    a.part# = p.product#
               DO AddMaterial(p.product#, p.name, a.quantity);
                  AnalyzeOperations(product#);
                  AnalyzeProductStructure(a.part#,level + 1)
               END
      END
END AnalyzeProductStructure;

BEGIN Empty(ReqOperations); Empty(ReqMaterials);
      WriteHead(product#);
      AnalyzeProductStructure(product#,0);
      WriteOperations;
      WriteMaterials
END PartsAndLabor.
```

Exercises

(1) Aggregation and Generalization

(i) The purpose of this exercise is to model the criminal-court application environment (see (Brodie and Ridjanović, 1984b)), using aggregation and generalization abstractions. The chosen application environment is presented in terms of its objects and their structure. The reader is invited to complete the object-oriented model at each development step in terms of actions, definition, and implementation modules.

(ii) The fundamental entity type of this application is CASE. Apart from simple attributes, components of this object are also other objects: JUDGE, PROSECUTOR, and DEFENSE. This decomposition is presented below:

(iii) DEFENSE is also a composite object. Its decomposition (in terms of aggregation) is given in the following diagram:

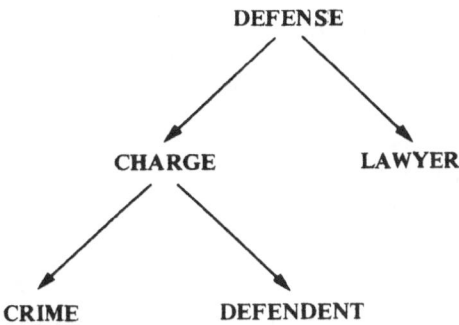

(iv) The object type LAWYER may be further decomposed into two subtypes (specialization), COURT-LAWYER and NON-COURT-LAWYER, according to the diagram below:

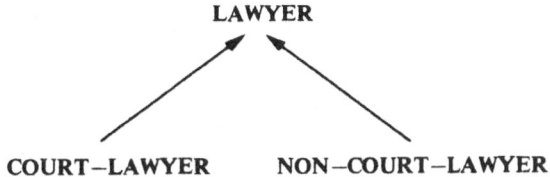

(v) Objects JUDGE, PROSECUTOR, and COURT-LAWYER are in fact subtypes of their generic object type COURT-EMPLOYEE:

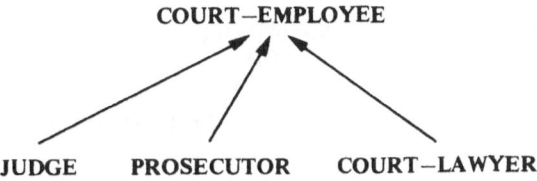

(vi) The result of the overall development is now presented in a single diagram:

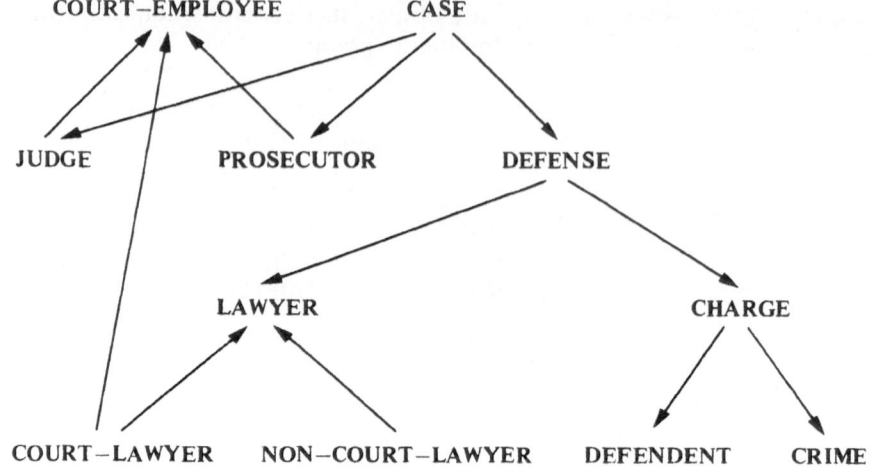

(2) Covering and Generalization

(i) Consider the following conceptual view of a convoy monitoring application environment (see (Codd, 1979)):

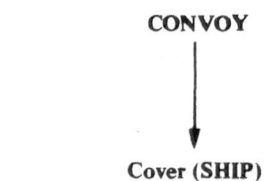

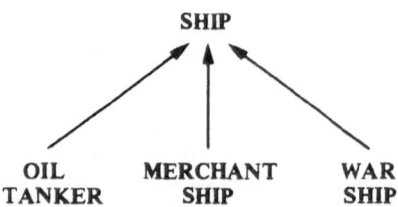

(ii) Analyze possible object-oriented and relational representations of the above conceptual view.

(iii) Outline specifications of the definition and implementation modules for the proposed representations.

(iv) Develop fully (in terms of the definition and the implementation modules) the most appropriate one.

(3) Aggregation and Generalization

(i) Consider the following conceptual view of an application subenvironment expressed in terms of the aggregation and generalization abstractions:

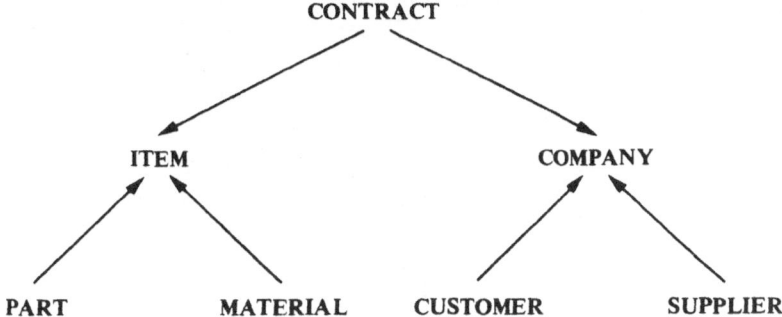

(ii) Choose appropriate attributes and actions of the above object types and specify their definition modules.

(4) Molecular Abstraction

(i) Four-input gates are built using two-input gates, as in the example below (see (Batory and Kim, 1985)):

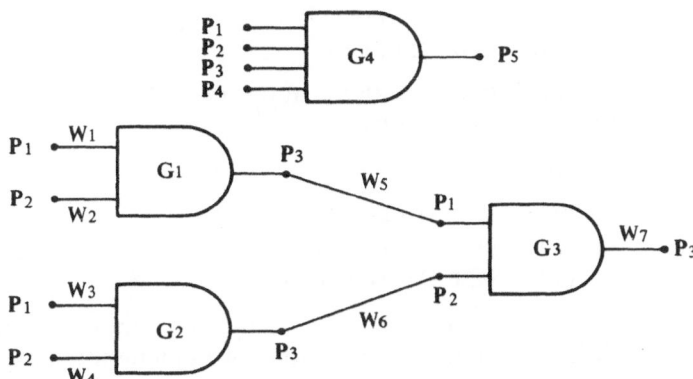

(ii) The above composition can be expressed in terms of standard abstractions, as follows:

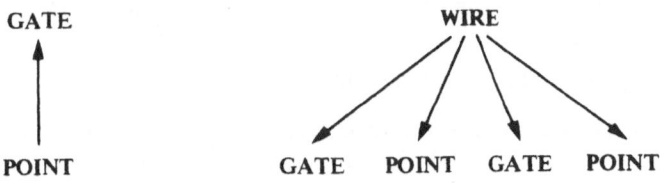

(iii) A possible relational representation of the above model may be based on the following description of the above object types:

```
TYPE PointId    = (P1,P2,P3,P4,P5);

     GateType  = RECORD Gate#:      GateId;
                        GType:      (TwoInput,FourInput);
                        Function:   (AndGate,OrGate);
                        Parent#:    GateId
                 END;

     PointType = RECORD Gate#:      GateId;
                        Point#:     PointId;
                        Role:       (Input,Output);
                        Parent#:    GateId
                 END;

     WireType  = RECORD Wire#:      WireId;
                        StartGate#: GateId;
                        StartPoint#: PointId;
                        EndGate#:   GateId;
                        EndPoint#:  PointId;
                        Parent#:    PointId
                 END
```

The purpose of the attribute Parent# is to tie together two-input gates that are connected in a four-input gate.

(iv) Specify the actual relations with the above described structure for the particular example given in step (i).

(v) Three entity sets

```
VAR Gates:  ENTITY SET OF GateType;
    Points: ENTITY SET OF PointType;
    Wires:  ENTITY SET OF WireType
```

specify the actual connection of the two-input gates into four-input gates. As such, they in fact contain specifications of implementations of four-input gates in terms of two-input gates. Specify the definition and the implementation modules of the four-input gate object type.

(5) Hidden Relational Representation

(i) Consider the following object-oriented specification of the assembly of the products database:

DEFINITION MODULE AssemblyOfProducts;

EXPORT QUALIFIED ProductId, ProductType, SetOfParts,
                 InsertProduct, DeleteProduct,
                 UpdateQuantity, UpdatePrice,

```
                        AddPart, DropPart,
                        DisplayProduct, DisplayParts,
                        DisplayProductStructure;

TYPE ProductId     = String7;
     ProductType   = RECORD product#:       ProductId;
                            name:           String30;
                            quantity, price: Real
                     END;
```

.
.
.

END AssemblyOfProducts.

(ii) Observe the action-oriented representation of the product structure. The users of the object type AssemblyOfProducts have access to that structure in terms of actions that may be performed upon it (AddPart, DropPart, DisplayParts, DisplayProductStructure). The actual representation of the assembly of products is hidden in the corresponding definition module. Such a representation in the relational approach is given below:

IMPLEMENTATION MODULE AssemblyOfProducts;

```
TYPE AssemblyType     = RECORD product#: ProductId;
                               part#:     ProductId
                        END;

     AssemblySetType = ENTITY SET OF AssemblyType;
     ProductSetType  = ENTITY SET OF ProductType;

VAR AssemblySet: AssemblySetType;
    ProductSet: ProductSetType
```

.
.
.

END AssemblyOfProducts.

(iii) Write the procedure declarations required in the above implementation module. Procedures AddPart and DropPart are intended to establish and erase an instance of a product-part relationship so that both product and part must already exist in the database in both cases. The procedure DisplayParts prints out immediate parts of a product, and the recursive procedure DisplayProductStructure prints out the entire product structure in terms of its immediate and indirect components (parts).

(6) Opaque Export

(i) When a type is exported from a definition module and a complete specification of that type is given in that module, we say that the export is *transparent*. The details of such a type are then visible to the clients of the module. For example, if a record type is exported transparently, all identifiers of its attributes are exported as well. If an enumeration type is exported, all identifiers of its elements are also exported.

If the details of a type should be hidden from users, then the definition module contains only the identifier of that type that is also exported. This sort of export is called *opaque*. An example of opaque export follows:

DEFINITION MODULE Product;

EXPORT QUALIFIED ProductId, ProductType,
                 ReadProduct, WriteProduct,
                 InsertProduct, DeleteProduct,
                 UpdateQuantity, UpdatePrice,
                 AddPart, DropPart,
                 DisplayProduct,
                 DisplayProductStructure;

TYPE ProductId = String7;
     ProductType;

PROCEDURE ReadProduct(VAR product: ProductType);
PROCEDURE WriteProduct(product: ProductType);
PROCEDURE InsertProduct(product: ProductType);
PROCEDURE DeleteProduct(product#: ProductId);
PROCEDURE UpdateQuantity(product#: ProductId;
                         NewQuantity: Real);
PROCEDURE UpdatePrice(product#: ProductId;
                      NewPrice: Real);
PROCEDURE AddPart(product#: ProductId;
                  part#: ProductId);
PROCEDURE DropPart(product#: ProductId;
                   part#: ProductId);
PROCEDURE DisplayProduct(product#: ProductId);
PROCEDURE DisplayProductStructure(product#: ProductId);

END Product.

(ii) When opaque export is used, the actual specification of the type exported in that way must appear in the corresponding implementation module. Since that type is known to the users by its name only and all its properties are hidden from them, procedures operating on operands of this type and on its components must be defined in the same implementation module that hides the properties of that type. In view of this requirement, choose an appropriate representation of ProductType, and write up a complete specification of the implementation module based on that representation.

(iii) Give examples of client modules of the module AssemblyOfProducts specified in step (i)

(7) Standard Abstractions

(i) The assembly of the products application could be further generalized so that its conceptual model contains all the standard abstractions discussed thus far (classification, aggregation, generalization, covering, and recursion). The object type PRODUCT is in fact the generic type of two subtypes—PART and MATERIAL—as in the following diagram:

On the other hand, PRODUCT is defined as an aggregation of its attributes. In addition to the simple attributes of this object type, its attributes are also

(a) set of parts,
(b) set of working operations, and
(c) set of tools,

each required in manufacturing a product. This means that PRODUCT is the cover (aggregation) of its associated member types PART, OPERATION, and TOOL as in the diagram below:

PART, however, is already established as a subtype of PRODUCT, so that we also have the recursion abstraction.

(ii) Develop full specification in terms of the definition and the implementation modules of the above described conceptual model.

(8) Generic Objects as Views

(i) The purpose of this exercise is to present another approach to the representation of generic objects, and to explore the possibilities and limitations of modules in that respect. The approach is based on the representation of object subtypes in such a way that they explicitly have the attributes inherited from their common generic object type, as well as the attributes specific to those subtypes. The generic object type is then defined with the attributes that are common to all the subtypes. The actual set of tuples representing the generic object type is meant to be derived from the sets of tuples representing its subtypes.

(ii) Specify the definition and the implementation modules of the object subtypes Graduate and Undergraduate so that they have the following attributes:

TYPE ProgramType   = (MSc,PhD);

```
GraduateType = RECORD student#:   String10;
                      name:       String30;
                      address:    String50;
                      phone:      String7;
                      program:    ProgramType;
                      department: String20
             END
```

TYPE SchoolType = (Arts, Sciences, Engineering, Medicine);
     YearType   = (freshman, junior, sophomore, senior);

```
UndergraduateType = RECORD student#: String10;
                           name:     String30;
                           address:  String50;
                           phone:    String7;
                           school:   SchoolType;
                           year:     YearType
                  END
```

(iii) Explore the possibilities and limitations of modules in the representation of the generic object type Student as a view over the object types Graduate and Undergraduate so that Student has the following attributes:

TYPE LevelType   = (undergraduate,graduate);

```
StudentType = RECORD student#: String10;
                     name:     String30;
                     address:  String50;
                     phone:    String7;
                     level:    LevelType
            END
```

Bibliographical Notes

The notions of aggregation and generalization as database abstractions were first introduced by Smith and Smith (1977a, 1977b). The object-action-oriented approach to these abstractions based on modules is novel and appears first in this book. It was partly motivated by former work of Brodie and Ridjanović (1984a). Aggregation, generalization, and covering abstractions in the extended relational framework are presented by Codd (1979). The algebraic approach to these abstractions that is used informally throughout the book comes from a much more rigorous approach of Alagić (1986). The section in recursion and covering does not rely on any particular references. Among the references on traversal recursion, we mention (Dayal et al. 1985) and (Rosenthal et al. 1986). The example from exercise (1) is adapted from (Brodie and Ridjanović 1984b), and the example in exercise (2) is based on (Codd, 1979). The example in exercise (4) is due to Batory and Kim (1985).

CHAPTER 5
Input/Output Programming

1 Standard Input/Output Programming

Input and output are nice examples of application of the abstraction that permits classification of seemingly quite different objects into the same object type. As usual, differences among such objects are suppressed and their common, abstract properties are defined in such a way that those objects may be viewed as instances of the same abstract (object) type. What is more important and interesting is that those common properties in case of input and output are in fact actions and nothing else. In other words, the desired abstraction is achieved by the specification of the common actions applicable to input and output.

First consider standard input. Two prime examples of interest to us are the input from a terminal keyboard and the input from a file. Although these input objects are quite different, they can both be classified in the same object type using the input stream abstraction. This abstraction views both of them as a sequence of characters (a *text stream*). The length of that sequence is not known and not bounded a priori, and if it is empty, we have an *empty input stream*.

The only action associated with the input stream is reading its current element, which is determined by the stream's position. The Read action advances the position by one element. In this process, when the end of the stream is reached, the Read action sets the variable Exception to *true*. Reading beyond the end of the input stream makes no sense, and an attempt to do so will abort the program.

The input stream is normally (by default) associated with the user's terminal. To redirect it to a file, the action OpenInput is used. This action requires specification of the name of the input file. To redirect the input to the terminal, the action CloseInput is invoked.

The most important cases of standard output are also represented by a single abstraction of the output stream. Types of output captured by this abstraction are terminal screen output, printer output, and output to a file. In spite of obvious differences among these output devices, the most important common abstract view of all of them is again a text stream. The basic action associated with the output stream is appending a new element to its end. This action is called *writing*.

The output stream abstraction also captures an important abstract property of all the above three prime examples of standard output—the fact that those text streams are typically (and in the case of terminal screen and printer necessarily) structured into lines. Controlling the line structure of the output stream is achieved by the action WriteLn, which terminates the current output line.

As with the input stream, the output stream is by default associated with the user's terminal. To redirect it to a file, the OpenOutput action, which requires specification of the output file, is invoked. When this action is successfully executed (i.e., the value of the variable Exception is set to *false*), subsequent output is written to the specified file. To redirect the output back to the user's terminal, the CloseOutput action is invoked.

DEFINITION MODULE InputStream;

EXPORT QUALIFIED Exception, OpenInput, CloseInput, ReadCh;

 VAR Exception: Boolean;

PROCEDURE OpenInput (s: String);
PROCEDURE CloseInput;
PROCEDURE ReadCh(VAR ch: Char);

END InputStream.

DEFINITION MODULE OutputStream;

EXPORT QUALIFIED Exception, OpenOutput, CloseOutput,
              WriteCh, WriteLn;

 VAR Exception: Boolean;

PROCEDURE OpenOutput(s: String);
PROCEDURE CloseOutput;
PROCEDURE WriteCh(ch: Char);
PROCEDURE WriteLn;

END OutputStream.

The text stream abstraction is very successful, but, at the same time, very basic as well. A higher-level abstraction is developed by observing the fact that particular sequences of characters in the input and output streams in fact represent values of types Integer, Cardinal, Real, and String. These types are typical for attributes of a vast majority of objects (entities) from application environments considered in this book. To capture typed (formatted) input and output of this sort, higher level actions are associated with the input and output streams. These actions operate with sequences of characters in the input and output streams that, according to the programming language syntax, represent values of types Integer, Cardinal, Real, and String. Thus, we obtain five types of Read actions associated with the input stream,

—ReadCh(x),
—ReadString(x),
—ReadInt(x),
—ReadCard(x), and
—ReadReal(x),

each of which attempts to recognize an external representation of the value of the corresponding type in the sequence of characters in the input stream. If such an action succeeds (which means that the input sequence is a correct representation of a value of the expected type), the conversion to the internal representation is performed, and the result value is assigned to the variable x.

Likewise, we have five types of Write actions associated with the output stream.

—WriteCh(x),
—WriteString(x),
—WriteInt(x, n),
—WriteCard(x, n), and
—WriteReal(x, n).

These actions generate the external representation of the value x as a sequence of characters according to the programming language syntax. The generated sequence is appended to the output stream. The parameter n is of the type Cardinal and determines the least number of digits required in the character representation of the numeric value x.

DEFINITION MODULE FormattedInput;

EXPORT QUALIFIED OpenInput, CloseInput,
                  ReadCh, ReadString,
                  ReadInt, ReadCard, ReadReal,
                  Exception;

  VAR Exception: Boolean;

PROCEDURE OpenInput(s: String);
PROCEDURE CloseInput;
PROCEDURE ReadCh(VAR c: Char);
PROCEDURE ReadString(VAR text: String);

```
PROCEDURE ReadInt(VAR x: Integer);
PROCEDURE ReadCard(VAR x: Cardinal);
PROCEDURE ReadReal (VAR x: Real);
```

END FormattedInput.

DEFINITION MODULE FormattedOutput;

```
EXPORT QUALIFIED OpenOutput, CloseOutput, WriteLn,
                 WriteCh, WriteString,
                 WriteInt, WriteCard, WriteReal,
                 Exception;
```

   VAR Exception: Boolean;

```
PROCEDURE OpenOutput(s: String);
PROCEDURE CloseOutput;
PROCEDURE WriteCh(c: Char);
PROCEDURE WriteString(s: String);
PROCEDURE WriteInt(x: Integer; n: Cardinal);
PROCEDURE WriteCard(x: Cardinal; n: Cardinal);
PROCEDURE WriteReal(x: Real; n: Cardinal);
PROCEDURE WriteLn;
```

END FormattedOutput.

   The I/O conversion is illustrated below for the type Cardinal:

```
PROCEDURE ReadCard(VAR x: Cardinal);
  VAR i: Cardinal; Ch: Char;
BEGIN i : = 0;
      REPEAT ReadCh(Ch)
      UNTIL (Ch > =  "0") AND (Ch < =  "9");
      REPEAT i : =  10 * i + (Ord(Ch) − Ord("0"));
             ReadCh(Ch)
      UNTIL   (Ch <  "0") OR (Ch >  "9");
      x : = i
END ReadCard;
```

```
PROCEDURE WriteCard(x,n: Cardinal);
  CONST MaxDigits = 10;
  VAR i: Cardinal;
      buffer: ARRAY [1..MaxDigits] OF Cardinal;
BEGIN i : = 0;
      REPEAT buffer [i] : =  x MOD 10;
             i : = i + 1;
             x : = x DIV 10
      UNTIL   x = 0;
      WHILE   n > i DO
```

```
        WriteCh (" "); n := n - 1
    END;
    REPEAT WriteCh(Chr(buffer[i] + Ord("0")));
            i := i - 1
    UNTIL  i = 0
END Write Card
```

The fundamental I/O abstractions were introduced separately, but for convenience, all the primitives for standard input and output are specified in one module, as follows:

DEFINITION MODULE StandardIO;

EXPORT QUALIFIED OpenInput, CloseInput,
                 OpenOutput, CloseOutput,
                 ReadCh, WriteCh,
                 ReadString, ReadInt, ReadCard, ReadReal,
                 WriteString, WriteInt, WriteCard, WriteReal,
                 WriteLn,
                 IOException;

  VAR IOException: Boolean;

PROCEDURE OpenInput(s:String);
PROCEDURE CloseInput;
PROCEDURE OpenOutput(s:String);
PROCEDURE CloseOutput;

PROCEDURE ReadCh(VAR ch: Char);
PROCEDURE ReadString(VAR text: String);
PROCEDURE ReadInt(VAR x: Integer);
PROCEDURE ReadCard(VAR x: Cardinal);
PROCEDURE ReadReal(VAR x: Real);

PROCEDURE WriteCh(ch: Char);
PROCEDURE WriteString(s: String);
PROCEDURE WriteInt(x: Integer; n: Cardinal);
PROCEDURE WriteCard(x: Cardinal; n: Cardinal);
PROCEDURE WriteReal(x: Real; n: Cardinal);
PROCEDURE WriteLn;

END StandardIO.

I/O conversion. Procedures that perform explicit conversion to/from standard numeric types are specified in the following definition module:

DEFINITION MODULE Conversion;
EXPORT QUALIFIED StringToCard, StringToInt, StringToReal,
                 CardToString, IntToSting, RealToString,
                 Done;

VAR Done: Boolean;

```
PROCEDURE StringToCard (str: ARRAY OF Char;
                        VAR num: Cardinal);
PROCEDURE StringToInt   (str: ARRAY OF Char;
                        VAR num: Integer);
PROCEDURE StringToReal (str: ARRAY OF Char;
                        VAR r: Real);
PROCEDURE CardToString (num:Cardinal;
                        VAR str: ARRAY OF Char;
                        width: Cardinal);
PROCEDURE IntToString   (num:Integer;
                        VAR str: ARRAY OF Char;
                        width: Cardinal);
PROCEDURE RealToString (r: Real;
                        VAR str: ARRAY OF Char;
                        digits, width: Integer);
END Conversion.
```

In the above procedures, the parameter width denotes the width of the output (string) representation. If that representation requires less than width characters, blanks are added to the left. The parameter digits denote the number of digits to the right of the decimal point in the floating-point representation of a real number. If the number is less than zero, then the exponent representation of a real number is assumed. The variable Done indicates whether a successful conversion took place. Various exception-handling conventions are possible. For example, if the output string is too small, CardToString and IntToString truncate the output without raising an exception. On the other hand, RealToString returns the empty string in that case and sets the variable Done to *false*. There are, of course, other conventions related to the above procedures, but since they tend to be implementation dependent, we do not present them here.

Terminal I/O. Now consider terminal I/O more carefully. Character-oriented output is captured by the abstraction Display specified as follows:

```
DEFINITION MODULE Display;

EXPORT QUALIFIED WriteCh, WriteLn;

PROCEDURE WriteCh(ch: Char);
PROCEDURE WriteLn;

END Display.
```

Character-oriented input is specified by the following definition of the abstract object Keyboard:

```
DEFINITION MODULE Keyboard;
```

EXPORT QUALIFIED ReadCh, KeyPressed;

PROCEDURE ReadCh(VAR ch: Char);
PROCEDURE KeyPressed ( ): Boolean;

END Keyboard.

The action KeyPressed tests whether a character is available from the keyboard, and the action ReadCh waits, if necessary, for a character to be entered.

The definition of the high level abstract object Terminal is now based on the abstract definitions of its abstract components Display and Keyboard:

DEFINITION MODULE Terminal;

EXPORT QUALIFIED ReadCh, KeyPressed, ReadAgain, ReadString,
                WriteCh, WriteString, WriteLn;

PROCEDURE ReadCh(VAR ch: Char);

PROCEDURE KeyPressed( ): Boolean;

PROCEDURE ReadAgain;

PROCEDURE ReadString(VAR s: ARRAY OF Char);

PROCEDURE WriteCh(Ch: Char);

PROCEDURE WriteString(s: ARRAY OF Char);

PROCEDURE WriteLn;

END Terminal.

The above definition module makes it clear that its implementation module is written on the basis of the already introduced abstractions Display and Keyboard. A further level of generality in the definition of the abstract object Terminal is achieved by introducing actions AssignRead and AssignWrite. These two actions assign specific Read and Write actions to the abstract object Terminal. In addition, AssignRead also assigns a specific status procedure that tests whether a character is available to read. The abstraction obtained this way is called VirtualTerminal. It permits not only selection of private procedures with special interpretation of input and ouput characters, but also redirection of input to be taken from a file and output to be written to a file. So the I/O abstract object is indeed a virtual terminal. In reality, it does not have to be a terminal at all.

The above described level of generality is achieved by procedure types ReadProcedure, StatusProcedure, and WriteProcedure, where the first two are parameter types of the procedure AssignRead, and the third of the procedure AssignWrite. Procedures Keyboard.ReadCh, Keyboard.Keypressed, and Display.WriteCh are, respectively, assigned by default.

DEFINITION MODULE VirtualTerminal;

EXPORT QUALIFIED ReadProcedure, StatusProcedure,
                 WriteProcedure, AssignRead, AssignWrite,
                 UnAssignRead, UnAssignWrite, ReadCh,
                 KeyPressed, WriteCh, Exception;

```
TYPE ReadProcedure   = PROCEDURE(VAR Char);
     StatusProcedure = PROCEDURE( ): Boolean;
     WriteProcedure  = PROCEDURE(Char);
```

VAR Exception: Boolean;

```
PROCEDURE AssignRead (r:  ReadProcedure;
                      s:  StatusProcedure);
PROCEDURE AssignWrite (w:  WriteProcedure);

PROCEDURE UnAssignRead;

PROCEDURE UnAssignWrite;

PROCEDURE ReadCh(VAR Ch: Char);

PROCEDURE KeyPressed( ): Boolean;

PROCEDURE WriteCh(ch: Char);
```

END VirtualTerminal.

2 Input Data Validation

The fundamental importance of verifying correctness of data to be inserted in the database is obvious. Achieving the ideal situation in which the input data are checked for all possible errors is not simple at all. The integrity constraints at the programming language level are enforced procedurally (e.g., uniqueness of object identifiers). In addition to these higher level constraints, which are discussed many times in this book, there are also many lower level, lexical type of errors that must also be checked before the input data are processed against the database. Throughout this book we in fact assume those checks have been made. In this section we discuss one characteristic case in order to show what these lower level checks are and how they are performed.

Consider the following type definition:

```
TYPE PersonType  =  RECORD Name:String30;
                            Sex: Char;
                            DateOfBirth: String11
          END
```

This illustrates nicely one of the pitfalls of the basic relational model, which in its normalized version permits only simple types (including strings of characters) of attributes. This is precisely the reason why the type of the attribute DateOfBirth is specified as String11. This specification hides the actual structure and semantics of the type of this attribute, which should be specified as follows:

```
TYPE DateType  =  RECORD Month:  String3;
                          Day:    String2;
                          Year:   String4
          END
```

The above specification is not permitted by the normalized basic relational model. Indeed, we should now have the following definition of the entity type PERSON:

```
TYPE PersonType  =  RECORD Name:String30;
                            Sex:  Char;
                            DateOfBirth:
                            RECORD Month:String3;
                                    Day:  String2;
                                    Year: String4
                        END
          END
```

The above definition, although very natural and customary in the programming language notation, is not permitted by the basic relational model. To get around the severe restrictions of the normal forms, one could represent the entity type DATE as a separate relation, called *property relation* in the extended relational model (RM/T). But this is quite often unnatural and cumbersome and, in many cases, inefficient as well. Of course, the basic relational model permits the following representation:

```
TYPE PersonType  =  RECORD Name:         String30;
                            Sex:          Char;
                            MonthOfBirth: String3;
                            DayOfBirth:   String2;
                            YearOfBirth:  String4
          END
```

However, this representation does not properly separate semantic levels (levels of abstraction). Indeed, Name, Sex, and DateOfBirth belong to the same level, quite opposite to the last representation.

Given these restrictions, we are faced with the problem of properly handling the representation of the type of the attribute DateOfBirth as String11, in which we assume that single blanks are used in order to separate the three attributes actually hidden in this representation. In particular, when input of a date as a string of 11 characters is performed, we have to check that the input string is lexically a correct representation of a date. This task is performed by the function procedure CorrectDate. Although the procedure is conceptually very simple, it illustrates not only some typical input-data validation actions, but also actions on one-dimensional arrays (strings of characters) using FOR statements and complex conditional statements.

To perform the required check, month, year, and day portions must be extracted from the input date string. These simple actions (projections) are defined as procedures ExtractMonth, ExtractDay, and ExtractYear. It is also necessary to check the overall format of the input string that requires blanks in the fourth and the seventh position. This action is specified by the Boolean function procedure CorrectFormat.

Checking the month portion of the input date string is performed by the Boolean function procedure CorrectMonth in such a way that a string of all months is formed first and then the input month is compared with appropriate portions of the months string using FOR statement whose increment value (step) of the control variable is 3. Of course, an alternative approach would be to specify the type of the variable AllMonths as ARRAY[1..12] OF ARRAY[1..3] OF Char. Checking the day portion of the input string (Boolean function procedure CorrectDay) is straightforward and amounts to the verification of that portion to be a string of two digits in the range 1 to 31. We assume the range of relevant years is 1920..1999. The Boolean function procedure CorrectYear checks whether the first two digits in the year portion of the input date string are 19 and then that the next two are in the range 20..99.

Having checked the month, day, and year portions of the input date string separately, we have to verify an overall integrity constraint that relates all three of them. Indeed, to check whether the number of days is correct, we have to check whether that number equals "31" if the specified month is April, June, September, or November. Furthermore, if the input month is February, some more subtle checking must be performed. Invalid numbers of days are certainly 30 and 31, but to check whether the input number of days 29 is valid or not, we have to check whether the input year is leap year. The required Boolean function procedure LeapYear is defined as a local procedure of the Boolean function procedure CorrectNumberOfDays. The procedure LeapYear contains a local procedure Convert that converts the input year string into an integer value that is then used to check whether the year is leap year.

The body of the procedure CorrectDate is then a straightforward conditional composition whose Boolean expression is specified using the described Boolean function procedures.

```
PROCEDURE CorrectDate(Date:String11): Boolean;

  VAR  Month: String3;
       Day:   String2;
       Year:  String4;

PROCEDURE ExtractMonth (Date:          String11;
                               VAR Month: String3);
  VAR i: Cardinal;
BEGIN FOR i : = 1 TO 3 DO
      Month[i] : = Date[i]
      END
END    ExtractMonth;

PROCEDURE ExtractDay (Date: String11:
                             VAR Day: String2);
  VAR i: Cardinal;
BEGIN FOR i : = 1 TO 2 DO
      Day[i] : = Date [i + 4]
      END
END    ExtractDay;

PROCEDURE ExtractYear (Date:          String11;
                              VAR Year: String4);
  VAR i: Cardinal;
BEGIN FOR i :  = 1 TO 4 DO
      Year[i] : = Date[i + 7]
      END
END    ExtractYear;

PROCEDURE CorrectFormat(Date: String11): Boolean;
BEGIN IF      (Date[4] =  " ") AND
              (Date[7] =  " ")
      THEN Return(true)
      ELSE Return(false)
      END
END    CorrectFormat;

PROCEDURE CorrectMonth(Month: String3): Boolean;

  VAR AllMonths: String36; NextMonth: String3;
      i: Cardinal;
PROCEDURE ExtractNextMonth (AllMonths:          String36;
                            index:              Cardinal;
                            VAR NextMonth: String3);
  VAR i: Cardinal;
BEGIN FOR i : = index TO index + 3 DO
      NextMonth[i] : = AllMonths[i]
      END
END    ExtractNextMonth;
```

```
BEGIN AllMonths := "JanFebMarAprMayJunJulAugSepOctNovDec";
      FOR i := 1 TO 12 BY 3 DO
        ExtractNextMonth(AllMonths,i,NextMonth);
        IF NextMonth = Month THEN
          Return(true)
        END
      END;
      Return(false)
END   CorrectMonth;

PROCEDURE CorrectDay(Day: String2): Boolean;
BEGIN IF      (Day[1] < "1") AND (Day[1]<>" ") OR
              (Day[1] > "3")
      THEN Return(false)
      ELSIF (Day[2] < "0") OR
            (Day[2] > "9")
      THEN Return(false)
      ELSIF (Day[1] = "3") AND
            (Day[2] > "1")
      THEN Return(false)
      ELSE Return(true)
      END
END   CorrectDay;

PROCEDURE CorrectYear(Year: String4): Boolean;
BEGIN IF     Year [1] <> "1" THEN Return(false)
      ELSIF Year [2] <> "9" THEN Return(false)
      ELSIF Year [3] < "2" THEN Return(false)
      ELSIF Year[3] > "9" THEN Return(false)
      ELSIF Year[4] < "0" THEN Return(false)
      ELSIF Year[4] > "9" THEN Return(false)
      ELSE  Return(true) END
END   CorrectYear;

PROCEDURE CorrectNumberOfDays (Year: String4; Month: String3;
                                      Day: String2): Boolean;

  PROCEDURE LeapYear(Year: String4): Boolean;

    VAR YearOrd: Cardinal;
    PROCEDURE Convert (Year: String4;
                          VAR YearOrd: Cardinal);
    VAR i: Cardinal;
    BEGIN   i := 4; YearOrd := 0;
    REPEAT YearOrd := 10 * YearOrd +
            (Ord (Year[i]) - Ord("0"));
            i := i-1
```

```
      UNTIL   i = 1
END         Convert;
  BEGIN Convert(Year, YearOrd);
         IF (YearOrd MOD 4 = 0)
         THEN Return(true)
         ELSE Return(false) END
  END    LeapYear;

BEGIN IF      (Month =  "Feb") AND (DAY =  "30") THEN Return(false)
      ELSIF (Month =  "Feb") AND (DAY =  "31") THEN Return(false)
      ELSIF (Month =  "Feb") AND LeapYear(Year)
                                 AND (Day =  "28") THEN Return(false)
      ELSIF (Month =  "Apr") AND (DAY =  "31") THEN Return(false)
      ELSIF (Month =  "Jun") AND (DAY =  "31") THEN Return(false)
      ELSIF (Month =  "Sep") AND (DAY =  "31") THEN Return(false)
      ELSIF (Month =  "Nov") AND (DAY =  "31") THEN Return(false)
      ELSE  Return(true)          END
END CorrectNumberOfDays;

BEGIN (* Main *)
      ExtractMonth(Date,Month);
      ExtractDay(Date,Day);
      ExtractYear(Date,Year);
      IF      CorrectFormat(Date) AND
              CorrectMonth(Month) AND
              CorrectDay(Day) AND
              CorrectYear(Year) AND
              CorrectNumberOfDays(Year, Month, Day)
      THEN Return(true)
      ELSE Return(false)
      END
END    CorrectDate
```

3 Screen-Oriented I/O

Standard input and output as captured by the stream abstraction is not
adequate for many typical end users in database application environments.
They require a much more attractive type of input and output commonly
achieved using terminal screen-management facilities. To provide an object-oriented framework for such a case, we have to generalize further
the terminal abstraction. Rather than using the output stream, we now

have a two-dimensional output area—a matrix with MaxRow rows and MaxColumn columns. This matrix could be described in the programming language notation as follows:

VAR Screen: ARRAY [1..MaxRow] OF
            ARRAY [1..MaxColumn] OF Char

or equivalently

VAR Screen: ARRAY [1..MaxRow,1..MaxColumn] OF Char

The concept of the current output position still applies, but now is a point in the two-dimensional output coordinate system whose graphical representation is given below:

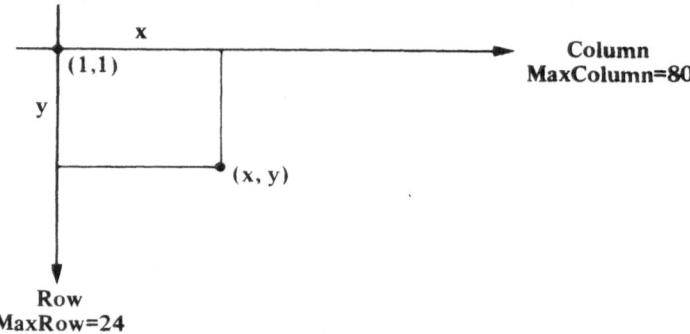

The output sequence of characters generated by output actions will be placed in the two-dimensional output area relative to the current output position. The first character is placed at the current output position, and each subsequent character at the next position in the same row (if possible). The current position is advanced by one column (if possible) with each generated output character. This means that the relevant description of the output area in the programming language notation is as follows:

VAR Screen: ARRAY [1..MaxRow] OF
            ARRAY [1..MaxColumn] OF Char

In addition to all the similarities with the output stream abstraction, a fundamental difference comes from an additional set of actions associated with the screen output that permit explicit control of the current output position. The current output position and its management are captured in the cursor abstraction specified below in the programming language notation:

DEFINITION MODULE Cursor;

EXPORT QUALIFIED MaxRow, MaxColumn, Exception,
                 SetCursor, CursorRow, CursorColumn;

CONST MaxRow = 24; MaxColumn = 80;

TYPE ExceptionType = (None, InvalidRow, InvalidColumn);

```
    ExceptionSetType = SET OF ExceptionType;
  VAR Exception: ExceptionSetType;

PROCEDURE SetCursor(Row, Column: Cardinal);
PROCEDURE CursorRow( ): Cardinal;
PROCEDURE CursorColumn( ): Cardinal;

END Cursor.
```

The cursor abstraction is obviously based on the following, although not explicitly given, view of the screen:

VAR Screen: ARRAY [1..MaxRow, 1..MaxColumn] OF Char

The action SetCursor sets the current cursor position to the point whose coordinates are given by its parameters Row and Column. Function procedures CursorRow and CursorColumn return as their result the corresponding coordinate of the current output position. The exceptions occur when the action SetCursor is invoked with a parameter that is out of the specified bounds for the row and column position.

Note that the above described management of the cursor position also affects the position of the displayed input sequences of characters that are typed from the terminal keyboard.

Example. A rather typical example of the use of cursor actions is given below. It assumes that various messages to the terminal user (e.g., error messages) are displayed at the bottom of the screen, for example, in the 22nd row. When such a message is needed, the current position of the cursor is saved, the cursor is set to the beginning of the message row, the desired message is displayed, and the previous cursor position is restored:

```
PROCEDURE ErrorMessage;

CONST MessageRow = 22; MessageColumn = 10;
VAR CurrentRow, CurrentColumn: Cardinal;

BEGIN CurrentRow := CursorRow( );
        CurrentColumn := CursorColumn( );
        SetCursor(MessageRow, MessageColumn);
        WriteString("ERROR!!!");
        SetCursor(CurrentRow, CurrentColumn)
END ErrorMessage
```

Note that the procedure ErrorMessage does not "know" the current cursor position and is applicable irrespectively of where the cursor is positioned at the time when the need for the error message occurs.

Controlling the placement of the output sequences of characters on the screen is one way of making the output more attractive and meaningful to end users of database systems. Another way is the selection of the video attributes of those characters. Choosing double-width, double-width and double-height, blinking, bold, underline, or reverse video (negative) characters may improve the quality of the end-user interface dramatically, making the semantics of the output much more obvious. The necessary primitives are given below in the form of a definition module called VideoDisplay, which also contains some other actions affecting entire rectangular areas of the screen.

DEFINITION MODULE VideoDisplay;

EXPORT QUALIFIED CharType, VideoType, VideoSetType,
                  ExceptionType,
                  ExceptionSetType, DirectionType,

                  ClearDisplay, RepaintDisplay,

                  SaveDisplay, RestoreDisplay,
                  SelectCharType, SetVideoAttributes,

                  EraseArea, ScrollArea,

                  BeginDisplayUpdate, EndDisplayUpdate;

TYPE CharType = (Normal, Wide, HighWide);

     VideoType = (blink, bold, reverse, underline);
     VideoSetType = SET OF VideoType;

     ExceptionType = (None, InvalidStartRow, InvalidStartColumn,
                  InvalidEndRow, InvalidEndColumn,
                  CountOverflow, InvalidDisplayId);
     ExceptionSetType = SET OF ExceptionType;
     DirectionType = (up, down, right, left);

PROCEDURE ClearDisplay;
PROCEDURE RepaintDisplay;

PROCEDURE SaveDisplay(DisplayId: Cardinal);
PROCEDURE RestoreDisplay(DisplayId: Cardinal);

PROCEDURE SelectCharType(Mode: CharType);

PROCEDURE SetVideoAttributes(StartRow, StartColumn: Cardinal;
                  EndRow, EndColumn: Cardinal;
                  VideoAttr: VideoSetType);
PROCEDURE EraseArea(StartRow, StartColumn,
                  EndRow, EndColumn: Cardinal);

PROCEDURE ScrollArea(StartRow, StartColumn,
                  EndRow, EndColumn: Cardinal;
                  Direction: DirectionType;
                  Count: Cardinal);

PROCEDURE BeginDisplayUpdate;
PROCEDURE EndDisplayUpdate;

END VideoDisplay.

Further enhancement of the screen-oriented output is achieved by adding some simple graphic primitives to it. Of course, those features are
heavily dependent on the underlying terminal type. We restrict ourselves
to those graphic primitives that are sufficient for standard applications
such as those handled appropriately by the relational model. Consequently,
the only graphic primitives are dot, line, and rectangle, where only horizontal and vertical lines are permitted. These primitives are easily sup-
ported by any terminal type, and sufficient for producing tabular type of
output with simple rectangular drawings. Note that we define the semantics
of the actions DrawDot, DrawLine, and DrawRectangle in such a way
that these actions do not affect the cursor position.

DEFINITION MODULE LineDrawing;

EXPORT QUALIFIED DrawDot, DrawLine, DrawRectangle,
                 ExceptionType, ExceptionSetType, Exception;

TYPE ExceptionType = (None, InvalidStartRow, InvalidStartColumn,
                 InvalidEndRow, InvalidEndColumn,
                 DiagonalLine);
     ExceptionSetType = SET OF ExceptionType;

VAR Exception: ExceptionSetType;

PROCEDURE DrawDot(Row, Column: Cardinal);

PROCEDURE DrawLine(StartRow, StartColumn,
                 EndRow, EndColumn: Cardinal);

PROCEDURE DrawRectangle(TopLeftRow, TopLeftColumn,
                 BottomRightRow, BottomRightColumn:
                 Cardinal);

END LineDrawing.

All the necessary primitives associated with a video terminal are
now defined in a single module, given below:

DEFINITION MODULE VideoTerminal;

EXPORT QUALIFIED MaxRow,MaxColumn,
                 Exception, ExceptionType, ExceptionSetType,
                 SetCursor, CursorRow, CursorColumn,
                 CharType, VideoType, VideoSetType,
                 DirectionType,
                 SelectCharType, SetVideoAttributes,
                 ReadString, WriteString,
                 DrawDot, DrawLine, DrawRectangle,
                 ClearDisplay, RepaintDisplay,
                 SaveDisplay, RestoreDisplay,
                 EraseArea, ScrollArea,
                 BeginDisplayUpdate, EndDisplayUpdate;

```
CONST MaxRow = 24; MaxColumn = 80;

TYPE CharType = (Normal, Wide, HighWide);

     VideoType = (blink, bold, reverse, underline);
     VideoSetType = SET OF VideoType;

     ExceptionType = (None, InvalidStartRow,
                      InvalidStartColumn, InvalidEndRow,
                      InvalidEndColumn, CountOverflow,
                      DiagonalLine,InvalidDisplayId);
     ExceptionSetType = SET OF ExceptionType;

     DirectionType = (up, down, right, left);

VAR Exception: ExceptionSetType;

PROCEDURE ClearDisplay;
PROCEDURE RepaintDisplay;

PROCEDURE SaveDisplay(DisplayId: Cardinal);
PROCEDURE RestoreDisplay(DisplayId: Cardinal);

PROCEDURE SetCursor(Row, Column: Cardinal);
PROCEDURE CursorRow( ): Cardinal;
PROCEDURE CursorColumn( ): Cardinal;

PROCEDURE SelectCharType(Mode: CharType);

PROCEDURE ReadString(VAR s: String);
PROCEDURE WriteString(s: String);

PROCEDURE SetVideoAttributes(StartRow, StartColumn: Cardinal;
                             EndRow, EndColumn: Cardinal:
                             VideoAttr: VideoSetType);
PROCEDURE EraseArea(StartRow, StartColumn,
                    EndRow, EndColumn: Cardinal);

PROCEDURE ScrollArea(StartRow, StartColumn,
                     EndRow, EndColumn: Cardinal;
                     Direction: DirectionType;
                     Count: Cardinal);

PROCEDURE BeginDisplayUpdate;
PROCEDURE EndDisplayUpdate;

PROCEDURE DrawDot(Row, Column: Cardinal);
PROCEDURE DrawLine(StartRow, StartColumn,
                   EndRow, EndColumn: Cardinal);
PROCEDURE DrawRectangle(TopLeftRow, TopLeftColumn,
```

> BottomRightRow, BottomRightColumn:
> Cardinal);

END VideoTerminal.

Example. Suppose we have a boardered rectangular output area whose top left corner coordinates are (Row6, Column20) and bottom right corner coordinates are (Row20, Column60). This output area is used for the display of passengers, starting from Row8. Passengers are displayed in every second row so that six of them can fit in the display area whose last row for the display of a passenger is Row18. Passenger attributes are name, whose length is 30 characters at most, and sex, which is represented by a single character in Column58. When a passenger is displayed, the cursor row is incremented by 2, and its column set to Column22. However, when a passenger is displayed in Row18, no more passengers can fit in the specified output area, which is scrolled up for two rows in order to make room for the next passenger.

```
+-------------------------------------------+
| XXXXXXXXXXXXXXXXXXXXXXXXXXXXXX      X      |
| XXXXXXXXXXXXXXXXXXXXXXXXXXXXXX      X      |
| XXXXXXXXXXXXXXXXXXXXXXXXXXXXXX      X      |
| XXXXXXXXXXXXXXXXXXXXXXXXXXXXXX      X      |
| XXXXXXXXXXXXXXXXXXXXXXXXXXXXXX      X      |
| XXXXXXXXXXXXXXXXXXXXXXXXXXXXXX      X      |
+-------------------------------------------+
```

Example

MODULE DisplayPassengers;

FROM Passenger IMPORT PassengerType, PassengerSetType,
                      PassengerSet;

FROM VideoTerminal IMPORT SetCursor, CursorRow, CursorColumn,
                          ScrollArea, DrawRectangle,
                          DirectionType,
                          WriteString;

CONST Row6 = 6; Row8 = 8; Row18 = 18; Row 20 = 20;
      Column20 = 20; Column22 = 22; Column58 = 58;
      Column60 = 60;
      TwoLines = 2;

VAR p: PassengerType;

```
BEGIN DrawRectangle(Row6, Column20, Row20, Column60);
      SetCursor(Row8, Column22);
      FOREACH p IN PassengerSet
      DO WriteString(p.name);
         SetCursor(CursorRow( ), Column58);
         WriteString(p.sex);
         IF CursorRow( ) = 18 THEN
            ScrollArea(Row8, Column20, Row18, Column58, Up,
                                                    TwoLines);
         ELSE SetCursor(CursorRow( ) + 2, Column22)
         END
      END
END DisplayPassengers.
```

Now consider a rather frequent situation in which a set of tuples selected according to some predicate is presented to the end user at the terminal and the user is expected to choose one of them. For example, there are usually many flights with the given source, destination, and departure date. Given values of these attributes, the application program will typically present possible flights at the terminal that activated the program. Having looked at the possibilities, the terminal user will select one of them. Since most of the screen will thus be occupied for the display of candidate flights, the bottom of the screen will be reserved for the communication between the application program and the user. The user will be interrogated by a message like "SELECTED? Y/N" and expected to reply with Y or N. Any other response by the terminal user will activate the terminal bell or buzzer, and an error message like "WRONG ANSWER" will be displayed at the next line. To make the communication lines more visible, they are displayed in reverse video. The procedure function Selected given below is written according to the above assumption:

```
PROCEDURE Selected( ): Boolean;

CONST Row22 = 22; Row23 = 23;
      Column1 = 1; Column2 = 2; Column15 = 15;
      Column20 = 20; Column21 = 21; Column80 = 80;
      TwoTimes = 2;
VAR   Ch: Char;
      Row, Column: Cardinal;

BEGIN Row := CursorRow( ); Column := CursorColumn( );
      SetCursor(Row22, Column2);
      SetVideoAttributes(Row22, Column2, Row22, Column15,
                                                    reverse);
      WriteString(" SELECTED? Y/N ");
      SetCursor(Row22, Column20);
      ReadString(Ch);
```

```
        WHILE (Ch < > "Y") AND (Ch < > "y") AND
              (Ch < > "N") AND (Ch < > "n")
        DO RingBell(TwoTimes);
             SetCursor(Row23, Column2);
             SetVideoAttributes(Row23, Column2,
                                Row23, Column15,
                                reverse);
             WriteString("WRONG ANSWER!");
             Erase(Row23, Column2, Row22, Column80);
             Erase(Row22, Column20, Row22, Column21);
             ReadString(Ch)
        END;
        Erase(Row22, Column1, Row22, Column80);
        SetCursor(Row, Column);
        IF (Ch = "Y") OR (Ch = "y") THEN Return(true)
        ELSE Return(false) END

END Selected
```

4 Sample I/O Programming: Flight-Reservation Application

We conclude our discussion of screen-management programming with three typical procedures for the flight-reservation application. The relational model of this application has already been developed using the top-down, incremental design methodology. The model is repeated here with slight modifications: The application programs perform the following actions:

(i) insertion of a new passenger into the database,
(ii) display of all passengers of a given departure of a given flight, and
(iii) update of attributes of a given departure of a given flight.

The emphasis in the programs that follow is on appropriate handling of input and output using the screen-management facilities introduced thus far. Attractive screen forms obviously play an important role in achieving high quality in the terminal user interface.

(i) *Insert a passenger.* This application program performs three I/O actions prior to the actual insertion of a passenger record. The first action displays an appropriate header (procedure WriteHeader) to the screen that clarifies what the currently performed action is. The second output action (procedure DisplayPassengerTemplete) displays an appropriate screen form that indicates the names of the passenger attributes, and the empty slots in reverse video for typing in their values. In this way the length of the attributes is also indicated. Finally, the third I/O action reads the actual attribute values (procedure ReadPassengerData) from the terminal. This action moves the cursor from one attribute value slot to the next, requesting input for each slot. Thus, the terminal user is in fact asked to fill out a predefined screen form. Only the final action is performed upon the database—the insertion of the passenger data.

```
PROCEDURE InsertPassenger;

   VAR NewPassenger: PassengerType;

PROCEDURE WriteHeader;
(* block *)
PROCEDURE DisplayPassengerTemplete;
(* block *)
PROCEDURE ReadPassengerData(VAR p: PassengerType);
(* block *)

BEGIN WriteHeader;
       DisplayPassengerTemplete;
       ReadPassengerData(NewPassenger);
       IF NOT PassengerExists(NewPassenger.Passenger#)
       THEN   Insert(NewPassenger, Passenger)
       END
END InsertPassenger
```

The above global structure of the procedure InsertPassenger in which the decompositions of its local procedures WriteHeader, DisplayPassenger-Templete, and ReadPassenger are not yet specified, is now completed with the declarations of those procedures.

INSERT PASSENGER

NAME	XXXXXXXXXXXXXXXXXXXXXXXXXXXXXXXX
SEX	X
PHONE	XXXXXXXXXX
ADDRESS	XXXXXXXXXXXXXXXXXXXXXXXXXXXXXXXX
ID	XXXXXXXXXXXX

```
PROCEDURE WriteHeader;

   CONST Row2 = 2; Row3 = 3;
         Column24 = 24; Column55 = 55;

BEGIN    SetCursor(Row3, Column24);
         SelectCharType(HighWide);
         SetVideoAttributes (Row2, Column24, Row3, Column55,
            reverse);
```

```
                WriteString(" INSERT PASSENGER")
END WriteHeader;

PROCEDURE DisplayPassengerTemplete;

CONST   Row7 = 7; Row9 = 9; Row11 = 11;
        Row13 = 13; Row15 = 15;
        Column3 = 3; Column21 = 21; Column31 = 31;
        Column32 = 32; Column51 = 51;

BEGIN   SetCursor(Row7, Column3);
        SelectCharType(Normal);
        WriteString(" NAME");
        SetVideoAttributes(Row7, Column21, Row7, Column51,
                                                       reverse);

        SetCursor(Row9, Column3);
        WriteString(" SEX");
        SetVideoAttributes(Row9, Column21, Row9, Column21,
                                                       reverse);

        SetCursor(Row11, Column3);
        WriteString(" PHONE");
        SetVideoAttributes(Row11, Column21, Row11, Column31,
                                                       reverse);

        SetCursor(Row13, Column3);
        WriteString(" ADDRESS");
        SetVideoAttributes(Row13, Column21, Row13, Column51,
                                                       reverse);

        SetCursor(Row15, Column3); WriteString(" ID");
        SetVideoAttributes(Row15, Column21, Row15, Column32,
                                                       reverse)

END DisplayPassengerTemplete;

PROCEDURE ReadPassengerData(VAR p: PassengerType);
CONST Row7 = 7; Row9 = 9; Row11 = 11; Row13 = 13;
      Row15 = 15; Column21 = 21;

BEGIN   SetCursor(Row7, Column21);
        ReadString(p.Name);
        SetCursor(Row9, Column21);
        ReadString(p.Sex);
        SetCursor(Row11, Column21);
        ReadString(p.Phone);
        SetCursor(Row13, Column21);
        ReadString(p.Address);
        SetCursor (Row15, Column21);
        ReadString(p.Passenger#)

END ReadPassengerData
```

(ii) *Display passengers on a given flight.* This action is specified as a procedure with two parameters: flight identifier and departure date. Given these two parameters, a complex query is executed first (procedure SelectPassengers) that selects the names and sexes of all passengers on the specified departure. This is actually the only action on the database. The output set is accumulated in the local entity set SelectedPassengers. The next action outputs an appropriate screen header that includes the flight identifier, and the departure date. The next action sets up the output screen area (procedure InitializeOutputArea), which contains the names of the output attributes and empty slots for their values in reverse video. The final action is output of the selected passengers in the specified output rectangular area. Since only four passengers can fit in that area, the procedure WritePassenger requires an appropriate scrolling action.

As in the previous example, the global structure of the procedure DisplayPassenger, which exhibits the headings of its local procedures and the main body, is given first, and the complete declarations of those local procedures are given afterwards.

```
PROCEDURE DisplayPassengers(Flight#: String8;
                            Date:    String8);

TYPE  OutputAttributes = RECORD Name: String30;
                                Sex:  Char;
                         END;
      OutputSetType   = ENTITY  SET OF OutputAttributes;

  VAR SelectedPassengers: OutputSetType;
      p:                  OutputAttributes;
PROCEDURE SelectPassengers(Flight#: String8;
                           Date: String8;
                           VAR OutputSet: OutputSetType);
(* block *)
PROCEDURE WriteHeader(Flight#: String8; Date: String8);
(* block *)
PROCEDURE InitializeOutputArea;
(* block *)
PROCEDURE WritePassenger(p: OutputAttributes);
(* block *)

BEGIN WriteHeader(Flight#, Date); InitializeOutputArea;
      SelectPassengers(Flight#, Date, SelectedPassengers);
      FOREACH p IN SelectedPassengers
      DO WritePassenger(p)
      END
END DisplayPassengers
```

FLIGHT   XXXXXXXX

DATE   XXXXXXXX

PASSENGERS:

                        NAME   **SEX**

```
XXXXXXXXXXXXXXXXXXXXXXXXXXXXXXXXX          X

XXXXXXXXXXXXXXXXXXXXXXXXXXXXXXXXX          X

XXXXXXXXXXXXXXXXXXXXXXXXXXXXXXXXX          X

XXXXXXXXXXXXXXXXXXXXXXXXXXXXXXX            X
```

```
PROCEDURE SelectPassengers (Flight#:          String8;
                            Date:             String8;
                            VAR OutputSet:OutputSetType);

    VAR d:   Departure Type; r: ReservationType;
        p:   PassengerType;
        out: OutputAttributes;

BEGIN FOREACH d IN Departure
      WHERE    (d.Flight# = Flight#)
      AND      (d.Date = Date)
      DO       FOREACH  r IN Reservation
               WHERE    r.Departure# = d.Departure#
               DO       FOREACH p IN Passenger
                        WHERE    p.Passenger# = r. Passenger#
                        DO       out.Name : = p.Name;
                                 out.Sex : = p.Sex;
                                 Insert(out,OutputSet)
                        END
               END
      END
END SelectPassengers;

PROCEDURE WriteHeader(flight#: String8; date: String8);

CONST Row3 = 3; Row5 = 5, Row8 = 8;
      Column5 = 5; Column18 = 18;
BEGIN SelectCharType(Normal);
      SetCursor(Row3, Column5);
      WriteString(" FLIGHT ");
      SetCursor(Row3, Column18);
```

```
                WriteString(flight#);
                SetCursor(Row5, Column5);
                WriteString("DATE");
                SetCursor(Row5, Column18);
                WriteString(date);
                SetCursor(Row8, Column5);
                SelectCharType(Wide);
                WriteString("PASSENGERS:")
END     WriteHeader;

PROCEDURE InitializeOutputArea;

   CONST Row10 = 10; Row11 = 11; Row13 = 13;
           Column18 = 18; Column21 = 21; Column30 = 30;
           Column54 = 54; Column60 = 60;
   VAR    i: Cardinal;
BEGIN     SelectCharType(Normal);
          SetCursor(Row10, Column30);
          WriteString("NAME");
          SetCursor(Row10, Column54);
          WriteString("SEX");
          DrawRectangle(Row11, Column18, Row21, Column60);
          FOR i := 13 TO 19 BY 2 DO
             SetVideoAttributes(i, 21, i, 51, reverse);
             SetVideoAttributes(i, 55, i, 55, reverse)
          END;
          SetCursor(Row13, Column21)
END InitializeOutputArea;

PROCEDURE WritePassenger(p: OutputAttributes);

   CONST TwoLines = 2;
          Row11 = 11; Row13 = 13; Row19 = 19; Row20 = 20;
          Column19 = 19; Column21 = 21; Column55 = 55;
BEGIN     IF CursorRow( ) = Row19 THEN
              ScrollArea (Row13, Column21,
                          Row19, Column55, up, TwoLines)
          END;
          WriteString(p.Name);
          SetCursor(CursorRow( ), Column55);
          WriteString(p.Sex)
END WritePassenger
```

(iii) *Update departure.* This action is specified as a procedure, Re-ScheduleDeparture, with two parameters: a flight record and a departure record. The latter is necessarily a variable parameter since the result of this procedure apart from its visibility on the screen will in fact be communicated to the calling environment returning an updated departure record. The actions WriteHeader and DisplayFlight display the required general attributes of this action (its effect, flight, source, and destination). The action DisplayDeparture displays the given departure record in a rectangular update area where the values of the departure attributes are presented in reverse video. Finally, UpdateDeparture action is similar to ReadPassengerData except that the slots for the attribute values are not empty. The cursor is moved to the date slot first, and the user is requested to overwrite the existing (old) date. The same is repeated for the departure and arrival-time attributes.

```
PROCEDURE ReScheduleDeparture (f: FlightType;
                                 VAR d: DepartureType);

  PROCEDURE WriteHeader;
  (* block *)
  PROCEDURE DisplayFlight(f: FlightType);
  (* block *)
  PROCEDURE DisplayDeparture(d: DepartureType);
  (* block *)
  PROCEDURE UpdateDeparture(VAR d: DepartureType);
  (* block *)

BEGIN WriteHeader;
      DisplayFlight(f);
      DisplayDeparture(d);
      UpdateDeparture(d)
END ReScheduleDeparture
```

```
                         ┌────────────────────────┐
                         │   DEPARTURE UPDATE      │
                         └────────────────────────┘


                         ┌──────────────────────────────┐
                         │  FLIGHT#   XXXXXXXX            │
                         │                               │
                         │  SOURCE    XXX                │
                         │                               │
                         │  DESTINATION      XXX         │
                         └──────────────────────────────┘


    ┌──────────────────────────────────────┐
    │  DATE                 XXXXXXXX         │
    │  DAY                  XXX              │
    │  DEPARTURE TIME       XXXXX            │
    │  ARRIVAL TIME         XXXXX            │
    └──────────────────────────────────────┘
```

```
PROCEDURE WriteHeader;
  CONST Row2 = 2; Row3 = 3; Row4 = 4;
        Column32 = 32; Column33 = 33; Column49 = 49;
```

```
BEGIN     DrawRectangle(Row2, Column32, Row4, Column49);
          SetCursor(Row3, Column33);
          WriteString("DEPARTURE UPDATE")
END WriteHeader;

PROCEDURE DisplayFlight(f: FlightType);

   CONST Row5 = 5; Row6 = 6; Row8 = 8; Row10 = 10; Row11 = 11;
         Column29 = 29; Column30 = 30; Column39 = 39;
         Column41 = 41; Column44 = 44; Column46 = 46; Column47 = 47;

BEGIN     DrawRectangle(Row5, Column29, Row11, Column47);
          SetCursor(Row6, Column30);
          WriteString("FLIGHT#");
          SetCursor(Row6, Column39);
          SetVideoAttributes(Row6, Column39, Row6, Column46, reverse);
          WriteString(f.Flight#);
          SetCursor(Row8, Column30);
          WriteString("SOURCE");
          SetCursor(Row8, Column39);
          SetVideoAttributes(Row8, Column39, Row8, Column41, reverse);
          WriteString(f.Source);
          SetCursor(Row10, Column30);
          WriteString("DESTINATION");
          SetCursor(Row10, Column44);
          SetVideoAttributes(Row10, Column44, Row10, Column46, reverse);
          WriteString(f.Destination)
END DisplayFlight;

PROCEDURE DisplayDeparture(d:DepartureType);

CONST Row13 = 13; Row14 = 14; Row15 = 15; Row16 = 16;
      Row17 = 17;
      Column8 = 8; Column10 = 10; Column29 = 29;
      Column31 = 31;
      Column33 = 33; Column36 = 36; Column38 = 38;

BEGIN DrawRectangle(Row13, Column8, Row18, Column38);
      SetCursor(Row14, Column10);
      WriteString("DATE");
      SetCursor(Row14, Column29);
      SetVideoAttributes(Row14, Column29, Row14, Column36,
                                                       reverse);
      WriteString(d.Date);
      SetCursor(Row15, Column10);
      WriteString("DAY");
      SetCursor(Row15, Column29);
```

```
            SetVideoAttributes(Row15, Column29, Row15, Column31,
                                                              reverse);
            WriteString(d.Day);
            SetCursor(Row16, Column10);
            WriteString(" DEPARTURE TIME ");
            SetCursor(Row16, Column29);
            SetVideoAttributes(Row16, Column29, Row16, Column33,
                                                              reverse);
            WriteString(d.DepartureTime);
            SetCursor(Row17, Column10);
            WriteString(" ARRIVAL TIME ")'
            SetCursor(Row17, Column29);
            SetVideoAttributes(Row17, Column29, Row17, Column33,
                                                              reverse);
            WriteString(d.ArrivalTime)
END    DisplayDeparture;

PROCEDURE UpdateDeparture(VAR d: DepartureType);

CONST Row16 = 16; Row18 = 18; Row20 = 20;
      Column29 = 29;

BEGIN SetCursor(Row14, Column29);
      ReadString(d.Date);
      SetCursor(Row15, Column29);
      ReadString(d.Day);
      SetCursor(Row16, Column29);
      ReadString(d.DepartureTime);
      SetCursor(Row17, Column29);
      ReadString(d.ArrivalTime)
END    UpdateDeparture
```

5 Sequential Files

A *sequential file* is an object type whose instances are variable-length sequences of records of the same type. Such a sequence can grow in only one, very specific way: by appending new records to its end. Accessing particular records of a sequential file is possible only in the order in which they appear in the sequence. Only one record of a sequential file is immediately accessible. That record is determined by the current position of a sequential file. Actions associated with the sequential file type perform appropriate updates of the current position. Arbitrary insertions and deletions are not allowed. The sequential ordering of records and severe restrictions on the types of actions applicable to such sequences are designed so that the following two typical composite actions are easily expressed:

(i) *Reading records.* The action Reset is performed to set the current position to the beginning of the file. The action ReadRec is applied repeatedly to access successive records of a file until the end of the file (EOF) is reached. ReadRec advances the current file position.
(ii) *Writing records.* The empty sequence of records is assigned to a file by the action Rewrite. As expected, this action establishes the condition EOF. The action WriteRec is applied repeatedly to append records to the file, where the records are taken from some source, for example, from a terminal or another file.

A composition of composite actions (i) and (ii) may be used to establish the condition EOF using (i), and then to append new records using (ii). However, a much more efficient way is to apply the action GetEOF, which sets the file position to the file end, and then to append new records. Note that the precondition for the action ReadRec is NOT EOF and the precondition of WriteRec is EOF. If the required precondition is not satisfied, an exception is raised. Since such an exception is a fatal error, the sequential file handler terminates execution so that the test EOF is used appropriately to avoid such situations.

A correct sequence of actions on a sequential file starts with the action OpenFile and ends with the action CloseFile. None of the above described actions may be applied if a file is not already open. Unexpected effects and, in particular, violations of various types of integrity constraints may occur if a file is not closed after completion of the desired actions. All these requirements make a sequence of actions on a file that starts with OpenFile and ends with CloseFile very close to the notion of a transaction.

Apart from introducing the sequential file abstraction, the module SeqFile is important for two other reasons: One is relaxed conditions on type compatibility, and the other is an exception handling technique that we have not used so far.

The problems of type compatibility occur in the actions ReadRec and WriteRec. These actions have the file record as their parameter. But how do we specify the type of that record in the module SeqFile so that the chosen specification applies to any record type? The framework developed so far does not offer a solution to that problem, and thus, we rely on some low-level facilities of Modula-2 and specify the types of the actions ReadRec and WriteRec as follow:

```
PROCEDURE ReadRec(VAR f: File;
                  VAR rec: ARRAY OF Word);

PROCEDURE WriteRec(VAR f: File;
                   VAR rec: ARRAY OF Word);
```

Word is a type of basic storage units and, as such, is imported from the module SYSTEM. No actions except assignment are defined on this type. If a formal parameter is of this type, then the corresponding actual parameter may be of any type that requires one storage word in the given implementation. Typical examples of such types are Cardinal and Integer. If the type of a formal parameter is ARRAY OF Word, then the corresponding actual parameter may be of any type. In particular, it may be a record type, which is then interpreted as an array of words. This flexibility is achieved sacrificing type safety. The feature must be used with care since bypassing type checking may lead to some very unpleasant errors. It is up to the programmer to avoid such errors by properly using the above described feature.

Let us now consider the exception-handling approach applied to the SeqFile object. The definition module of this object contains an enumeration of possible exceptions that may occur during execution of actions specified in that module. Rather than testing the variable Exception after every action on a file, an error-handling procedure is invoked automatically whenever an exception occurs. The error-handling procedure is supplied by a user of a sequential file, invoking the action AssignFileHandler of the module SeqFile. All of this is explained in the following definitions:

```
TYPE FileStatus = (FileOK, FileNotFound, EndOfFile,
                   NameError, FileNotOpen, FileNotClosed,
                   FileLocked, WrongFileType, DeviceError);

     FileHandler = PROCEDURE(FileStatus);

PROCEDURE AssignFileHandler(handler: FileHandler;
                            VAR f: File);
```

The advantages of this approach to exception handling are its generality and flexibility. Perhaps more importantly this approach avoides explicit checking of exceptions after every action on a file. The clients' modules exhibit a much more attractive structure that reflects only the normal sequence of events, rather than frequent checking of exceptional events using conditional (IF) or selective (CASE) actions. This point is illustrated by a client module ListEmployees:

```
DEFINITION MODULE SeqFile;

FROM Files IMPORT File;
FROM System IMPORT Word;

EXPORT QUALIFIED FileStatus, FileHandler, AssignFileHandler,
                 CreateFile, OpenFile, CloseFile, AccessMode,
                 DeleteFile, ReleaseFile, RenameFile,
                 Reset, Rewrite, EOF, GetEOF,
                 ReadRec, WriteRec, RecSize;
```

```
TYPE FileStatus = (FileOK, FileNotFound, EndOfFile,
                   NameError, FileNotOpen, FileNotClosed,
                   FileLocked, WrongFileType,
                   DeviceError);

TYPE FileHandler = PROCEDURE(FileStatus);

PROCEDURE AssignFileHandler(handler: FileHandler;
                            VAR f: File);

PROCEDURE CreateFile(name: ARRAY OF Char;
                     RecordSize: Cardinal;
                     VAR f: File);

TYPE AccessMode = (ReadMode, WriteMode);

PROCEDURE OpenFile(name: ARRAY OF Char;
                   access: AccessMode;
                   VAR f: File);
PROCEDURE CloseFile(VAR f: File);
PROCEDURE DeleteFile(name: ARRAY OF Char);
PROCEDURE RenameFile(oldname, newname: ARRAY OF Char);
PROCEDURE ReleaseFile(VAR f: File);
PROCEDURE ReadRec(VAR f: File; VAR rec: ARRAY OF Word);
PROCEDURE WriteRec(VAR f: File; VAR rec: ARRAY OF Word);
PROCEDURE EOF(f: File): Boolean;
PROCEDURE GetEOF(VAR f: File);
PROCEDURE Reset(VAR f: File);
PROCEDURE ReWrite (VAR f: File);
PROCEDURE RecSize(f: File): Cardinal;

END SeqFile.

MODULE ListEmployees;

FROM Employee IMPORT EmployeeType, WriteEmployee;
FROM Files IMPORT File;

FROM SeqFile IMPORT FileStatus, FileHandler, AssignFileHandler,
                    OpenFile, CloseFile, Reset,
                    AccessMode, ReadRec,
                    EOF;

VAR EmpRecord: EmployeeType;
    EmpFile: File;

PROCEDURE FileHandler(Status: FileStatus): Boolean;
(* block *)

BEGIN AssignFileHandler(FileHandler, EmpFile);
      OpenFile("Employee", ReadMode, EmpFile);
```

```
        Reset(EmpFile);
        WHILE NOT EOF(EmpFile) DO
          ReadRec(EmpFile, EmpRecord);
          WriteEmployee(EmpRecord)
        END;
        CloseFile(EmpFile)
END ListEmployees.
```

6 Files, Images, and Streams

A sequential file is a particular case of a much more general notion represented by the type File. This generality has to do with a more complex structure, and more subtle access and concurrency control options. While a sequential file is a sequence of records, a file is, in general, equipped with a number of such logical orderings of records. These orderings are called *images*. An image of a file is defined for a sequence of attributes of that file. The image attributes determine a logical ordering of file records. If A are image attributes, and r_1 and r_2 file records, then

$$r1 <= r2 \quad \text{if and only if} \quad r1.A <= r2.A$$

where $r.A$ denotes projection of the tuple r on attributes A. An image of a file permits access to the records of that file in the order determined by the image. In addition, an image permits selection of a particular position in its ordering that corresponds to a given value of the image attributes. The above described actions of selective and sequential access to a file via its images and the fact that a file may have a number of images make such files suitable low-level representations for sets of objects of the same type. This will be clarified with the examples of low-level programming given later in this chapter.

An image is implemented as a dynamic index, and actions associated with an image as actions on such indexes. When an image is defined, then a number of logical conditions may be associated with it determining the image type, defined as follows:

```
ImageOptions = (Unique, Clustering, NoChange, NoNull);
ImageType    = SET OF ImageOptions
```

An image is unique if the image attributes contain a key. If, in addition, we do not permit undefined values (NoNull) of image attributes, then a unique image may serve to implement an ordering based on a primary key (object identifier). A further restriction (integrity constraint) does not permit any changes of values of image attributes (NoChange). Among the images of a file, one may have the clustering property. Such an image corresponds to the physical ordering of records in the file.

A file with a set of images may be represented by the following diagram:

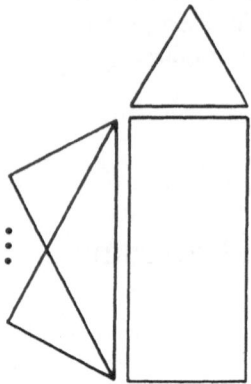

Specification of image attributes at the level of abstraction chosen for this section includes some low-level features:

```
AttributeType    = (ints, cards, chars, strings);
AttributeBlock   = RECORD attrtype: AttributeType;
                          offset:   Cardinal;
                          size:     Cardinal
                 END;
ImageAttributes = ARRAY OF AttributeBlock
```

In the above specification, low-level properties are the physical offset and the physical size of an attribute. Both are computed using the function TSize (type size), which is defined in the module SYSTEM and determines the physical size of any type.

The actions associated with the type Image in the definition module Images permit creation and deletion of an image (CreateImage and DropImage) of a file, and lookup of an existing image (FindImage). Other actions permit selection of image attributes (ImageFile, ImageName, TypeOfImage, ImageAttributes). The actual representation of the type Image is completely hidden in the implementation module Images so that only its identifier appears in the definition module Images. Export of that identifier appears in the definition module Images. Export of that identifier is called *opaque* since the clients of the module Images have no knowledge of the actual representation of that type. The definition of that type is thus strictly action oriented so that, in particular, to find out what the properties of an image are a client must invoke the above described actions that supply the desired data.

A particular case of a clustering image is a sorted file, and thus, the module Images contains the specification of the sorting actions whose parameters are the input and the output files, and an array of attributes on which the sorting is to be performed.

DEFINITION MODULE Images;

FROM Files IMPORT File;

EXPORT QUALIFIED Image, ImageOptions, ImageType,
                 AttributeType, AttributeBlock,
                 CreateImage, DropImage, FindImage,
                 SortFile,
                 ImageFile, ImageName, TypeOfImage,
                 ImageAttributes,
                 ImageStatus, ImageState;

TYPE Image;

```
     ImageOptions   = (Unique, Clustering, NoChange, NoNull);
     ImageType      = SET OF ImageOptions;
     AttributeType  = (ints, cards, chars, strings);
     AttributeBlock = RECORD Attribute: AttributeType;
                             offset:    Cardinal;
                             size:      Cardinal
             END;
```

PROCEDURE CreateImage(VAR f: File; VAR im: Image;
                      name: ARRAY OF Char;
                      attributes: ARRAY OF AttributeBlock;
                      Kind: ImageType);
PROCEDURE DropImage(im: Image);

PROCEDURE FindImage(name: ARRAY OF Char;
                    VAR im: Image);
PROCEDURE ImageFile(im:Image;
                    VAR f: File);
PROCEDURE ImageName(im: Image;
                    VAR name: ARRAY OF Char);
PROCEDURE TypeOfImage(im:Image): ImageType;
PROCEDURE ImageAttributes(im: Image;
                          VAR attributes: ARRAY OF
                          AttributeBlock);

PROCEDURE SortFile(InputFile, OutputFile: File;
                   attribute: ARRAY OF AttributeBlock);

TYPE ImageStatus = (ImageOk, ImageNotFound, FileNotFound,
                    WrongImageType);
   VAR ImageState: ImageStatus;

END Images.

The previously described actions of sequential and selective access to a file via its image are not associated with the type Image. Rather, these actions as well as the actions of reading, writing, and updating a record belong to the abstraction called *record stream*. Such a stream is created and connected to an image in order to access records of a file via that image and to perform appropriate actions upon them, and thus, such actions are not associated with the object type File either.

Now consider the definition of the object type File. This type is exported in the opaque manner, just as the type Image was and for the same reasons. Indeed, the actual implementation of both objects is very elaborate and with a number of low-level details that are of no concern to the users of such objects.

The exception-handling technique chosen for the object type File is identical to the technique chosen for sequential files. The number of possible exceptions is, of course, larger.

A file equipped with a nonempty set of images is specified as *indexed*. Two other possible file organizations are *sequential and relative*. In a relative file, records may be accessed via the record's ordinal number; for example, it is possible to access and rewrite (update) the *n*th file record of a relative file.

The only low-level feature appearing in the definition module Files and SeqFiles is *record size*. This parameter is computed from the record type using the system function TSize.

The definition of the object type File includes more subtle concurrency control options to be applied in multiuser environments. When a file is open, the type of access is specified according to the following options:

```
TYPE AccessOptions = (FPut, FGet, FDelete, FUpdate);
     AccessType    = SET OF AccessOptions
```

Subsequent actions (until the file is closed) must be in accordance with the specified access type. In addition, the action OpenFile specifies the level of sharing of that file with other, concurrent users. This is done in such a way that permissible actions of other, concurrent users are specified in the OpenFile action according to the following type specification:

```
TYPE SharingOptions = (ShrPut, ShrGet, ShrDelete,
                       ShrUpd, ShrMStream, ShrNil);
     SharingType    = SET OF SharingOptions
```

For example, ShrMStream permits a number of streams (multistream) of one or more users to be currently active on the same image of a file, and ShrNil permits no sharing whatsoever (i.e., OpenFile requires exclusive access to the file). If a file is successfully open, this in addition to other things, indicates that the specified access and sharing types are compatible with those of currently active users of that file. Subsequent file actions are performed (until the file is closed) under the chosen access and concurrency control options.

DEFINITION MODULE Files;

EXPORT QUALIFIED File, FileState, FileStatus,
                  FileHandler, AssignFileHandler,
                  OrgType, AccessOptions, AccessType,
                  SharingOptions, SharingType,
                  OpenFile, CreateFile, CloseFile,
                  ReleaseFile, RenameFile, DeleteFile,
                  LookupFile, FileName, RecordSize,
                  FileOrganization, FileAccess, FileSharing,
                  FileImages;

TYPE File;

    FileStatus   = (FileOk, FileNotFound, FileNotOpen,
                  FileLocked, NameError, RecordError,
                  AccessViolation, SharingViolation,
                  ProtectionViolation, DeviceError);
    FileState   = SET OF FileStatus;

TYPE FileHandler = PROCEDURE (FileState);
PROCEDURE AssignFileHandler(f: File;
                            handler: FileHandler);

TYPE OrgType = (sequential, relative, indexed);

PROCEDURE CreateFile (name: ARRAY OF Char;
                      RecordSize: Cardinal;
                      organization: OrgType;
                      VAR f: File);

TYPE AccessOptions = (FPut, FGet, FDelete, FUpdate);
    AccessType   = SET OF AccessOptions;

    SharingOptions = (ShrPut, ShrGet, ShrDelete,
                     ShrUpdate, ShrMStream,
                     ShrNil);
    SharingType   = SET OF SharingOptions;

PROCEDURE OpenFile(name: ARRAY OF Char;
                   access: AccessType;
                   sharing: SharingType;
                   VAR f: File);
PROCEDURE CloseFile(f: File);

PROCEDURE DeleteFile(f: File);
PROCEDURE RenameFile(VAR f: File;
                     NewName: ARRAY OF Char);
PROCEDURE ReleaseFile(VAR f: File);

```
PROCEDURE LookupFile(name: ARRAY OF Char;
                          VAR f: File);
PROCEDURE FileName(f: File;
                          VAR name: ARRAY OF Char);
PROCEDURE RecordSize(f: File): Cardinal;
PROCEDURE FileOrganization(f: File): OrgType;
PROCEDURE FileAcccess(f: File;
                          VAR access: AccessType);
PROCEDURE FileSharing(f: File;
                          VAR sharing: SharingType);
PROCEDURE FileImages(f: File;
                          VAR images: ARRAY OF ARRAY OF
                          Char);

END Files.
```

As an illustration, the client module CreateEmployee is given below. This module creates the Employee file with two images: one on the employee identifier, and the other on the department identifier.

```
MODULE CreateEmployee;

FROM Employee   IMPORT EmployeeType, EmployeeId, NameType,
                       JobType, SalaryType, DepartmentId;

FROM Files      IMPORT File, FileStatus, FileState, FileHandler,
                       AssignFileHandler;

FROM Images     IMPORT Image, CreateImage, ImageStatus,
                       ImageState, AttributeBlock,
                       AttributeType;

FROM System     IMPORT TSize;

FROM StandardIO IMPORT WriteString;

VAR EmpFile: File;
    EmpIdImage, EmpDeptImage: Image;

    ImageAtt: ARRAY [0..0] OF AttributeBlock;

PROCEDURE CheckFileError(State: FileState);
BEGIN IF    State < > FileState { } THEN
            WriteLn;
            IF NameError IN State
            THEN WriteString("Name")
            ELSIF RecordError IN State
            THEN WriteString("Record")
            ELSIF DeviceError IN State
            THEN WriteString("Device")
```

```
            ELSE WriteString(" File ") END;
            WriteString(" error(msg from Files)");
            Halt
      END
END CheckFileError;

BEGIN AssignFileHandler(EmpFile, CheckFileError);
      CreateFile(" Employee ",
               TSize(EmployeeType),
               indexed, EmpFile);

      WITH ImageAtt[0] DO
        attribute : = strings; offset : = 0;
        size : = TSize(EmployeeId);
      END;

      CreateImage(EmpFile, EmpIdImage,
                " EmpId ", ImageAtt,
                ImageType{Unique, Clustering, NoChange,
                NoNull});

      WITH ImageAtt[0] DO
        attribute : = strings;
        offset : = TSize(EmployeeId) + TSize(NameType) +
                TSize(JobType) + TSize(SalaryType);
        size   : = TSize(DepartmentId)
      END;

      CreateImage(EmpFile, EmpDeptImage,
                " EmpDept ", ImageAtt,
                ImageType{NoNull})

END CreateEmployee.
```

To perform actions on particular file records, a user must create (open) a record stream associated with an image of that file. When the desired sequence of actions is performed, the stream is closed. A stream has a position that determines the currently accessible file record and that may be set to the first record of the image (ResetStream), moved to the next record of the image (NextRec), and, most importantly, set to the first record of the image with a given value of image attributes (SelectPosition). When a file is processed sequentially in the order determined by its image, the EOS condition is necessary for testing whether the last record of the chosen ordering has been reached. The test Found is also useful for similar purposes such as for testing whether a record with a given value of image attributes was found by the action SelectPosition.

The types RStream and Position are both exported in the opaque manner. The type Position is equipped with actions SavePosition and Restore-

Position, which are used for composite actions in which it is necessary to return to a previously established position.

The actual actions on records associated with the type RStream are GetRec, PutRec, UpdateRec, and DeleteRec. These actions refer to the record determined by the current stream position. GetRec simply delivers that record and does not change the position, DeleteRec deletes the current record of the stream, and UpdateRec performs replacement of the current record with the record supplied as the actual parameter of this action. PutRec performs insertion of the record given as its actual parameter. All these actions perform appropriate updates of file images. In other words, the effect of those actions is immediately visible in all the images of that file.

```
DEFINITION MODULE RStreams;

FROM Files IMPORT File;

FROM Images IMPORT Image;

FROM System IMPORT Word, Address;

EXPORT QUALIFIED RStream, Position,
                 OpenStream, CloseStream,
                 SelectPosition, SetPosition,
                 SavePosition, RestorePosition,
                 ResetStream, NextRec, Found, EOS,
                 GetRec, PutRec, UpdateRec, DeleteRec,
                 RStreamException, RecordException;

TYPE RStream;
     Position;
     RStreamException = (RecordOk, FileError, ConnectError,
                         RecordLocked, EndOfStream,
                         RecordNotFound);

VAR  RecordException: RStreamException;

PROCEDURE OpenStream(VAR f: File; VAR i: Image;
                     VAR s: RStream);

PROCEDURE CloseStream(VAR s: RStream);

PROCEDURE ResetStream(VAR s: RStream);

PROCEDURE NextRec(VAR s: RStream);

PROCEDURE EOS(s: RStream): Boolean;

PROCEDURE Found(s: RStream): Boolean;

PROCEDURE GetRec(VAR s: RStream;
                 VAR buffer: ARRAY OF Word);
PROCEDURE PutRec(VAR s: RStream;
                 VAR buffer: ARRAY OF Word);
```

```
PROCEDURE UpdateRec (VAR s: RStream;
                            VAR buffer: ARRAY OF Word);
PROCEDURE DeleteRec(VAR s: RStream);

PROCEDURE SelectPosition(VAR s: RStream;
                            key: ARRAY OF Word);

PROCEDURE SetPosition(RecNum: Cardinal;
                            VAR s: RStream);

PROCEDURE SavePosition(s: RStream;
                            VAR p: Position);

PROCEDURE RestorePosition(s: Position;
                            VAR s: RStream);

END.
```

7 Low-Level Application-Oriented Programming

Here we present three client modules illustrating low-level representations of complex actions (transactions) on Employee and Department object types represented as indexed files.

The first module performs an extensive update of salaries of all employees. Access and Update actions on particular records are performed via a record stream associated with the image on the employee identifier. This decision is based on the assumption that this image is the clustering one. In general, a transaction acting on a large number of file records should operate on a record stream associated with the clustering image of that file, if at all possible. In this example, we update all records of the employee file.

```
MODULE UpdateSalaries;

FROM Employee   IMPORT EmployeeType;

FROM Files      IMPORT File, OpenFile, CloseFile,
                       AccessType, SharingType,
                       FileState, FileHandler,
                       AssignFileHandler;

FROM Images     IMPORT Image, FindImage;

FROM RStreams   IMPORT RStream,
                       OpenStream, CloseStream,
                       ResetStream, EOS,
                       GetRec, NextRec, UpdateRec;
```

```
FROM StandardIO IMPORT WriteLn, WriteString, ReadReal;

VAR EmpRec:      EmployeeType;
    EmpFile:     File;
    IdImage:     Image;
    EmpStream: RStream;
    Percent:     Real;

PROCEDURE FileError(Status: FileState);
(* block *)

PROCEDURE ReadPercentage(VAR percentage: Real);

BEGIN WriteLn;
      WriteString(" Percentage of salary increase?> ");
      ReadReal(percentage)
END    ReadPercentage;

BEGIN ReadPercentage(Percent);
      AssignFileHandler(EmpFile, FileError);
      OpenFile(" Employee ", AccessType{FGet, FUpdate},
               SharingType{ShrNil}, EmpFile);
      FindImage(" EmpId ", IdImage);
      OpenStream(EmpFile, IdImage, EmpStream);

      ResetStream(EmpStream);
      WHILE NOT EOS(EmpStream) DO
        GetRec(EmpStream, EmpRec);
        WITH EmpRec DO salary := salary + salary * Percent/100.0
        END;
        UpdateRec(EmpStream, EmpRec);
        NextRec(EmpStream)
      END;

      CloseStream(EmpStream);
      CloseFile(EmpFile)
END    UpdateSalaries.
```

The next example is more complex since it involves selective rather than extensive access to the employee file. The module performs update of salaries of employees of a given department. This transaction is performed via a record stream associated with the image on the department identifier of the employee file. Selective access on this stream is performed first to locate the first employee from a given department. Then, subsequent employees of the same department are accessed using the action NextRec on the same stream until the first employee record with a different department identifier is reached. The attribute salary of all the employee records located in the above manner is updated appropriately.

```
MODULE UpdateSalaries;

FROM Employee IMPORT EmployeeType, DepartmentId;

FROM Files      IMPORT File, OpenFile, CloseFile,
                       AccessType, SharingType,
                       FileState, FileHandler, AssignFileHandler;

FROM Images     IMPORT Image, FindImage;

FROM RStreams IMPORT RStream, Found, EOS,
                     OpenStream, CloseStream,
                     SelectPosition, GetRec, NextRec,
                     UpdateRec;

VAR EmpRecord:  EmployeeType;
    EmpFile:    File;
    DeptImage:  Image;
    EmpStream:  RStream;
    department#: DepartmentId;
    Percentage: Real;

PROCEDURE ReadDepartment;
(* block *)
PROCEDURE ReadPercentage;
(* block *)

PROCEDURE FileError (Status: FileState);
(* block *)

BEGIN ReadDepartment; ReadPercentage;
      AssignFileHandler(EmpFile, FileError);

      OpenFile("Employee", AccessType{FGet, FUpdate},
              SharingType{ShrGet});

      FindImage("EmpDept", DeptImage);
      OpenStream(EmpFile, DeptImage, EmpStream);

      SelectPosition(EmpStream, department#);

      LOOP IF NOT Found(EmpStream)
           THEN Exit END;
           GetRec(EmpStream, EmpRecord);
           WITH EmpRecord DO
             IF Department# < >
                department# THEN
                Exit
             ELSE Salary := Salary +
                  Salary * Percentage/100.0;
                  UpdateRec(EmpStream, EmpRecord)
```

```
            END
          END;
          NextRec(EmpStream)
     END;

     CloseStream(EmpStream);
     CloseFile(EmpFile)
END UpdateSalaries.
```

Our third example is a module that performs a join of the files Employee and Department in order to print out the names of employees together with the names of their departments. The join algorithm is based on two loops: The outer loop operates on the stream associated with the image on the department identifier of the file Department. This image is assumed to be clustering, and the file Department is processed extensively in the order determined by this image. For each department record encountered via this stream, selective access is performed on the stream associated with the image on the department identifier of the file Employee. The inner loop of the join algorithm operates on this second stream in order to access all employees with a given department identifier.

```
MODULE FileJoin;

FROM Employee     IMPORT EmployeeType;

FROM Department IMPORT DepartmentType;

FROM Files         IMPORT File, OpenFile, CloseFile,
                          AccessType, SharingType,
                          FileState, FileHandler,
                          AssignFileHandler;

FROM Images        IMPORT FindImage;

FROM RStreams      IMPORT RStream, Found, EOS,
                          OpenStream, CloseStream,
                          SelectPosition, GetRec, NextRec,
                          UpdateRec;

VAR EmpRec: EmployeeType; DeptRec: DepartmentType;
    EmpFile, DeptFile: File;
    EmpDeptImage, DeptIdImage: Image;
    EmpStream, DeptStream: Stream;

PROCEDURE FileError(Status: FileState);
(* block *)

BEGIN AssignFileHandler(EmpFile, FileError);
      AssignFileHandler(DeptFile, FileError);

         OpenFile(" Employee ", AccessType{FGet},
                  SharingType{ShrGet}, EmpFile);
```

```
OpenFile("Department", AccessType{FGet},
            SharingType{ShrGet}, DeptFile);

FindImage("EmpDept", EmpDeptImage);
FindImage("DeptId", DeptIdImage);

OpenStream(EmpFile, EmpDeptImage, EmpStream);
OpenStream(DeptFile, DeptIdImage, DeptStream);
ResetStream(DeptStream);
WHILE NOT EOS(DeptStream) DO
  GetRec(DeptStream, DeptRec);
  SelectPosition(EmpStream, DeptRec.Department#);
  LOOP IF NOT Found(EmpStream)
        THEN Exit END;
        GetRec(EmpStream, EmpRec);
        IF    EmpRec.department# < >
              DeptRec.department#
        THEN Exit
        ELSE WriteLn;
              WriteString(EmpRec.Name);
              WriteCh(" ");
              WriteString(DeptRec.Name)
        END;
        NextRec(EmpStream)
  END;
  NextRec(DeptStream)
END;

CloseStream(EmpStream); CloseStream(DeptStream);
CloseFile(EmpFile); CloseFile(DeptFile)

END FileJoin.
```

Exercises

(1) Line Input

Specify an implementation module for the following definition module:

DEFINITION MODULE LineInput;

EXPORT QUALIFIED ReadCh, NewLine, NewFile,
                   EOLN, EOF, Lno;

```
VAR Lno: Cardinal; (* line number *)
    EOLN, EOF: Boolean; (* end of line,
                          end of file *)
```

PROCEDURE NewFile;
PROCEDURE NewLine;
PROCEDURE ReadCh(VAR x: Char)

END LineInput.

This module is meant to be used for copying a text structured into lines from the input to the output character sequence. The file and line structure of the input is ignored when the output is written. Characters in the input sequence that represent file separator (FS) and line separator (LF) are translated into a blank, and Boolean variables EOF and EOLN are set respectively. FS is assumed to be preceded by LF. Observe that the desired implementation module requires import of the constants LF (line feed), CR (carriage return), and FS (file separator) from the module ASCII and procedures ReadCh and WriteCh from the module StandardIO.

(2) Character Stream

(i) A particular case of the stream abstraction is a *character stream*. A character stream is associated with a file of characters (text file). A *text file* is a fundamental abstraction and, as such, is predefined in languages like Pascal. Actions on text files have peculiarities of their own, but on the other hand, the type of their element is predefined so that we do not have the problem of relaxed type checking as we did with record streams. The character-stream abstraction is represented in the definition module given below. Note that this module is frequently used in such a way that appropriate symbolic constants are imported from the module ASCII such as ASCII.EOL, ASCII.FF, and ASCII.CR.

DEFINITION MODULE CharStream;

FROM Files IMPORT File;

EXPORT QUALIFIED ChStream, Connect, Disconnect,
                 Reset, ReadCh, WriteCh,
                 ExceptionType, Exception, EOS;

TYPE ChStream;
     ExceptionType = (None, FileError, ConnectError, EndOfStream,
                      FormatError);
VAR Exception: ExceptionType;

PROCEDURE Connect(f: File; VAR s: ChStream);
PROCEDURE Disconnect(f: File; VAR s: ChStream);

PROCEDURE ReadCh(s: ChStream; VAR Ch: Char);
PROCEDURE WriteCh(s: ChStream; Ch: Char);

PROCEDURE Reset(s: ChStream)
PROCEDURE EOS(s: ChStream): Boolean;

END CharStream.

(ii) Write up a module that performs the following actions:

—assigns appropriate file handlers to the input and the output text files;
—opens both of them, and creates appropriate character streams;
—reads the input file, interpreting it as a sequence of characters, and copies the character sequence from the input to the output with a given left margin and a given right margin without breaking up the input words; and
—closes properly the streams and the files.

(3) Text files

(i) The fundamental importance of the text abstraction justifies the definition and implementation of the module Texts (see (Knepley and Platt, 1986)), which performs opaque export of type Text together with the associated actions. The type Text permits a much higher level of type safety that makes the application of text-oriented actions to a file that is not of the appropriate type (i.e., that is not a text file) impossible. Analyze the appropriateness of the definition module Texts given below:

DEFINITION MODULE Texts;

FROM Files IMPORT File;

EXPORT QUALIFIED Text, input, output,
                 Connect, Disconnect,
                 EOT, EOL,
                 TextStatus, TextState,
                 TextHandler, AssignTextHandler,
                 Read, ReadLn, ReadAgain,
                 Write, WriteString, WriteLn;

TYPE Text;

VAR input, output, Text;

PROCEDURE EOT(t: Text): Boolean;
PROCEDURE EOL(t: Text): Boolean;

TYPE TextState = (TextOk, FormatError, FileError, ConnectError);

PROCEDURE TextStatus(t: Text): TextState;

TYPE TextHandler = PROCEDURE(TextState);

PROCEDURE AssignTextHandler(t: Text;
                            handler: TextHandler);

PROCEDURE Connect(VAR t: Text;
                  f: File): TextState;
PROCEDURE DisConnect(VAR t: Text;
                     f: File): TextState;

```
PROCEDURE Read(t: Text; VAR ch: Char);
PROCEDURE ReadLn(t: Text; VAR s: ARRAY OF Char);
PROCEDURE ReadAgain(t: Text);
PROCEDURE Write(t: Text; ch: Char);
PROCEDURE WriteString(t: Text; s: ARRAY OF Char);
PROCEDURE WriteLn(t: Text)
```

END Texts.

(ii) Using the module Texts, as well as other required modules, write-up a program module that performs text formatting. The input text is read and the output text produced with given left, right, top, and bottom margins. In addition, each output page has a header (a line of text), as well as the page number. The following is an illustration of a possible main algorithm:

```
BEGIN PageNum := 0; LineNum := 0;
      LOOP GetLine(line);
            IF    EOT(InText) THEN
                  Exit
            END;
            IF    LineNum = 0 THEN
                  PageTop
            END;
            PutLine(line)
      END
END Copy
```

(iii) Revise the definition of the module Texts in such a way that all the necessary primitives for processing a text file are available in that module so that, in particular, client modules do not have to rely on the module Files. This, for example, means that Texts will contain actions such as CreateText, OpenText, and CloseText.

(4) Access Rights

(i) In a multiuser environment, various groups of users have different access rights with respect to the objects in their common database. Access rights of a user with respect to an object determine the types of actions the user may perform on that object. One possible specification of access rights and a possible classification of users in a multiuser environment are given in the following type definitions:

```
TYPE Right  = (ReadRight, WriteRight, DeleteRight);
     Rights = SET OF Right;

TYPE User   = (System, Owner, Group, Public)
```

When an object is created, its creator assigns appropriate rights to the four classes of users: the system, the owner, the users belonging to the same group as the creator, and all other users (public).

(ii) Specify the definition module AccessRights, which is used to associate access rights with a file. The specification should follow these guidelines:

—The module imports the type File and exports the type Protection in the opaque manner.
—Actions CreateProtection and DeleteProtection connect and disconnect an object of type Protection with a file.
—The action SetRights assigns access rights of a particular class of users to an object of type Protection. Default rights are assigned when a protection object is connected to a file.
—The action GetRights applied to a particular Protection object and a particular class of users returns the access rights of that class of users.
—The action GetProtection applied to a file returns the protection object of that file. Observe that this action may be associated with the type File.

(5) Nonstandard I/O Devices

(i) A *mouse* is an input device, handheld and moved around on a plane related to the screen (see (Wirth, 1983a)). More specifically, a mouse has the following properties:

—The mouse has its position in terms of x and y coordinates.
—The mouse's position may be made visible on the screen by a specific cursor.
—The mouse's cursor can be positioned at any screen (raster) element. This condition determines the required resolution of this particular type of input device.
—A small set of keys is associated with the mouse in such a way that their state can also be tested in a program.

(ii) Specify the definition module of the object Mouse under the above assumptions. Three basic actions are meant to be associated with this object in its definition module: CursorOn, CursorOff, and TrackMouse. CursorOn and CursorOff determine whether the cursor is displayed on the screen or not. TrackMouse reads the mouse's position and draws the cursor accordingly. Its position is assigned to the variables exported from the desired definition module. The following example is an illustration of use of the above two actions:

```
InitializeScreen;
CursorOn;
LOOP TrackCursor;
        IF      MouseKeyPressed AND MouseHasMoved
        THEN CursorOff;
                PerformAction;
                CursorOn
        END;
```

```
IF      KeyPressed ( ) THEN
        Read (ch);
        IF ch = EscapeChar THEN
            Exit END
   END
END;
ClearScreen
```

(iii) A mouse is particularly useful in selecting an item from a menu on the screen. Give examples of such a use for the definition module specified in step (ii). Consider, for example, the flight reservation application.

(6) Pasteboards and Virtual Displays

(i) The purpose of this exercise is to generalize the screen-management facilities presented in this chapter, write up the required definition modules, and give examples of their use. The generalization is based on the abstract objects called *pasteboards* and *virtual displays*.

(ii) A pasteboard is a logical coordinate system associated with a physical screen. The associated actions are as follows:

CreatePasteboard, DeletePasteboard, ErasePasteboard, GetPasteboardAttributes, ChangePasteboardAttributes,

The action CreatePasteboard associates a pasteboard with a physical device, and returns the identifier of the created pasteboard and the number of rows and columns available on that device. A pasteboard is deleted and disassociated from a particular device by the action DeletePasteboard. GetPasteboardAttributes delivers the attributes of a pasteboard, and ChangePasteboardAttributes changes those attributes, for example, from 80 to 132 columns. ErasePasteboard clears the associated screen.

(iii) Specify the definition module Pasteboard according to the above description.

(iv) A virtual display is a rectangular area of the terminal screen used to output images on the screen. The associated actions are as follows:

CreateVirtualDisplay, DeleteVirtualDisplay, GetDisplayAttributes, ChangeDisplayAttributes, PasteVirtualDisplay, UnpasteVirtualDisplay, RepasteVirtualDisplay, MoveVirtualDisplay, PopVirtualDisplay, CheckForOcclusion

The action CreateVirtualDisplay creates a virtual display with selected video attributes and character type. The action returns the identifier of the created display, which is used to refer to that display, for example, in the action DeleteVirtualDisplay.

PasteVirtualDisplay positions the display at the given coordinates of the pasteboard so that the display is visible on the screen. Of course, a module can paste a number of virtual displays on the same pasteboard. Their occlusion depends on the order in which they are pasted. In other words, virtual displays indeed behave like sheets of paper on a pasteboard. On the other hand, a single virtual display may be pasted to more than one pasteboard at a time. A virtual display may be repasted (on top) or simply moved without changing the pasting order. The actions Repaste-VirtualDisplay and MoveVirtualDisplay thus produce different effects in terms of occlusion of the pasted virtual displays. PopVirtualDisplay removes a virtual display, as well as all displays pasted after it.

(v) Output actions are now always related to a virtual display that has its associated logical cursor. This cursor determines the position at which the output occurs and is affected by actions on the virtual display such as moving the cursor, and writing and erasing characters. Of course, only one of the cursors associated with virtual displays on the screen corresponds to the physical cursor.

(vi) Write up the definition module VirtualDisplay according to the above description.

(vii) Express the examples of screen management for the flight reservation application in this generalized framework (i.e., using virtual displays).

(7) Complex Screen Management

(i) The actions SaveDisplay and RestoreDisplay of the module VideoDisplay perform saving and restoring of (usually complex) screen images. The saved display is identified by a unique cardinal number and subsequently restored using that number. An example in which this feature may be useful is the ExtendReservation recursive algorithm of Section 6 of Chapter 3. The reason for this is the backtracking nature of the algorithm. Extend this algorithm, as well as the overall BookItinerary procedure, with appropriate screen-management actions—SaveDisplay and RestoreDisplay, in particular.

(ii) The actions BeginDisplayUpdate and EndDisplayUpdate of the module VideoDisplay permit batching of screen-management actions that appear among these two actions. In this case, intermediate steps of complex screen updating are not visible—only the final effect is. Give examples of the use of these features using the flight booking example.

(8) Images and Efficiency of Recursive Algorithms

(i) The existence of appropriate images dramatically affects the efficiency of a number of algorithms presented in this book. The purpose of this exercise is to point out some algorithms in which these effects are particularly critical, such as

—display product structure, and part and labor analysis of Section 3 of Chapter 4.

—traversal recursion examples of Exercises (2.1), (2.2), and (2.8);

—optimal selection and stable marriage problems of Exercises (2.1), (2.2), and (2.8); and

—extend reservation algorithm of Section 6 of Chapter 3.

(ii) Observe that all the chosen examples are recursive. The existence of appropriate images affects the above algorithms, as well as most others, because of the role the action SelectPosition of the record stream abstraction has in the low-level representation of these algorithms generated by the compiler. Give some estimates of the number of executions of the action SelectPosition in the above algorithms. Specify the appropriate images that, when implemented as indexes, affect critically the above algorithms because of the efficiency of the SelectPosition action in that case. The second module UpdateSalaries of Section 6 of Chapter 5 is instructive in better understanding the problems of low-level decomposition of the above algorithms, and the effects of efficiency of actions associated with images and streams.

(9) File Handlers

(i) The file handlers as specified in the modules SeqFile, Files, and Texts (exercise (3)) do not know the identity of the file whose error conditions they handle, and thus, the error messages from those handlers cannot refer to the file name. Provide a more general specification of a file handler that has access to the actual file, and not only to its error conditions.

(ii) The file handlers FileError in the low-level application-oriented examples of Section 6 are left unspecified. Provide appropriate specifications for those handlers.

(iii) Consider specifications of file handlers in multiuser environments. Specify appropriate actions when file status such as FileLocked, SharingViolation, AccessViolation, and ProtectionViolation occur.

Bibliographical Notes

The formatted I/O as defined in Modula-2 (Wirth, 1983a, 1983b) is not suitable for database environments and thus somewhat different in our approach. The same applies to I/O conversions. The terminal I/O as presented here follows (Wirth, 1983a) and Logitech Modula-2/86. The input data validation example is adapted from (Stuart, 1987). The approach to screen-oriented I/O is an abstraction motivated by various publications such as DEC's screen management for VAX. Our approach to the concepts of files, images, and streams presented in this chapter explain the underlying support of the MODULEX system. It was influenced to some extent by RMS for VAX, but of course, the abstraction presented here is ours. Exercises (4) and (6) are motivated by relevant DEC publications. Exercises (1) and (5) are based on (Wirth 1983a, 1983b), and exercise (3) on (Knepley and Platt, (1986). These last references explain file handling in Modula-2.

Selected Bibliography

Alagić, S. (1985): Relational Pascal database programming environment. Information Systems Conference, Tokyo University.

Alagić, S. (1986): *Relational Database Technology*. Springer-Verlag, New York.

Alagić, S. (1988): Object-oriented database programming in a relational environment extended with modules. Tech. Rep., Software Laboratory, Faculty of Electrical Engineering, University of Sarajevo, Yugoslavia.

Alagić, S., and Arbib, M.A. (1978): *The Design of Well-Structured and Correct Programs*. Springer-Verlag, New York.

Alagić, S., and Kulenović, A. (1981): Relational Pascal database interface. *Computer Journal*, Vol. 24, No. 2, 112–117.

Alagić, S. (1986): Conceptual modelling: The arrow-theoretic perspective. Tech. Rep., Dept. of Informatics, Faculty of Electrical Engineering, University of Sarajevo, Yugoslavia.

Albano, A., Cardelli, L., and Orsini, R. (1985): Galileo: A strongly typed, interactive conceptual language. *ACM Transactions on Database Systems*, Vol. 10, No. 2 (June), 230–260.

Atkinson, M.P., and Buneman, P.O. (1987): Types and persistence in database programming languages. *ACM Computing Surveys*, Vol. 19, No. 2 (June), 105–190.

Bancilhon, F., and Khoshafian, S. (1986): A calculus for complex objects. ACM Conference on Principles of Database Systems, ACM, New York.

Bancilhon, F., and Ramakrishnan, R. (1986): An amateur's introduction to recursive query processing strategies. In *Proceedings of the ACM–SIGMOD 86 Annual Conference* (Washington, D.C.). ACM, New York.

Batory, D.S., and Kim, W. (1985): Modelling concepts for VLSI CAD objects. *ACM Transactions on Database Systems*, Vol. 10, No. 3 (Sept.), 322–346.

Beeri, C., Bernstein, P.A. (1979): Computational problems related to the design of normal form relational schemas. *ACM Transactions on Database Systems*, Vol. 4, No. 1 (Mar.), 30–59.

Bernstein, P.A. (1976): Synthesizing third normal form relations from functional dependencies. *ACM Transactions on Database Systems*, Vol. 1, No. 4 (Dec.), 277–298.

Borgida, A. (1986a): Language features for flexible handling of exceptions in information systems. *AMC Transactions on Database Systems,* Vol. 10, No. 4 (Dec.), 565–603.

Borgida, A. (1986b): Conceptual modelling of information systems. In M.L. Brodie, and J. Mylopoulos, Eds. *On Knowledge Base Management Systems.* Springer-Verlag, New York, pp. 461–469.

Borgida, A., Mitchell, T., and Williamson, K.E. (1986): Learning improved integrity constraints and schemas from exceptions in data and knowledge bases. In M.L. Brodie, and J. Mylopoulos, Eds. *On Knowledge Base Management Systems.* Springer-Verlag, New York, pp. 259–286.

Borgida, A., Mylopoulos, J., and Wong, H.K.T. (1984): Generalization/specialization as a basis for software specification. In M.L. Brodie, J. Mylopoulos, and J.W. Schmidt, Eds. *On Conceptual Modelling.* Springer-Verlag, New York, pp. 87–117.

Borgida, A., Jarke, M., Mylopoulos, J., Schmidt, J.W. and Vassiliou, Y. (1987) The software development environment as a knowledge base management system. Technical report, ESPRIT project 892 (DAIDA).

Brodie, M.L., and Mylopoulos, J., Eds. (1986): *On Knowledge Base Management Systems.* Springer-Verlag, New York.

Brodie, M.L., and Ridjanović, Dž. (1984a): On the design and specification of database transactions. In M.L., Brodie, J. Mylopoulos, and J.W. Schmidt, Eds. *On Conceptual Modelling.* Springer-Verlag, New York, pp. 277–312.

Brodie, M.L., and Ridjanović, Dž. (1984b): A strict database transaction design methodology. Tech. Rep, Computer Corporation of America, Cambridge, Mass.

Brodie, M.L., Mylopoulos, J., and Schmidt, J.W., Eds. (1985): *On Conceptual Modelling.* Springer-Verlag, New York, pp. 277–312.

Buneman, P., and Atkinson, M. (1986): Inheritance and persistance in database programming languages. In *Proceedings of the ACM–SIGMOD 86 Annual Conference* (Washington, D.C.). ACM, New York.

Cardelli, L. (1988): Types for data-oriented languages. In *Advances in Database Technology—EDBT 88.* Lecture Notes in Computer Science, Vol. 303. Springer-Verlag, New York, pp. 1–15.

Cardelli, L., and Wegner, P. (1985): On understanding types, data abstraction and polymorphism. *Computing Surveys,* Vol. 17., No. 4 (Dec.), 471–522.

Claybrook, B.G., and Claybrook, A.M. (1985): Defining database views as data abstractions. *IEEE Transactions on Software Engineering,* Vol. SE-11, No. 1, (Jan.), pp. 3–14.

Codd, E.F. (1971a): Further normalization of the relational database model. Database Systems. *Courant Computer Science Symposia 6* (R. Rustin, Ed.). Prentice-Hall, Englewood Cliffs, N.J., pp. 33–64.

Codd, E.F. (1971b): Relational completeness of database sublanguages. Database Systems. Courant Computer Science Symposia 6 (R. Rustin, Ed). Prentice-Hall, Englewood Cliffs, N.J., pp. 65–93.

Codd, E.F. (1979): Extending the database relational model to capture more meaning. *ACM Transactions on Database Systems,* Vol. 4, No. 4 (Dec.), 397–434.

Dadam, P., et al. (1986): A DBMS prototype to support extended NF2-relations: An integrated view on flat tables and hierarchies. In *Proceedings of the ACM–SIGMOD Conference on Management of Data* (Washington, D.C.). ACM, New York.

Dayal, U., and Smith, J.M. (1986): Probe: A knowledge-oriented management system. In M.L. Brodie, and J. Mylopoulos, Eds. *On Knowledge Base Management Systems.* Springer-Verlag, New York.

Dayal, U., Buchmann, A., Goldhirsch, D. Heiler, S., Manola, F.A., Ornestein, J.A., and Rosenthal, A.L. (1985): Probe—A research project in knowledge-oriented database systems: Preliminary analysis. Tech. Rep. CCA-85-03, Computer Corporation of America, Cambridge, Mass.,

Eckhardt, J., Edelmann, J., Koch, J., Mall, M., and Schmidt, J.W. (1985): Draft report on the database programming language DBPL. Fachbereich Informatik, J.W. Goethe Universitat, Frankfurt.

Greenspan, S.J., Borgida, A., and Mylopoulos, J. (1985): A requirements modelling language and its logic. In M.L. Brodie and J. Mylopoulos Eds. *On Knowledge Base Management Systems*. Springer-Verlag, New York.

Guting, R.H. (1987): Geo-Relational Algebra: A model and query language for database systems. In *Advances in Database Technology—EDBT88*. Lecture Notes in Computer Science, Vol. 303. Springer-Verlag, New York, pp. 506–527.

Hoare, C.A.R., and Wirth, N. (1973): An axiomatic definition of the programming language Pascal. *Acta Informatica*, Vol. 3, 135–153.

Kemper, A., Lockemann, P.C., and Wallrath, M. (1987): An object-oriented database system for engineering applications. In *Proceedings of the ACM–SIGMOD 87 Annual Conference*. ACM, New York.

Knepley, E., and Platt, R. (1986): *Modula-2 Programming*. Reston Publishing Company, Reston, Va.

Logitech (1984): *Modula2/86*. Springer-Verlag, New York.

Mall, M., Reimer, M., and Schmidt, J.W. (1984): Data selection, sharing, and access control in a relational scenario. In M.L. Brodie, J. Mylopoulos, and J.W. Schmidt, Eds. *On Conceptual Modelling*. Springer-Verlag, New York, pp. 411–436.

Manola, F.A., and Orenstein, J.A. (1986): Toward a general spatial data model for an object-oriented DBMS. In *Proceedings of the 12th International Conference on Very Large Databases* (Kyoto, Japan).

Mylopoulos, J. Bernstein, P.A., and Wong, H.K.T. (1980): A language facility for designing database intensive applications. *ACM Transactions on Database Systems*, Vol. 5, No. 2 (June), 185–207.

Osborn, S., and Heaven, T.E. (1986): The design of a relational database system with abstract data types for domains. *ACM Transactions on Database Systems*, Vol. 11., No. 3 (Sept.), 357–373.

Reimer, M. (1984): Implementation of the database programming language Modula/R on the personal computer Lilith, *Software Practice & Experience*, Vol. 14, No. 10 (Oct.), 945–956.

Rosenthal, A., Heiler, S., Dayal, U., and Manola, F. (1986): Traversal recursion: A practical approach to supporting recursive applications. Tech. Rep., Computer Corporation of America, Cambridge, Mass.

Rowe, L.A., and Shones, K.A. (1979): Data abstractions, views and updates in Rigel. ACM SIGMOD International Conference on Management of Data, Boston.

Schek, H.J., and Pistor, P. (1982): Data structures for an integrated database management and information retrieval system. *Proceedings of the VLDB Conference* (Mexico City).

Schmidt, J.W. (1977): Some high-level language constructs for data of type relation. *ACM Transactions on Database Systems*, Vol. 2, No. 3 (Sept.), 247–261.

Smith, J.M., and Smith, D.C.P. (1977a): Database abstractions: Aggregation. *Communications of the ACM*, Vol. 20, No. 6 (June), 405–413.

Smith, J.M., and Smith, D.C.P. (1977b): Database abstractions: Aggregation and generalization. *ACM Transactions on Database Systems*, Vol. 2, No. 2 (June), 105–133.

Stemple, D., Mazudar, S. and Sheard, T. (1987): On the modes and meaning of feedback to transaction designers. In *Proceedings of the ACM–SIGMOD 87 Annual Conference* (San Francisco, Calif.) ACM, New York.

Stonebraker, M., and Rowe, L. (1986): The design of POSTGRESS. *Proceedings of the ACM–SIGMOD 86 Annual Conference* (Washington, D.C.). ACM, New York.

Stonebraker, M., Anton, J., and Hanson, E. (1987): Extending a database system with procedures. *ACM Transactions on Database Systems*, Vol. 12, No. 2 (Sept.), 350–376.

Stuart, A. (1987): *Screen Input/Output Programming Techniques Using Turbo Pascal*. Management Information Press, Portland, Oreg.

Ulman, J.D. (1980): *Principles of Database Systems*. Computer Science Press, Rockville, Md.

Weber, H., and Ehrig, H. (1986): Specification of modular systems. *IEEE Transactions on Software Engineering*, Vol. SE-12, No. 7 (July), 784–798.

Wirth, N. (1971): Program development by stepwise refinement. *Communications of the ACM*, Vol 14, No. 4 (Apr.), 221–227.

Wirth, N., Ed. (1983a): *Programming in Modula-2*. Springer-Verlag, New York. pp. 1–138

Wirth, N. (1983b): Report on the programming language Modula-2. In N. Wirth, *Programming in Modula-2*. Springer-Verlag, New York, pp. 139–170.

Wirth, N. (1986): *Algorithms + Data Structures*. Prentice-Hall, Englewood Cliffs, N.J.

Author Index

Subject Index